CREATIVITY AND ART

Margaret Boden presents a series of essays in which she explores the nature of creativity in a wide range of art forms. Creativity in general is the generation of novel, surprising and valuable ideas (conceptual, theoretical, musical, literary, or visual). Boden identifies three forms of creativity: combinational, exploratory, and transformational. These elicit differing forms of surprise, and are defined by the different kinds of psychological process that generate the new ideas. Boden examines creativity not only in traditional fine art, but also in craftworks, and some less orthodox approaches—namely, conceptual art and several types of computer art. Her introduction draws out the conceptual links between the various case-studies, showing how they express a coherent view of creativity in art.

For Nick & Ayla,

with all best wishes,

Maggie

Creativity and Art

Three Roads to Surprise

MARGARET A. BODEN

UNIVERSITY PRESS

OXFORD
UNIVERSITY PRESS

Great Clarendon Street, Oxford OX2 6DP
United Kingdom

Oxford University Press is a department of the University of Oxford.
It furthers the University's objective of excellence in research, scholarship,
and education by publishing worldwide. Oxford is a registered trade mark of
Oxford University Press in the UK and in certain other countries

© in this volume Margaret A. Boden 2010

The moral rights of the author have been asserted

First published 2010
First published in paperback 2012

All rights reserved. No part of this publication may be reproduced, stored in
a retrieval system, or transmitted, in any form or by any means, without the
prior permission in writing of Oxford University Press, or as expressly permitted
by law, by licence or under terms agreed with the appropriate reprographics
rights organization. Enquiries concerning reproduction outside the scope of the
above should be sent to the Rights Department, Oxford University Press, at the
address above

You must not circulate this work in any other form
and you must impose this same condition on any acquirer

British Library Cataloguing in Publication Data
Data available

Library of Congress Cataloging in Publication Data
Data available

ISBN 978–0–19–959073–5 (Hbk)
ISBN 978–0–19–965939–5 (Pbk)

Printed in the United Kingdom by
Lightning source UK Ltd., Milton Keynes

For Elke, Kit, and Tusia
—and in memory of Ron Crocombe (1929–2009).

Preface

These essays explore creativity within a wide range of art. Many of the examples discussed lie within traditional fine art, or in familiar kinds of craftwork. Some are drawn from movements explicitly contrasted with orthodox art, such as conceptual art. Yet others are instances of computer art, which has been developing, and diversifying, since the late 1950s. (The taxonomy in Chapter 7 provides an introduction to the field.)

Creativity is not the only philosophically problematic concept raised by computer art. Others include autonomy, authenticity, authorship . . . and occasionally even life. The philosophical problems differ according to the type of computer art being discussed. So do the aesthetic criteria that are regarded as relevant—some of which are applied also to traditional fine art.

Two papers are published here for the first time (Chapters 6 and 11), and two are extended versions of very brief earlier pieces (Chapters 9 and 10). The originals appeared in widely diverse publications—focused on art, philosophy, education, and science. Nevertheless, the chapters are unified by a particular theoretical approach, summarized in Chapter 2. The Introduction indicates the conceptual links between them, showing how they express a coherent view of creativity in art.

M.A.B.

Brighton, October 2009

Acknowledgements

I am grateful to the following publishers for their permission to reprint material here:

Chapter 2 ('Creativity in a Nutshell') was originally published as the introduction to the second edition of my book *The Creative Mind: Myths and Mechanisms* (London: Routledge, 2004), 1–10.

Chapter 3 ('Are Autodidacts Creative?') was written for J. Solomon (ed.), *The Passion to Learn: An Inquiry Into Autodidactism* (London: RoutledgeFalmer, 2003), 24–31.

Chapter 4 ('Crafts, Perception, and the Possibilities of the Body') is a slightly extended version of a paper of the same title in *British Journal of Aesthetics*, 40 (2000), 289–301.

Chapter 5 ('Creativity and Conceptual Art') first appeared in P. Goldie and E. Schellekens (eds.), *Philosophy and Conceptual Art* (Oxford: OUP, 2007), 216–37.

Chapter 7 ('What is Generative Art?'), co-authored with Ernest A. Edmonds, was published in *Digital Creativity*, 20/1–2 (2009), 21–46.

Chapter 8 ('Agents and Creativity') is drawn from *Communications of the Association of Computing Machinery* (special issue on Agents, ed. D. Riecken), 37/7 (1994), 117–21.

An earlier version of Chapter 9 ('Autonomy, Integrity, and Computer Art') appeared as a brief piece on 'Stillness as Autonomy', in S. Worden, L. Green, and P. Thomas (eds.), *Proceedings of Computers in Art and Design Education (CADE) Conference*, Stillness (Perth), September 2007; published as a CD–ROM (ISBN 1 74067 530 4).

Chapter 10 ('Authenticity and Computer Art') is an extended version of a paper of the same title in *Digital Creativity*, 18/1 (2007), 3–10. Parts of this chapter are based on section 13.iv.b of my book *Mind as Machine: A History of Cognitive Science* (Oxford: Clarendon Press, 2006).

Lastly, Chapter 12 ('Is Metabolism Necessary?') is reprinted from *British Journal for the Philosophy of Science*, 50/2 (1999), 231–48.

I am grateful also to the Arts and Humanities Research Council, for support during the writing of Chapters 5, 6, 7, 9, 10, and 11 (AHRC Grant no. B/RG/AN8285/APN19307: "Computational Intelligence, Creativity, and Cognition: A Multidisciplinary Investigation"). Support for Chapter 7 was received, too, from the Australasian CRC for Interaction Design, established and supported under the Australian Government's Research Centres Programme.

Finally, I thank Alan Sutcliffe, for suggesting that I collect these essays together in the first place.

Contents

1. Introduction — 1
2. Creativity in a Nutshell — 29
3. Are Autodidacts Creative? — 41
4. Crafts, Perception, and the Possibilities of the Body — 50
5. Creativity and Conceptual Art — 70
6. Personal Signatures in Art — 92
7. What Is Generative Art? — 125
8. Agents and Creativity — 164
9. Autonomy, Integrity, and Computer Art — 175
10. Authenticity and Computer Art — 193
11. Aesthetics and Interactive Art — 210
12. Is Metabolism Necessary? — 235

Index — 255

There is sometimes a greater judgment shewn in deviating from the rules of art, than in adhering to them; and . . . there is more beauty in the works of a great genius who is ignorant of all the rules of art, than in the works of a little genius, who not only knows but scrupulously observes them.

Joseph Addison (1714)

1
Introduction

The three roads to surprise are the three forms of creativity: combinational, exploratory, and transformational. In previous writings, I've illustrated these by examples drawn from many different specialist domains, and from everyday life too (Boden 2004). Here, I relate them to art (as understood in the post-medieval Western tradition), and especially to the visual arts. Besides many references to traditional fine art, I also discuss some less orthodox approaches—namely, conceptual art and several types of computer art. Craftworks of various kinds are also considered, in the context of a new account of the distinction between art and craft.

A brief statement of my threefold theory of creativity, which underlies this collection as a whole, is given in Chapter 2 ('Creativity in a Nutshell'). Creativity in general is the generation of novel, surprising, and valuable ideas. "Ideas", here, is a catch-all term covering not only concepts and theories but also (for example) music and literature, and artefacts such as architecture, sculpture, and paintings. The three types of creativity, which elicit differing forms of surprise, are defined by the different kinds of psychological process that generate the new structures.

As it happens, those processes have been greatly clarified by computer models of creativity. But that fact is *not* a core theme of this collection. If and when computers are mentioned here, it is in the context of computer art, not computer modelling. Computer modelling is a form of science, and most computer artists never engage in it. Like their fellow artists working in other genres, they have no particular interest in detailing the processes that may go on in human minds. (The leading exception is Harold Cohen, who in the late 1960s—when already a highly acclaimed abstract painter—embarked on his AARON suite of programs in order to throw light on his own creativity: Cohen 1981, 1995, 2002.) So the remarks in Chapter 2 that note the scientific value of computer models of creativity are not followed up in the other chapters (but see Boden 2004: chs. 5–8 and 12).

The first road to surprise that's identified in Chapter 2 is *combinational* creativity: the generation of unfamiliar combinations of familiar ideas. Most discussions of creativity, even in the specialist psychological literature (e.g. Sternberg 1988, 1999), consider only this type. (Of the roughly sixty definitions of creativity that had been offered by experts twenty years ago, almost all boiled down to this: Taylor 1988.) The combinational way of generating surprise is indeed important. It underlies most spontaneous jokes and wordplay, and is the key source of poetic/literary imagery and visual collage—and (as argued in Chapter 5) of conceptual art, too.

But my account allows also for two other sorts of creativity. As explained in Chapter 2, these involve the *exploration* and *transformation* of familiar conceptual spaces—such as artistic styles. A style is a (culturally favoured) space of structural possibilities: not a painting, but *a way* of painting. Or *a way* of sculpting, or of composing fugues . . . and so on.

It's partly because of these thinking styles that creativity has an ambiguous relationship with freedom. On the one hand, it's commonly thought of as being the very opposite of disciplined, or rule-governed, behaviour. Creative ideas are surprising because they are unpredictable (and that is so for several reasons—Boden 2004: ch. 9). Some are so surprising that they strike us as outrageous (think of the unfamiliar combinations within the literary conceits in *Finnegan's Wake*). Indeed, some are deliberately intended to be outrageous (conceptual art, again). And transformational creativity, by definition, amends/ignores some normally respected constraints. So there's a tempting launchpad, here, for neo-Romantic stories of the divine spark of creative freedom.

On the other hand, all three types of creativity exploit stylistic and/or conceptual constraints. In exploratory creativity it's especially clear that "artistic discipline" is not a contradiction in terms. But even the transformational variety preserves much of the preceding style. And even the most surprising visual juxtapositions (surrealism, perhaps), and the most challenging poetic imagery, have a connecting thread of intelligibility. (This is lacking, for instance, in the undisciplined outpourings of a schizophrenic's 'word-salad'—which, despite being unpredictable and occasionally suggestive to eavesdroppers, is not in itself an exercise of creative thinking.) That intelligibility is grounded in the rich network of conceptual structures in an adult's mind (Boden 2004: chs. 5–6)—which structures are recognized by combinational creativity, not ignored by it.

These remarks imply that creativity also has an ambiguous position with respect to education, and in particular to autodidacts. For the "one hand" cited above suggests that a lack of conventional education need be no barrier to creativity—indeed, it's commonly held that education may actually inhibit it. But the "other hand" stresses the importance of stylistic constraints that may require many years, and the help of dutiful tutors, to learn. So perhaps autodidacts, contrary to common belief, are actually at a disadvantage when it comes to creative thinking?

In Chapter 3 ('Are Autodidacts Creative?'), I outline the complex pattern of relationships between original thinking and self-education. As well as saying a little more about the three types of creativity, I distinguish three types of autodidact. The 3 × 3 matrix implied by these distinctions defines a variety of interrelationships between creativity and autodidacticism, sometimes mutually supportive and sometimes not.

Most of those interrelationships apply irrespective of the domain concerned. In other words, art and science here are in much the same boat. Indeed, the threefold account of creativity sketched in Chapters 2 and 3 applies to both, and some scientific examples are mentioned there. The next eight chapters, however, focus on art.

In 'Crafts, Perception, and the Possibilities of the Body' (Chapter 4), I compare creativity in the fine arts with craftsmanship. I also take up the old problem of distinguishing "art" from "craft". In one sense, I avoid that problem, for I don't offer mutually exclusive *definitions* of these terms. Nor are satisfactory definitions available in the literature: quite apart from the hugely controversial question "What is art?", one historian has identified many competing interpretations of "craft", none of which is entirely apt (Harrod 1999: 10). Instead of offering definitions, I refer to many specific examples that are normally labelled as one or the other, and ask what are the differences between the two classes.

My answer distinguishes the practices of art and craft, but also explains *why* they aren't always clearly separable. That is, the difficulty of definition here goes beyond the fact that all everyday concepts are fuzzy, allowing for borderline cases and anomalies. There is a specific (psychological) reason why it is impossible to assign every relevant artefact to *only one* of these categories.

The crafts are grounded in biologically evolved human tendencies to respond to certain things in particular ways. The psychologist's jargon, here, is "affordances" (Gibson 1966). A pot or a textile, a chair or a sword, a box or a jewel, afford diverse opportunities for (fitness-related) action—which opportunities are readily, 'naturally', perceptible by *Homo sapiens*. The perception excites a disposition to act in a certain way: in general, to approach or to avoid the environmental feature concerned—so affordances embody basic *values*. (The play of affordances here is more complex than one might think: besides their more obvious functionalities, highly skilled craftworks—including the beautifully symmetrical, and unused, hand axes fashioned 1,400,000 years ago—are counters in the game of sexual selection, signalling their makers' physical strength, muscular control, perceptual acuity, power of concentration, and endurance: Miller 2000.)

In the case of craftworks, then, the value-criterion of creativity is grounded in our evolutionary biology. That's why the aesthetics of craft are more stable, and its appreciation more cross-cultural, than the aesthetics of fine art.

It's sometimes said that a pure craftsman, untainted by 'art-envy' (see below), isn't creative at all—merely skilled. I wouldn't go that far. To the contrary, I'd say that craftsmen rely on exploratory creativity. But this is of a relatively unadventurous kind. Even an internationally famous master potter (for instance) may be aiming to produce yet another—albeit more perfect—example of something located in a part of the possibility space that has been visited many times before. The result can be an artefact that amazes us, in its (affordance-based) power to engage our attention/valuation. But if gaining our attention and positive valuation is part of the point of the exercise, producing amazement (or anyway, amazement-at-novelty) is not.

In other words, the crafts downplay the role of surprise in creative work. Even the best examples typically display only minor novelty, and our wonder is elicited less by what is done than by its being done supremely well. The crafts aren't dependent on highly imaginative combinational creativity, nor driven by increasingly adventurous exploratory creativity, nor sporadically progressed by transformational creativity—as fine art is.

That's not to say, however, that craftwork *never* involves journeying on these three roads to surprise. It's true that the key mental capacities that underlie the generation (and appreciation) of craftwork differ from those which underlie fine art. The former relies on basic affordances, whereas the latter relies on the high-level psychological processes involved in learning, retaining, exploring, challenging, and (sometimes) transforming culturally specific concepts and/or artistic styles. But both types of mental process can occur within someone's mind simultaneously, with respect to different properties of a single artefact.

This psychological fact makes it possible for a potter, jeweller, or tapestry maker to exploit knowledge of specific fine-art styles in their work (various examples are given in Chapter 4). Indeed, it makes it possible for them to do this in order to raise their social status in a culture that values fine art over 'mere' crafts—hence my reference, above, to art-envy. Similarly, a professional craftsman irritated by unsympathetic cultural values may deliberately, and atypically, aim for surprise—by following one or more of the three roads I've distinguished. This explains why there can never be a definition of crafts that can unambiguously distinguish every individual craftwork from a work of art.

In saying that craftworks don't involve adventurous creativity, I've assumed that the craftworker is using already accepted techniques. But it is possible, of course, for someone to create (by combination, exploration, or transformation) a new way of firing pots, say, or of working metals.

An intriguing recent example of the creative (combinational) use of novel techniques in craftwork is 'digital jewellery'. Here, rings and bracelets are not only attractive physical adornments but also digital devices. Considered as items of jewellery, they afford [sic] the social communications for which jewellery has evolved (see Chapter 4). But they can do more, for impersonal digital techniques can be put to highly personal uses. For instance, digital jewellery may be connected with some remote location of personal significance to the wearer, such as their birthplace—where their family may still reside (Wallace et al. 2007). Instead of a Victorian locket containing a lover's likeness, or a mourning brooch woven from a dead spouse's hair, these baubles may display images/sounds drawn from the wearer's own past, or from their far-flung relatives' situation *at this very moment*.

The crafts, then, typically underplay surprise—and are often dismissed as being uncreative, accordingly. But if surprise is a key criterion of creativity, the 1970s movement known as conceptual art shouldn't suffer the same fate. On the contrary, it should be seen as highly creative. For to say that conceptual art is surprising is an understatement. It is shocking, bizarre, outrageous, challenging . . . so much so, that it's often said not to be *art* at all. In Chapter 5 ('Creativity and Conceptual Art'), I ask just which sort of creativity it involves. Which of the three roads leads to these artistic astonishments?

Prima facie, conceptual art may seem to be a case of transformational creativity. For its artworks are *very* different from traditional ones. Moreover, the conceptual artists were undoubtedly trying to effect a radical change in the public's ideas and expectations about "art". However, not every radical change counts as a "transformation", in the (stylistic) sense that I define this. Looked at more closely, conceptual art is an example—or rather, a set of highly various examples (many described in Chapter 5)—of combinational creativity.

Each of the individual artworks generated by this movement involves some unfamiliar, often highly challenging, juxtaposition of ideas. And "ideas" should be interpreted literally, here. For a conceptual artist, as opposed to an orthodox fine artist, the physical artefact is not the main point. Indeed, there may be no physical artefact, merely (for instance) a verbal injunction to imagine one. Even if there is, the artist may have ensured that it remains utterly invisible to the 'audience'—by being buried, for example.

The key aim, then, is not to generate intrinsically beautiful objects, nor disturbing ones either. Admittedly, Eduardo Kac outraged people by producing a genetically engineered albino rabbit that turned a fluorescent green in ultraviolet light. But even this was as much an idea as a thing: the notorious green image that sped around the world via the mass media was not an actual photograph, but a Photoshop-generated design; and the rabbit was never publicly exhibited, because fears about mad-cow disease prevented agricultural movements around the laboratory where it was born. Nor do conceptual artists aim to display hard-won painterly or sculptural skills (so they might well be autodidacts: see Chapter 3). Rather, they aim to raise a host of questions in the minds of the audience. Many of these concern the nature of "art" itself—and its twentieth-century social context, the art market.

Many of the conceptual artists were challenging the popular view of art wherein art is a highly personal matter: not merely effected by a person (not by a machine), but by some particular, unique, human individual. This view has its roots in the humanism of the Renaissance, but was strengthened by early nineteenth-century Romanticism. Coincidentally, the historical circumstances of the mid-nineteenth century led to a need (on the part of collectors and curators) for better ways of attributing old paintings or sculptures to one artist rather than another. And this, in turn, led pioneering art connoisseurs to identify the characteristic marks, or personal signatures, of different artists.

Chapter 6 ('Personal Signatures in Art') not only describes how this notion arose, but also asks why personal signatures exist in the first place. What is it about the creative process which makes personal signatures near-inevitable?

Even exploratory creativity, which is the most highly constrained of all three types, leaves many points for individual choice. Were that not so, each artistic style would allow only one instantiation: a single painting, sculpture, fugue... in that particular style. And because of certain general features of mental information-processing, necessitated by the finitude of our minds, it is highly probable that individual artists will develop idiosyncratic habits of working which distinguish their art from that of other artists—even those exploring the same style. Combinational creativity is more free, less predictable. But here too, general psychological features (affecting the perception of relevance, for example) will engender patterns of thought that are specific to the individual artist.

A further question raised in Chapter 6 is whether personal signatures are not merely highly probable, but wholly inevitable. Why have those fine artists who (in a twentieth-century reaction against Romanticism) have deliberately tried to avoid the personal signature been only partially successful at doing so? And why have they failed even when turning to impersonal machines for help?

In particular, is it possible for a human artist to lose his personal signature by engaging in a type of computer art wherein a robot is *evolved* (not specifically designed) to draw aesthetically acceptable marks that don't betray his authorship? One internationally famous artist is already trying to do precisely this—but it's by no means clear whether he will, or even could, succeed.

Using a robot, as opposed to a computer screen, is not mere gimmickry. For it makes it possible for serendipitous events to happen, wherein the robot interacts with some previously unconsidered aspect of its physical environment. In other words, the drawings that result needn't be wholly dependent on exploring the space of possibilities predefined by the program (including its mutation rules). In principle, some fundamental transformation could occur—comparable to evolving a first-time eye, not just an improved eye. (A first-time sensor has already been evolved *in practice*, by someone involved in the art-oriented robotics project being considered here: Bird and Layzell 2002.) In short, something deeply surprising could conceivably emerge from the evolutionary processes underlying the robot's behaviour (cf. Boden, in preparation). Such a result isn't guaranteed, and is even pretty improbable—but it is possible.

One might think that the desired loss of signature *must* be possible too. After all, the robot's final line-drawing behaviour will be the end point of a process involving myriad random mutations. Indeed, one might think that this randomness makes it impossible for the evolving robot *not* to lose the artist's telltale sign. Chapter 6 shows that this issue is not so easily decided.

The problem is that the signature-fleeing artist himself will have the final say in choosing the criteria of selection (the 'fitness function') that are used at each generation to pick the 'best' mutants for further evolution. His chances of success—that is, of enabling the robot to *lose* his personal mark—depend on the degree to which our (and his) aesthetic preferences rest on basic, culture-free, properties as opposed to culturally, or even personally, specific styles. These basic properties might include some of the affordances favoured in craftwork (see Chapter 4), but could also include other features that are fundamental to visual perception. Certain fractal properties, for instance, might be naturally attractive. In short, this project raises empirical psychological questions as well as philosophical ones.

Why "philosophical" ones? Well, references to robots making line drawings may raise the hackles of some readers: "These papers are supposed to be about creativity and art" they may grumble, "Robots, in principle, can have nothing to do with either". In other words, they believe that *there can be no such thing as computer creativity*, and (a different, though related, point) that *there can be no such thing as computer art*.

With respect to the latter claim, some philosophers justify their refusal to admit the possibility of computer art by defining "art" in exclusively human terms. Anthony O'Hear (1995), for example, insists that art involves some form of communication between one human being and another. For this to be possible, he says, artist and audience must share human experience.

He would be willing to admit that computer art exists in the sense in which watercolour art, or marble art, do: that is, a computer can be used as an artist's medium. He'd probably allow, also, that a computer can be an artist's tool, or aid—perhaps even an artist's assistant (although that is more questionable: see Chapter 8). But if any 'artwork' is generated by the computer itself, by means of processes that are largely beyond the human artist's control, then—for O'Hear—it isn't really an artwork at all. It may happen to be visually/aurally arresting, decorative, or even beautiful. But to respond to it as an artwork is, he says, to be deceived. Even to see it as aesthetically valuable, he says, is to be largely misled. On discovering its provenance, our aesthetic satisfaction would—and should—decrease, even evaporate. (I have witnessed people making this sudden shift of evaluative attitude on several occasions.)

O'Hear is not alone in such views. And the problem he raises remains even if one includes other ways, besides communication, in which human experience may be involved—for instance, where the artist aims to enable, facilitate, and/or arouse certain experiences, rather than communicate them. It remains, also, if the type of experience one regards as aesthetically crucial involves emotion (a very common view, broadly known as expressionism in aesthetics).

The problems remain because anyone who *defines* art in such a way that human experience and/or human creativity is essential to it must be sceptical about the notion of computer art. And the more the computer 'artwork' is generated by processes going on in the computer itself, the stronger their scepticism must be. At best, computer art will be seen as art at one remove, thanks entirely to its human instigation. Even if art is defined in terms of the *natural*, as opposed to the *human*, the notion of computer art will still be problematic. If, by contrast, art is defined in terms of properties of the art object that are not exclusively human and/or natural, talk of computer art might escape challenge.

However, I shan't offer any 'non-human' definition of art, designed to allow the inclusion of the computer-based varieties. Quite apart from the air of special pleading that would attend such a definition, it would require lengthy argument that would be out of place here. For the definition of art is a notoriously slippery matter, which often threatens to exclude works that many people regard as art—such as conceptual art, and certain items of craftwork: see Chapters 5 and 4, respectively. I'll rely instead on the (undefined) common usage of "art", and on paradigm cases of it—from Fra Angelico's delicate murals to Mark Rothko's glowing colour constructions. The more problematic cases can be accepted as art to the extent that they show similarities to and continuities with the commonly accepted examples.

One more point must be made before talk of *computer* art can be specifically defended. Namely, our intuitive concepts of art, if not our explicit definitions, typically see it as creative. Indeed, the link is so close that people often fail to realize, or anyway forget, that science and mathematics involve creativity too. This leads to a further problem in speaking of computer art, since many people insist that no computer can *really* be creative. They may be willing to grant that a machine may generate novel, surprising, and even arguably valuable results: lifelike and/or beautiful images, for example. But, they say, the creativity involved can be attributed only to the human being/s who made it behave in that way.

This claim is usually grounded in arguments involving one or more key philosophical concepts that are (plausibly) assumed to be essential for creativity. These concern consciousness, intentionality, the role of 'brain-stuff' and/or embodiment, and membership of the human moral community. I've argued elsewhere that although the brain-stuff argument can be rejected, each of the others remains highly problematic (Boden 2004: 286–300). What's more, they are problematic primarily because of the disagreements concerning these philosophical concepts themselves. If we understood intentionality better, or consciousness, we'd be in a better position to pronounce on whether or not computers can "really" be creative.

Since these notoriously controversial problems remain unsolved, I nowhere claim that computers are "really" creative. If and when I mention creativity in computers I am asking *what aesthetically interesting results can computers generate, and how?* and *Just what might lead someone to suggest that a particular computer system is creative, or that its functioning is somehow similar to creativity in human beings?* In that sense, I'm content to leave the question of "real" computer creativity open. And if art necessarily involves creativity—a reasonable, if not a strictly provable, view—then (in that sense) I must leave the question of "real" computer art open too.

So I shan't try to *prove* that computer art can exist because it fits some favoured (and tendentious?) definition of art and/or of creativity. Instead, I'll rely on two strategies to persuade sceptical readers that this isn't an empty class. On the one hand, I'll point out (in Chapters 7–11) many similarities and continuities between computer art and the more familiar varieties. On the other hand, I'll mention some examples where the work of computer artists is taken seriously *as art* by aesthetes of an orthodox kind. For instance, I remark in Chapter 7 that a computer artwork was included in the Washington DC exhibition mounted in 2007 to celebrate the sixtieth anniversary of the ColorField painters: Rothko, Clyfford Still, Kenneth Noland, and the like (Edmonds 2007).

Despite the welcome imprimatur of the Washington gallery (and many others, including the Tate), computer art is still largely unknown even to art lovers and aestheticians. So Chapter 7 ('What Is Generative Art?'), co-authored with Ernest Edmonds, offers a novel taxonomy of work in this genre—along with an indication of the philosophical issues that attend the various categories. As well as distinguishing significantly different types of computer art, this taxonomy displays several connections between computer art and more established forms. Chapter 7 can therefore act as an introduction to the field for readers who haven't yet encountered it—much as Chapter 5 can act as an introduction to conceptual art for those unfamiliar with it.

By different "types" of computer art, in the context of Chapter 7, I mean different techniques for producing computer artworks and/or different types of experience on encountering them. But one might also distinguish these artworks by the differences in their physical implementation—which cut across the generative distinctions used to draw up the taxonomy.

For instance, some computer artworks are framed 'pictures' hung on the wall. These may be unchanging images, both produced and printed by a computer program (e.g. Todd and Latham 1992). Or they may be ever-changing coloured patterns, the changes being prompted by the viewer's movements—thanks to a minicamera and minicomputer hidden in the square perspex frame (Edmonds 2007). As Chapter 6 implied, a few involve physical robots. Whether attached to walls or ceiling, or ranging free over the floor, their movements have some intrinsic interest and/or produce results, such as sounds or line drawings, that the audience finds intriguing. Others are interactive CD-ROMs, which provide differing experiences as a result of the viewer's input (Leggett 1996). Yet others are static or (more usually) dynamic video projections, perhaps presented on a computer monitor or perhaps filling an entire wall. And some of these are virtual reality environments, a millennial form of *trompe l'œil* (a genre employed by artists since Roman times: Grau 2004) often projected onto all four walls, and maybe floor and ceiling too. Occasionally, it's not only the audience's *eyes* that are deceived, but their ears and (if special gloves are worn) their fingertips too.

Whereas all of those examples are located inside a building, whether an art gallery or someone's home, others are exhibited in bustling city squares. In that case, the installations are typically huge: much more than human size. Being out-of-doors, their form may change as a result of weather conditions, as well as of the movements of the people passing by.

One must add, however, that some computer artworks aren't physically located at all. Rather, they exist on the Internet. (Thor Magnusson has suggested an additional entry for the taxonomy: N-Art, or Network art.) These works are accessed—and developed—by human beings located in physical space: staring at their PC screens, for instance, or using their mobile phones, or playing musical instruments while online. They may be altered, to some (highly variable) degree, by input coming from those individuals. But the artwork itself, even if there happens to be some physical installation at its core (which there may not be), isn't really located anywhere—except in cyberspace.

A prominent early case of Network art was Ken Goldberg's *Telegarden*. Developed at the University of Southern California in 1995, this was installed in the Ars Electronica Centre (now renamed the Museum of the Future) in Linz, Austria, a year later; it ran non-stop for nine years, until being switched off in 2004. Unlike many N-art works, it did have a physical core: a garden filled with living plants, which were planted and watered by means of a robot arm. The garden's progress could be monitored through images from an on-site camera. The movements of the robot arm were remotely directed by web-users all over the world: 9,000 people connected with it in its first year. Besides remarking on a wide range of ecological/environmental meditations prompted by this artwork (see <http://goldberg.berkeley.edu/garden/Ars/>), the users reported feelings of human community of a (distributed) type never experienced before (McLaughlin et al. 1997). The nearest analogy would be their prior experience, if any, of web-based 'games' involving huge numbers of players (Turkle 1995).

The *Telegarden* example shows us that tricky ontological questions arise with respect to some computer artworks. Is the garden the artwork?; or the community of human users that's been built up over the years?; or their comments and meditations, shared on the web alongside camera images of the plants?; or...? Again, consider the line-drawing robots mentioned in Chapter 6: are the robots the artwork, or is the artwork rather their drawings? Or perhaps both?

Conceptual art can engender similar conundrums (or conundra, if you prefer!). The work called *42nd Parallel* (described in Chapter 7) is said by its instigator—one can hardly say its maker—to consist in a geographically dispersed pattern of activity in the US postal system. As such, it isn't clearly located either. Of course, tricky ontological problems can arise with respect to much more familiar forms of art than this (a classic discussion is: Goodman 1968). So ontology is one of the various philosophical/aesthetic dimensions on which this new category of art is related to 'art as we know it'.

One difference noted in the taxonomy is that between computer-assisted or computer-aided art (CA-art) and computer-generated art (CG-art). (This distinction underlay my claim, above, that O'Hear might allow the possibility of computer-assisted art, though not of computer-generated art.) In CA-art, the human artist produces the artwork with some help from the computer, which is in principle non-essential. In CG-art, the artwork is produced by the computer itself, with minimal or zero interference from a human being.

The terms "computer-assisted" and "computer-aided" art are normally used interchangeably, and the category of CA-art covers both. But one might want to make a further distinction here. A tool (e.g. a paintbrush or chisel) that's wholly under the artist's control is more readily thought of as an *aid* than as an *assistant*. And indeed, the examples of CA-art given in Chapter 7 involve off-the-shelf programs (Photoshop and video editors) used by the artist as tools in the production of many different artworks. But Chapter 8 ('Agents and Creativity') suggests that CA-art could also involve specially written programs, containing AI "agents" for some particular style of art. As this label implies, these would be conceptualized—and experienced—by their human users less as mere tools than as semi-autonomous assistants, capable of cooperating [*sic*] in the task at hand.

AI agents in general have a significant degree of independence from the human being who is using the program. Indeed, they are often termed "autonomous" by AI researchers. There are two reasons for this. First, they are not deliberately called up by the human user, but are automatically triggered by specific cues: events occurring within the running of the program or in the environment (maybe including the user's actions). And second, they are not amenable to interference from the user once they have started to run.

Whereas some agents are relatively simple processes, comparable to a reflex knee-jerk, others are more like mini-minds. These can set and follow goals, and cooperate with partner-agents. For example, they can devise engagement schedules (avoiding conflicts with entries already in the user's diary), book hotel rooms, and arrange for flights and car-hire—perhaps without bothering the user, or perhaps making suggestions for human ratification (Norman 1994). Some can even learn how to do better in future by inferring, or being told, why their suggestion was rejected (Mitchell et al. 1994: 87). Where such 'mini-minds' are concerned, the user's illusion of having a quasi-intelligent assistant can be fairly strong.

Sometimes, the agent's action is to send a message to the user. This may be a warning, saying that he/she has made a mistake or that some danger point is being approached. Or it may be a suggestion about what to do next: perhaps how to rectify the mistake, or avoid the danger. The user can then decide whether or not to heed the agent's advice.

The *existing* computer-art programs that are mentioned in Chapter 8 do not contain agents: they exemplify CG-art, not CA-art. They include (exploratory) programs for designing Palladian villas or Frank Lloyd Wright's Prairie Houses, and for improvising jazz. Each of them, I suggest, could in principle be modified to form an agentive version. So too could large semantic networks—so as to help writers, whether comfortable in advertising studios or freezing in garrets, to find and develop conceptual associations (alias combinations). In practice, however, agent-based computer art is thin on the ground.

The reason, I suspect, is that (with a caveat mentioned below) the more strongly the human user identifies him/herself as a creative artist, the less likely that they will want to rely on AI agents as design crutches. They may be happy to bite the bullet—indeed, to swallow it whole—and go down the route of CG-art. But that's a different enterprise (one which could well involve agents working behind the scenes, like the diary-organizer mentioned above). In other words, CA-artists may feel that an agentive CA-system would compromise their own artistic autonomy, integrity, or authenticity: they want computer aids (tools), not computer assistants.

The caveat, here, is that some CA-artists might be perfectly happy to have the "A" mean "assistant", given that some *non-computer* artists rely heavily on human assistants in their work. Examples range from the Renaissance masters to conceptual artists such as Sol LeWitt and Jeff Koons (see Chapter 5). The sixteenth-century masters would sometimes merely sketch the outlines of the picture and paint the faces of the key people depicted in it, leaving the drapery and/or background to be executed by their apprentices. And the conceptual artists all underplayed the role of personal art-making skills, if not of creativity, in their work; Koons, for instance, became notorious for employing others to paint 'his' canvases. So for a CA-artist who sympathizes with that general art movement, there's no reason to avoid using computer agents as assistants.

Nor is there reason to avoid this if the creative activity is thought of as practical design, as opposed to art. For instance, the computer-assisted design (CAD) programs used today by professional engineers and jobbing architects can monitor the provisional decisions of the user, identifying mistakes and sometimes offering suggestions. If a design for a building had a potential structural weakness, for instance, an engineering-wise CAD program could warn the architect of that fact; it might also be able to suggest how the fault could be put right. Or suppose that an architect's client had requested a building like a Prairie House, and that there were no CG-art program capable of designing one entire: in that case, the architect might find it helpful [sic] to have a set of Prairie-agents, to be consulted at particular choice points during his design work. But the results wouldn't be presented to the world as "art". Moreover, no self-styled *creative* architect would be spending his/her time copying Lloyd Wright.

I said, above, that some computer artists may be loath to use computer assistants for fear of jeopardizing their own autonomy, integrity, or authenticity. And some readers will surely sympathize, feeling that concepts such as these can have no place in computer-based art—least of all, where the artwork is generated by wholly automatic processes. On their view, artists who adopt a CG-art methodology thereby abandon any claim to such epithets. The next two chapters address these issues.

As for the first member of the problematic trio of concepts, some computer artists justify the value of their work in part by citing the "autonomy" of the computerized system concerned. They have inherited that terminology from the AI researchers whose methods they are exploiting. We've seen, for example, that agents are commonly termed autonomous within the AI community. Critics may object that the fact that computer scientists speak in this way merely shows that their field doesn't foster sensitivity to natural language. However, even if we ignore that objection and focus instead on the nature of the systems themselves, we must recognize that there are significantly different senses of "autonomy". If autonomy does have any aesthetic value, we need to know what type of autonomy is in question in a given case.

Chapter 9 ('Autonomy, Integrity, and Computer Art') shows that the various senses of autonomy are distinguished not by mere nuances, but by differences that include some seemingly radical oppositions. So natural autonomy includes biological homeostasis, psycho-physiological reflexes, various kinds of animal behaviour, and human freedom. Likewise, the autonomy that characterizes (some) computer systems is comparable to those very different phenomena. (We've seen already that computerized agents are sometimes like reflexes, and sometimes like goal-seeking mini-minds.) Different types of computing methodology are best suited to achieve different types of autonomy.

It follows that to understand the vexed concept of autonomy we need to understand the differences that are involved. In the case of the natural autonomies, this requires biological and psychological knowledge. In the case of the seemingly paradoxical concept of computer autonomy, which some computer artists see as a key source of value in their work, it requires some knowledge about the details of the programs concerned. To ascribe (or to withhold) any particular sense of autonomy to/from a computer artwork therefore requires one to know something about *just how* the relevant program works. As remarked in Chapter 9, the epistemology of art is thus more taxing in the case of computer art than for more familiar forms.

Admittedly, knowledge of the details of art-making can enrich art criticism in conventional areas too. For instance, someone who understands *just how* to place paint on a surface is in a better position to appreciate certain aspects of paintings than someone who has never held a paintbrush. This is evident, for example, in a history of art written by the painter Julian Bell. Bell repeatedly points out virtues of artworks that result from the way in which the paint is applied, and often invites us to imagine the 'feel' that the artist would have experienced in making the work. For instance, he explains Rothko's colours that "pulse against one another—now drawing in, now glaring out" by referring to his ability to "coax big cloud-blocks of colour from the canvas with a soft glazing-brush" (Bell 2007: 415 f.). And in writing about Giorgione, he says that "[his] brushwork, for the first time, exploits the unevenness of canvas, a surface for paint . . . only recently adopted in Northern Italy. The definitiveness of brushmarks made on a perfectly flat wooden panel is gone, but something more alluring replaces it. A loaded brush quickly traversing canvas leaves traces on its "teeth", not its valleys: the viewer, induced to complete the intended line in the imagination, also enjoys by proxy the sensation of the action that produced it" (2007: 189). Even the art connoisseur Giovanni Morelli, whose loving knowledge of Giorgione's paintings is mentioned in Chapter 6, would not have picked up on that.

The second member of the trio, namely integrity, is a special case of autonomy—indeed, a special case of human freedom. It can arise only in adult human minds capable of holding, integrating, following, and also abandoning general principles of behaviour. These may be moral, political, religious . . . or aesthetic. In general, to have integrity is not merely to show consistency and coherence in following one's principles: it also involves resisting—while also recognizing—the temptation to follow an easier path, in which those principles would be betrayed. So integrity is not simple innocence. Honesty is here joined with a refusal to compromise, where it's evident that compromising would in some ways be more comfortable.

An artist can be praised for the integrity of the content of their work, and/or for the integrity of its observable style. By the same token, they can be criticized for lacking integrity in these matters. Such judgements are common in the traditional arts.

Computer artists are subject to these sorts of evaluation too. And, again like their more orthodox fellows, they can be criticized for lack of either moral/political or logical/structural integrity. So all the familiar disputes about the relation between morality and art can arise in this relatively unfamiliar context: think of violent, sadistic, or pornographic video installations (or computer games), for example. Similarly, a critic who praises Picasso for choosing to paint *Guernica*, or who condemns Jane Austen for her novels' silence on the Napoleonic wars, might complain of a lack of integrity in some computer artworks with a sociopolitical content.

But computer artists might also be judged in terms of the *technical* integrity of the computational methods they use to achieve their art. In such cases, the art critic must understand how the various methods are distinguished, and how they may be integrated [*sic*] within a single artwork.

Chapter 9 makes this point by reference to "hybrid" computer systems, in which two (or more) normally distinct approaches are combined. Methodologically, a hybrid system is less neat, less 'aesthetically' pure, than a single-method system. As such, it is comparable to a mixed-media work in art. If a hybrid computer artwork is not to be scorned as an inelegant ragbag of programming tricks, it needs to display a smooth switching between the various methods at appropriate points, and an overall result that is valuable in itself and which could not have been achieved in any other way. (Chapter 9 describes a psychological example: a hybrid system that models voluntary actions, and certain pathological disturbances of action caused by brain damage.)

Third, authenticity. This concept, too, is often used in critiques of the more familiar forms of art. Chapter 10 ('Authenticity and Computer

Art') distinguishes various senses of authenticity, and asks whether any can be satisfied by computer art.

Some critics argue that all computer art must be inauthentic—not even *bad* art: rather, not really art at all—because computers lack emotions. Others doubt its authenticity on the grounds that (non-interactive) computer artworks, even if they happen to be unique, are unlimited in quantity: in principle, they could be churned out for ever. Yet others refuse to respond to computer-generated works as anything but "computer output", not deserving the critical/appreciative thinking that greets traditional fine art. These negative responses are likely to be compounded if the computer can be seen as producing pastiches (even forgeries?) of the work of specific human individuals.

One renowned computer artist, the composer David Cope, has been so frustrated by these attitudes towards the results generated by his 'Emmy' program that he has recently destroyed the program's musical database, painstakingly built up over the last twenty-five years. For him, Emmy composes *music*, to be appreciated (or not, of course) as such. To consider it as mere computer output, on his view, is to miss the point.

People who refuse to treat Emmy's music as music (alias art) thereby threaten Cope's perceived status *as an artist*. This raises the question why anyone would want to do computer art in the first place. One of the three main reasons identified in Chapter 10 is to produce and exhibit works of art so as to gain a public reputation as an artist. If the "public" adamantly deny the authenticity of any computer art, that hope will be frustrated. A would-be artist who does not already have a reputation as a painter (like the young Cohen), or as a composer (like the young Cope), might think twice before embarking on this unfamiliar path. For if this public attitude persists, they will be honoured as an artist only by a relatively small group of people.

My own bet would be that this public attitude will not persist. Although much computer art is still confined to a niche market, some examples have been exhibited in prominent public spaces—from the Millennium Dome in London (see below) to busy squares in Melbourne or Washington. The Internet, of course, ensures that some computer art is displayed—and, in the case of Network art, made freely open for worldwide creative participation—on the web. And sometimes, as remarked above, computer art is deliberately placed in the same aesthetic space (under the same gallery theme) as the work of more orthodox artists, such as Rothko.

Conventional galleries/museums face many difficulties in exhibiting computer art: new curatorial practices, and some dedicated facilities, will be needed (Leggett 1999). Increasingly, however, people won't have to decide to enter one of the (still rare) galleries that regularly feature these types of art. They won't even have to decide to visit one of the occasional exhibitions held at the Tate and comparable venues. Rather, they will come across them willy-nilly—much as people today can't avoid seeing statuary in public places.

There's a caveat needed here, however. The continual invention of new types of interface doesn't merely present a practical problem for curators: some of the potential audience may become irritated and even bored by "the continually transitional character of the medium" (Kahn 1996: 30). Even the artists themselves may be discouraged by the amount of labour involved in adapting to yet another novel interface. (Not the young men, perhaps: "Meanwhile, computers are mobbed by adolescent males as if the mouse was a pimple-cream dispenser, and the whole scene is flanked by a smattering of art critics and journalists bent on asking *what's next?* or *so what?*"—Kahn 1996: 21.) In addition, computer artists face a problem similar to that facing librarians: computer technology fast becomes out-of-date, even *unusable*. Champions of art implemented on interactive CD-ROMS point out that these are relatively permanent, like the bronzes of old (Leggett 1996). Even so, a suitable (out-of-date) CD-player must still be available.

The next paper, Chapter 11 ('Aesthetics and Interactive Art'), turns to another category defined within the taxonomy of Chapter 7: interactive art. Here, the form/content of the artwork is significantly affected by the behaviour of the audience.

Such art need not involve computers. Interactive theatre, for example, does not. Indeed, Marcel Duchamp (1957) maintained that every artwork, even the *Mona Lisa*, is part-created by the observer, because in interpreting it they "add [their] contribution to the creative act". Nevertheless, computers have hugely enriched the potential of this type of art, because they enable one to specify an indefinite variety of interactions between audience and artwork. Most of these would have been impossible, even inconceivable, without the new technology.

To give just one example, Richard Brown's *Mimetic Starfish* (briefly mentioned in Chapter 9) delighted visitors to London's Millennium Exhibition, and was even described in *The Times* as "the best thing in the Dome". This seemed to be a huge multicoloured starfish, trapped inside a near-transparent table but managing to move nevertheless.

Moreover, it moved in very lifelike ways. And it did so in response to the actions of the visitors. Mostly, these movements suggested mere cautious interest on its part, but if someone shouted at it or approached it very suddenly it would 'freeze' as though in fear. In fact, it was a coloured image projected down onto the table from the ceiling, whose changes were generated by a self-organizing neural network (built by the computer scientist Igor Alexander) that was sensitive to various aspects of the visitors' behaviour.

Computerized interactive art has raised new aesthetic questions, for the aesthetic interest is focused less on the images and/or sounds that are produced than on the (hugely diverse) nature of the interaction itself. The 'artwork', one might say, is the interaction at the heart of the entire human-computer system, not just the visible/audible results. And here, there is a good deal of disagreement.

For example, these artists differ over what degree of predictability and/or personal control will afford the greatest interest or satisfaction to the human participant. They even disagree over the extent to which, and the speed at which, the person should be able to realize that they are actually affecting what is going on.

As implied in the previous paragraph, the term "participant" seems more appropriate here than "audience". Indeed, many interactive artists, irrespective of whether they use computers, have made a point of stressing the creative role of the person who would normally be called the audience, not just of the person whom one would naturally identify as the artist. Sometimes, this attitude is explicitly justified in postmodernist terms (citing "the death of the author"), and also in terms of democracy: everyone an artist (Ascott 2003). This ideological justification invites *a fairly high degree of participant-control* as an aesthetic criterion, for if one cannot deliberately change the display in particular ways then it's not clear that one can be seen as creating it. (Causing it, yes; but that's not the same thing. Conscious monitoring, if not conscious planning, is usually involved: hence the common insistence on consciousness as a mark of "real" creativity—see above.)

The shift from audience to participant means that characterizing and attributing the creativity involved can be tricky. In general, the gallery visitor explores [*sic*], more or less imaginatively, the space of possibilities implicitly defined by the system. But those possibilities can differ in kind, as we've seen.

For instance, suppose that a visual transformation occurs. The artist must have written the program so as to allow for this, but it would not have happened unless the audience/participant had behaved in a particular way. However, the gallery visitor may have had no intention of causing a transformation, and may not even recognize it as such once it has happened. In such a case, they are a cause—but hardly a creator. Again, the system may have been set up to enable creative exploration of a particular conceptual space, but the participant may or may not actively explore it. (Stamping one's feet a couple of times hardly counts as *exploration*.)

Similarly, if combinational creativity is the name of the game there are at least two people effecting the combinations: the designer-artist and the participant-creator (of which there may be several). If the artist is highly imaginative in the combinations that he/she allows, the audience may not be. In other words, the creative potential in the artwork may be much greater than is evident from this particular audience's interactions with it.

Yet another major category defined in Chapter 7 is evolutionary art (Evo-art). Here, the artwork is evolved by processes of random variation and selective reproduction that affect the art-generating program itself.

Some computer artists employ evolutionary methods for purely pragmatic reasons. Perhaps they want to maximize unpredictability (within certain boundaries) or, as explained in Chapter 6, to try to lose their personal signature. Perhaps they simply want to save on physical effort, by switching from part-random art produced by means of paper, pencil, and dice to Evo-art generated by computer (Todd and Latham 1992: 2–5). But many artists who use evolutionary programming do so largely, even primarily, because of evolution's close connection with *life*. Much as a painted landscape may be intended as a celebration of the sublimity of Nature, so an Evo-artwork may be intended as a salutation to the wondrous phenomenon of life.

All the living organisms we know about have evolved. Indeed, evolution is often taken to be a defining feature of life. Moreover, many of the scientists who write evolutionary programs do so in the context of artificial life, or A-Life. This area of research, using computer models and mathematics, aims to define the general principles of life in abstract, functionalist, terms: "life as it could be", not just "life as we know it" (Langton 1989/1996; cf. Boden 2006: ch. 15).

A-Life is not concerned only with evolution, nor reliant only on evolutionary methods of computing. For instance, it provided the simple algorithms that underlie the realistic animations in *Jurassic Park*, wherein each dinosaur in the flock follows its own idiosyncratic path but manages both to keep up with its fellows and to avoid bumping into them. A-Life has also provided models of cell formation; of the origin of naturalistic patterns (e.g. on the fur of dalmatians, leopards, cheetahs, and giraffes) from interacting waves of chemicals; of the ever-branching structures of plants; of the autonomous development of an initially random neural network into organized 'columns' of cells like those in visual cortex; of the emergence of cooperation within groups of minimally communicative robots... and so on.

This scientific field has inspired a number of computer artists, including animators and designers of virtual reality installations. For example, A-Life's stress on *autonomy* has drawn a variety of artists towards the field (see Chapter 9). Again, many CG-artists produce images by using an A-Life methodology called "cellular automata", in which each unit in a large array behaves in a way that's determined by the current states of its close neighbours. And some of these artists choose that approach partly because of the strong analogies between cellular automata and multi-cellular organisms—analogies which they regard as adding to the *value* of their creations. In this, they resemble a jeweller who chooses to work with pearls not just because they are beautiful but also because they are natural products of living animals, or a woodcarver who favours wood not only because of its material properties (colour, vein-patterns, carveability...) but also because of the fact that it was once a living thing. Such CG-artists see the value of their work, in part, as being an encomium to life itself.

Evo-artists, in particular, have been inspired by A-Life research on evolution (Whitelaw 2004). And some of them, in turn, have been especially excited by the claims of a small coterie of maverick A-Life scientists who hope to create life in computers.

In other words, whereas some Evo-artists simply wish to generate artworks that prompt the audience to meditate on the wonders of life, others go much further. They accept the claims of (some) A-Life researchers that life could be realized, not just simulated, in a computer. Believing that virtual life—life in cyberspace—would be genuine life (and therefore intrinsically valuable), they see their own art as, potentially, a step towards achieving it. This is evident in many interviews in which they describe their aesthetic motivations (Whitelaw 2004), and in claims that they require us "to consider the power of technology to create life, rather than simply represent it" and that their audiences are confronted by "the artificial creation of life and living systems" (Tofts 2005: 103).

To put this point in another way, these artists base their work on the assumption that "strong A-Life" is possible (compare "strong AI": Searle 1980). If they are wrong in that assumption, then their artworks—however visually/aurally engaging, and even intellectually stimulating, they may be—don't have the significance which they claim for them.

One couldn't say that their art is therefore fraudulent, for their belief in the possibility of virtual life is sincere. One couldn't even say that it is inauthentic, if authenticity is primarily a matter of honesty of intent (see Chapter 10). But one could call it inauthentic in the sense of being unrealistic, or even radically flawed—being based on a philosophical premiss that is mistaken. Whether that premiss is indeed mistaken is therefore a matter of interest to aesthetics, at least as regards this small corner of the art world. Chapter 12 ('Is Metabolism Necessary?') takes up that question.

At first sight, that chapter may seem to have no place in this collection. For it doesn't mention art, nor even "creativity" as defined above. However, it concerns something significantly akin to psychological creativity: namely, biological self-organization (also discussed in Chapter 9). Here, some higher level of structural order emerges spontaneously out of an origin that's ordered to a lesser degree. (Examples include cell formation, organ development, homeostasis, flocking, evolution . . . and metabolism.) Such self-organization isn't the same as what's normally meant by creativity, for it doesn't generate *ideas/artefacts* and nor is it goal-driven—still less, consciously monitored. But it does generate phenomena that are new, surprising, and valuable. It even does so by way of biological versions of the three types of artistic creativity: genetic combination (crossover), exploration by mutation, and transformation by mutation and/or interaction with the environment (Boden, in preparation).

In discussing this close cousin of creativity, Chapter 12 also addresss the specific query raised above: *Is virtual life possible?* My argument that it isn't depends on my analysis of the concept of metabolism. (Autopoiesis, a notion often explicitly endorsed by artists influenced by A-Life, is a similar concept—but it is also interestingly different: Boden 2000.) Metabolism is a form of self-organization which, as explained in Chapter 12, is reasonably regarded as a defining feature of life. And it is irreducibly physical. It can't be understood in purely functionalist terms, but only by reference to physical energy.

Proponents of strong A-Life will rush to point out that computers consume energy, too. But merely consuming energy—as computers certainly do—isn't enough to count as metabolism in the biologist's sense. Nor is individual energy-budgeting, wherein the amount of energy held by the system is finite and must be continually replenished if functioning is to continue (again, something that can be true of computers). When the term is used to describe/explain processes in living organisms, it also denotes the self-creation and maintenance of a physical unity, by means of interlocking biochemical cycles of some *necessary* complexity.

Manufactured computers, 'feeding' on energy from a battery or a plug in the wall, don't metabolize in this sense. Since they don't metabolize, they aren't alive. The idea that Evo-art could be a first step on the road to virtual life is therefore mistaken.

It doesn't follow that all the Evo-art inspired by this fond hope is worthless. One can appreciate a Fra Angelico Annunciation, or a sculptor's Madonna or Pieta, without being a Christian, or even a theist. Possibly, one's appreciation is less full, less nuanced, and less deeply felt than if one were a believer. Certainly, an atheist can't admire these creative artworks *as* genuine intimations of the divine, but must seek other values in them. That's relatively easy, however, for there are many ways in which the content of these religious paintings (not to mention the skill of their execution) can evoke a response in non-believers. That's because most non-Christians are broadly familiar with the Christian story, and all are intimately familiar with the general human themes of maternity and mourning.

By contrast, the notion of virtual life is highly unfamiliar. To understand what this subclass of Evo-artists are up to, we need to know what 'faith' is driving them, much as we need to know the Scriptures to understand what Fra Angelico was up to. That is the third reason why Chapter 12 has a place in this collection. And perhaps it is the most important reason: after all, it is the Gospel stories themselves, not our decisions about their truth or falsehood, which are key to what the Renaissance painters were doing.

Reference to Renaissance painting brings us back full circle to the more traditional, familiar, forms of art. As we've seen, to understand how creative artworks are *possible*, we need to understand the psychological differences between the three types of creativity. (In this project, computer modelling—as opposed to computer art—is helpful: see Chapter 2.) And to see them as *creative*, we also need to appreciate their value.

This requires us to situate them within a wide—and highly controversial—range of issues. We can probably all agree that *if* something were a powerful expression of a true story about divinity then it would be valuable, even though we may differ about whether any such story is credible. And probably most of us can be persuaded to agree that a certain painter had a fine (and perhaps historically original) grasp of perspective, or colour, or light-and-shadows, or facial expressions... etc. But even figurative painters can prompt very different evaluations, especially if they go out of their way to outrage their audience. Think of the disturbing oeuvres of Francis Bacon and Jean Dubuffet, for instance: the one saw painting as "purely the challenge of delivering an instant, visceral shock", and the other recommended his canvasses as "*art brut*", or "ugly art" (Bell 2007: 416, 419).

There's even less agreement about whether abstract art, or conceptual art, or interactive art, or computer-generated art is valuable. And in all those categories, there are distinct subclasses—which need not be valued equally. The works of the ColorField painters, for instance, are extreme examples of abstract art: someone could well be enamoured of much abstractionism, but draw the line at Rothko. Similarly, someone might appreciate some of the categories defined by the taxonomy of Chapter 7 more than others.

Our values change, of course. In part, they change because people gradually come to see—and to appreciate—the links and likenesses between the novel and the familiar. Indeed, the novel eventually becomes the familiar: Bacon's screaming Pope is now as acceptable, at least to art-lovers, as its seventeenth-century model (Diego Velázquez's portrait of Innocent X). Even computer art won't remain shocking for ever, especially if it continues to invade our public spaces. Some aesthetic values (as suggested in Chapter 4) may be enduring, because they are part of our biological heritage. But many are culturally based. Some of these are rooted in aspects of culture that are normally distinguished from art: religious beliefs, scientific theories, political ascendancies, economic conditions... even high-street fashion and haute couture. And some are subject to sudden changes triggered by intrinsically trivial events in the cultural milieu (what a celebrity chooses to wear to a paparazzo-infested party, for example).

Values in general, whether enduring or not, can't be justified—even though they may sometimes be explained—in scientific terms. In that sense, and in that sense alone, both creativity and art lie for ever beyond the reach of science.

With respect to how it's possible for novel ideas to arise, however, science does have something to say. The wondrous idiosyncracies of works of art cannot be fully detailed, although they can—up to a point—be intuitively appreciated by art-lovers willing to familiarize themselves with the style, and the artist, concerned. Human minds (and cultures) are so rich that psychologists will never be able to map out every narrow track, still less every footstep, that led to an individual artist's creative idea. (That isn't science's aim, anyway—Boden 2006: 7.iii.d.) But we can now descry the main paths of possibility: the three roads to wonder and surprise.

REFERENCES

Ascott, R. (2003), *Telematic Embrace: Visionary Theories of Art, Technology, and Consciousness* (Berkeley and Los Angeles: University of California Press).

Bell, J. (2007), *Mirror of the World: A New History of Art* (London: Thames and Hudson).

Bird, J., and Layzell, P. (2002), 'The Evolved Radio and its Implications for Modelling the Evolution of Novel Sensors', *Proceedings of Congress on Evolutionary Computation*, CEC-2002, 1836–41.

Boden, M. A. (2000), 'Autopoiesis and Life', *Cognitive Science Quarterly*, 1: 1–29.

—— (2004), *The Creative Mind: Myths and Mechanisms* (2nd edn., expanded/revised, London: Routledge) (1st edn., London: Weidenfeld and Nicolson, 1990).

—— (2006), *Mind and Machine: A History of Cognitive Science* (Oxford: Clarendon/Oxford University Press).

—— (in preparation), 'Can Evolutionary Art Provide Radical Novelty?', to appear in M. A. Boden and E. A. Edmonds, *From Fingers to Digits: Art for a New Age*.

Cohen, H. (1981), *On the Modelling of Creative Behavior*, RAND Paper P-6681 (Santa Monica, Calif.: RAND Corporation).

—— (1995), 'The Further Exploits of AARON Painter', in S. Franchi and G. Guzeldere (eds.), *Constructions of the Mind: Artificial Intelligence and the Humanities*, special edn. of *Stanford Humanities Review*, 4/2: 141–60.

—— (2002), 'A Million Millennial Medicis', in L. Candy and E. Edmonds (eds.), *Explorations in Art and Technology* (London: Springer), 91–104.

Duchamp, M. (1957), 'The Creative Act', in M. Sanouillet and E. Peterson (eds.), *The Essential Writings of Marcel Duchamp* (London: Thames and Hudson, 1975), 138–40.

Edmonds, E. (2007), *Shaping Form* (Sydney: Creativity and Cognition Press).

Gibson, J. J. (1966), *The Senses Considered as Perceptual Systems* (Boston: Houghton-Mifflin).

Goodman, N. (1968), *Languages of Art: An Approach to a Theory of Symbols*, John Locke Lectures, Oxford 1962 (Indianapolis: Bobbs-Merrill).
Grau, O. (2004), *Virtual Art: From Illusion to Immersion* (Cambridge, Mass.: MIT Press).
Harrod, T. (1999), *The Crafts in Britain in the Twentieth Century* (London: Yale University Press).
Kahn, D. (1996), 'What Now the Promise?', in M. Leggett and L. Michael (eds.), *Burning the Interface: International Artists' CD-ROM, 27 March–14 July* (Sydney: Museum of Contemporary Art), 21–30.
Koning, H., and Eizenberg, J. (1981), 'The Language of the Prairie: Frank Lloyd Wright's Prairie Houses', *Environment and Planning, B*, 8: 295–323.
Langton, C. G. (1989/96), 'Artificial Life', in C. G. Langton (ed.), *Artificial Life*, the Proceedings of an Interdisciplinary Workshop on the Synthesis and Simulation of Living Systems (held September 1987) (Redwood City, Calif.: Addison-Wesley), 1–47, rev. version in M. A. Boden (ed.), *The Philosophy of Artificial Life* (Oxford: Oxford University Press, 1996), 39–94.
Leggett, M. (1996), 'CD-ROM—The 21st Century Bronze?', in M. Leggett and L. Michael (eds.), *Burning the Interface: International Artists' CD-ROM, 27 March–14 July* (Sydney: Museum of Contemporary Art), pp. 31–42.
—— (1999), 'Electronic Space and Public Space: Museums, Galleries, and Digital Media', *Continuum: Journal of Media and Cultural Studies*, 13/2: 175–186.
McLaughlin, M. L., Osborne, K. K., and Ellison, N. N. (1997), 'Virtual Community in a Telepresence Environment', in S. Jones (ed.), *Virtual Culture* (London: Sage), 146–68.
Miller, G. F. (2000), *The Mating Mind: How Sexual Choice Shaped the Evolution of Human Nature* (London: William Heinemann).
Mitchell, T. M., Caruana, R., Freitag, D., McDermott, J., and Zabowski, D. (1994), 'Experience with a Learning Personal Assistant', in D. Riecken (ed.), *Agents* (special issue of *Communications of the Association for Computing Machinery*, 37/7), 81–91.
Norman, D. A. (1994), 'How Might People Interact with Agents', in D. Riecken (ed.), *Agents* (special issue of *Communications of the Association for Computing Machinery*, 37/7), 68–71.
O'Hear, A. (1995), 'Art and Technology: An Old Tension', in R. Fellows (ed.), *Philosophy and Technology* (Cambridge: Cambridge University Press), 143–58.
Searle, J. R. (1980), 'Minds, Brains, and Programs', *Behavioral and Brain Sciences*, 3: 417–57, includes peer commentaries, and reply.
Sternberg, R. J. (ed.) (1988), *The Nature of Creativity: Contemporary Psychological Perspectives* (Cambridge: Cambridge University Press).
Sternberg, R. J. (ed.) (1999), *Handbook of Creativity* (Cambridge: Cambridge University Press).

Taylor. C. W. (1988), 'Various Approaches to and Definitions of Creativity', in Sternberg (1988: 99–124).
Todd, S. C., and Latham, W. (1992), *Evolutionary Art and Computers* (London: Academic Press).
Tofts, D. (2005), 'Artificial Nature', in D. Tofts, *Interzone: Media Arts in Australia* (Fisherman's Bend, Victoria: Craftsman House), 80–103.
Turkle, S. (1995), *Life on the Screen: Identity in the Age of the Internet* (New York: Simon & Schuster).
Wallace, J., Dearden, A., and Fisher, T. (2007), 'The Significant Other: The Value of Jewellery in the Conception, Design and Experience of Body Focussed Digital Devices', *AI & Society*, 22/1: 53–62.
Whitelaw, M. (2004), *Metacreation: Art and Artificial Life* (London: MIT Press).

2
Creativity in a Nutshell

Creativity and computers: what could these possibly have to do with one another? "Nothing!", many people would say. Creativity is a marvel of the human mind. But computers, with all due apologies to Mario, Sonic, and friends, are basically just tin cans. It follows—doesn't it?—that the two are related only by utter incompatibility.

Well, no. Computers and creativity make interesting partners with respect to two different projects. One, which interests me the most, is understanding *human* creativity. The other is trying to produce machine creativity—or anyway, machine "creativity"—in which the computer at least *appears* to be creative, to some degree.

WHAT IS CREATIVITY?

First things first. Human creativity is something of a mystery, not to say a paradox. One new idea may be creative, while another is merely new. What's the difference? And how is creativity possible? Creative ideas are unpredictable. Sometimes, they even seem to be impossible—and yet they happen. How can that be explained? Could a scientific psychology help us to understand how creativity is possible?

Creativity is the ability to come up with ideas or artefacts that are *new, surprising, and valuable*. "Ideas", here, includes concepts, poems, musical compositions, scientific theories, cooking recipes, choreography, jokes... and so on, and on. "Artefacts" include paintings, sculpture, steam engines, vacuum cleaners, pottery, origami, penny whistles... and you can name many more.

As these highly diverse examples suggest, creativity enters into virtually every aspect of life. It's not a special "faculty", but an aspect of human intelligence in general. In other words, it's grounded in everyday abilities such as conceptual thinking, perception, memory, and reflective self-criticism. So it isn't confined to a tiny elite: every one of us is creative, to a degree.

Nor is it an all-or-none affair. Rather than asking "Is that idea creative, Yes or No?", we should ask "Just how creative is it, and in just which way(s)?" Asking that question will help us to appreciate the subtleties of the idea itself, and also to get a sense of just what sorts of psychological process could have brought it to mind in the first place.

Creative ideas, then, are new. But of course, there's new—and there's *new*. Ask a teacher, for instance. Children can come up with ideas that are new *to them*, even though they may have been in the textbooks for years. Someone who comes up with a bright idea is not necessarily less creative just because someone else had it before them. Indeed, if the person who had it first was Shakespeare, or Euclid, we'd think even more highly of the achievement.

Suppose a 12-year-old girl, who'd never read *Macbeth*, compared the healing power of sleep with someone knitting up a ravelled sleeve. Would you refuse to say she was creative, just because the Bard said it first? Perhaps, if you'd been talking around the topic with her, encouraging her to come up with non-literal ways of speaking, and even putting one or more of the three key ideas into the conversation. Otherwise, you'd have to acknowledge her remark as a truly imaginative one.

What you might do, and what I think you should do in this situation, is to make a distinction between "psychological" creativity and "historical" creativity. (P-creativity and H-creativity, for short.) P-creativity involves coming up with a surprising, valuable idea that's new *to the person who comes up with it*. It doesn't matter how many people have had that idea before. But if a new idea is H-creative, that means that (so far as we know) no one else has had it before: it has arisen for the first time in human history.

Clearly, H-creativity is a special case of P-creativity. For historians of art, science, and technology—and for encyclopaedia users, too—H-creativity is what's important. And in daily life, we appreciate it too: it really isn't true that "The old jokes are the best ones". But for someone who is trying to understand the *psychology* of creativity, it's P-creativity that's crucial. Never mind who thought of the idea first: how did *that* person manage to come up with it, given that *they* had never thought of it before?

If "new", in this context, has two importantly different meanings, "surprising" has three.

An idea may be surprising because it's unfamiliar, or even unlikely—like a 100-to-1 outsider winning the Derby. This sort of surprise goes against statistics.

The second sort of surprise is more interesting. An unexpected idea may "fit" into a style of thinking that you already had—but you're surprised because you hadn't realized that this particular idea was part of it. Maybe you're even intrigued to find that an idea *of this general type* fits into the familiar style.

And the third sort of surprise is more interesting still: this is the astonishment you feel on encountering an apparently *impossible* idea. It just *couldn't* have entered anyone's head, you feel—and yet it did. It may even engender other ideas which, yesterday, you'd have thought equally impossible. What on earth can be going on?

THE THREE WAYS OF CREATIVITY

"What is going on" isn't magic—and it's different in each type of case. For creativity can happen in three main ways, which correspond to the three sorts of surprise.

The first involves making unfamiliar combinations of familiar ideas. Examples include poetic imagery, collage in painting or textile art, and analogies. These new combinations can be generated either deliberately or, often, unconsciously. Think of a physicist comparing an atom to the solar system, for instance, or a journalist comparing a politician with a decidedly non-cuddly animal. Or call to mind some examples of creative associations in poetry or visual art.

In all these cases, making—and also appreciating—the novel combination requires a rich store of knowledge in the person's mind, and many different ways of moving around within it.

The journalist or newspaper-reader needs a host of concepts about both politics and animal behaviour, and some "personal" knowledge about the individual politician in question. Cartoonists who depict Ken Livingstone (the first publicly elected Mayor of London) as a newt are tapping into many different conceptual streams, including gossip about what he keeps in an aquarium in his home. The surprise you feel on looking at the cartoon is largely caused by seeing a human figure with a newt's crest and tail: a combination of ideas that's even less probable than the outsider winning the Derby.

If the novel combination is to be valued by us, it has to have some point. It may or (more usually) may not have been caused by some random process—like shaking marbles in a bag. But the ideas/marbles have to have some intelligible conceptual pathway between them for the combination to "make sense". The newt-human makes sense for many reasons, one of which is Ken's famed predilection for newts. (What are some of the others?) And (to return to the example from *Macbeth*) sleep is a healer, as knitting can be. Even if two ideas are put together randomly in the first place, which I suspect happens only rarely, they are retained/valued only if some such links can be found.

The other two types of creativity are interestingly different from the first. They involve the *exploration*, and in the most surprising cases the *transformation*, of conceptual spaces in people's minds.

EXPLORING CONCEPTUAL SPACES

Conceptual spaces are structured styles of thought. They're normally picked up from one's own culture or peer group, but are occasionally borrowed from other cultures. In either case, they're already there: they aren't originated by one individual mind. They include ways of writing prose or poetry; styles of sculpture, painting, or music; theories in chemistry or biology; fashions of couture or choreography, nouvelle cuisine and good old meat-and-two-veg... in short, any disciplined way of thinking that's familiar to (and valued by) a certain social group.

Within a given conceptual space, many thoughts are possible, only some of which may have been actually thought. Some spaces, of course, have a richer potential than others. Noughts and crosses is such a restricted style of game-playing that every possible move has already been made countless times. But that's not true of chess, where the number of possible moves, though finite, is astronomically large. And if some sub-areas of chemistry have been exhausted (every possible molecule of that type having been identified), the space of possible limericks, or sonnets, has not—and never will be.

Whatever the size of the space, someone who comes up with a new idea within that thinking style is being creative in the second, exploratory, sense. If the new idea is surprising not just in itself but as

Creativity in a Nutshell 33

an example of an unexpected general *type*, so much the better. And if it leads on to others (still within the same space) whose possibility was previously unsuspected, better still. Exploratory creativity is valuable because it can enable someone to see possibilities they hadn't glimpsed before. They may even start to ask *just what* limits, and *just what* potential, this style of thinking has.

We can compare this with driving into the country, with an Ordnance Survey map that you consult occasionally. You can keep to the motorways, and only look at the thick red lines on your map. But suppose, for some reason (a police diversion, or a call of nature), you drive off onto a smaller road. When you set out, you didn't even know it existed. But of course, if you unfold the map you'll see it marked there. And perhaps you ask yourself "I wonder what's round that corner?", and drive round it to find out. Maybe you come to a pretty village, or a council estate; or perhaps you end up in a cul-de-sac, or back on the motorway you came off in the first place. All these things were always possible (and they're all represented on the map). But you'd never noticed them before—and you wouldn't have done so now, if you hadn't got into an exploratory frame of mind.

In exploratory creativity, the "countryside" is a style of thinking. Instead of exploring a structured geographical space, you explore a structured conceptual space, mapped by a particular style of painting, perhaps, or a specific area of theoretical chemistry.

All professional artists and scientists do this sort of thing. Even the most mundane street artists in Leicester Square produce new portraits, or new caricatures, every day. They are exploring their space, though not necessarily in an adventurous way. Occasionally, they may realize that their sketching style enables them to do something (convey the set of the head, or the hint of a smile) better than they'd been doing before. They add a new trick to their repertoire, but in a real sense it's something that "fits" their established style: the potential was always there.

TRANSFORMING THE SPACE

What the street artist may also do is realize the *limitations* of their style. Then, they have an opportunity which the Sunday driver does not. Give or take a few years, and ignoring earthquake and flood, the country roads are fixed. Certainly, *you* can't change them. Your Ordnance

Survey map is reliable not only because it's right, but because it stays right. (Have you bothered to buy a new book of road maps within the last few years?) But the maps inside our heads, and favoured by our communities, can change—and it's creative thinking which changes them.

Some changes are relatively small and also relatively superficial. (Ask yourself: what's the difference?) The limits of the mental map, or of some particular aspect of it, are slightly pushed, slightly altered, gently tweaked. Compare the situation in geographical space: suppose everyone in that pretty village suddenly added a roof extension to their cottage. It may ruin the prettiness of the village, but it won't change the dimensions of the map. At most, the little "portrait" of the village (assuming that it's *that* sort of map) will have to be redrawn.

The street artist, then—or Picasso, in a similar position—has an opportunity. In principle, he (or, as always, she) could do the psychological equivalent of adding roof extensions, or building a new road (a new technique, leading to new possibilities), or even rerouting the motorway.

Rerouting the motorway (in "real life" as in the mind) is the most difficult of all. The surprises that would engender could be so great as to make the driver lose his bearings. He may wonder if he's been magically transported to a different county, or even a different country. Maybe he remembers a frustrating episode on his last trip, when he wanted to do something but his passenger scornfully said: "In England, motorways are like *this*: they simply don't allow you to do *that*. You want to do it? Tough! It's impossible."

A given style of thinking, no less than a road system, can render certain thoughts impossible—which is to say, unthinkable. The difference, as remarked above, is that thinking styles can be changed—sometimes, in the twinkling of an eye.

Someone skilfully writing a limerick won't find iambic pentameters dropping from their pen. But if you want to write a new sort of limerick, or a non-limerick somehow grounded in that familiar style, then maybe blank verse could play a role. The deepest cases of creativity involve someone's thinking something which, with respect to the conceptual spaces in their minds, they *couldn't* have thought before. The supposedly impossible idea can come about only if the creator changes the pre-existing style in some way. It must be tweaked, or even radically transformed, so that thoughts are now possible which previously (within the untransformed space) were literally inconceivable—But how can that possibly happen?

MACHINE-MAPS OF THE MIND

To understand how exploratory or transformational creativity can happen, we must know what conceptual spaces are, and what sorts of mental processes could explore and modify them.

Styles of thinking are studied by literary critics, musicologists, and historians of art, fashion, and science. And they are appreciated by us all. But intuitive appreciation, and even lifelong scholarship, may not make their structure clear. (An architectural historian, for instance, said of Frank Lloyd Wright's Prairie Houses that their "principle of unity" is "occult".)

This is the first point where computers are relevant. Conceptual spaces, and ways of exploring and transforming them, can be described by concepts drawn from artificial intelligence (AI).

AI-concepts enable us to do psychology in a new way, by allowing us to construct (and test) hypotheses about the structures and processes that may be involved in thought. For instance, the structure of tonal harmony, or the "grammar" of Prairie Houses, can be clearly expressed, and specific ways of exploring the space can be tried out. Methods for navigating, and changing, highly structured spaces can be compared.

Of course, there is always the additional question of whether the suggested structures and processes are actually implemented in human heads. And that question isn't always easy to answer. But the point, here, is that a computational approach gives us a way of coming up with scientific hypotheses about the rich subtleties of the human mind.

COMPUTER CREATIVITY?

What of the second link between machines and creativity? Can computers be creative? Or rather, can they at least appear to be creative?

Many people would argue that no computer could possibly be genuinely creative, *no matter what* its performance was like. Even if it far surpassed the humdrum scientist or street artist, it would not be counted as creative. It might produce theories as groundbreaking as Einstein's, or music as highly valued as McCartney's "Yesterday" or even Beethoven's Ninth... but still, for these people, it wouldn't *really* be creative.

Several different arguments are commonly used in support of that conclusion. For instance: it's the programmer's creativity that's at work here, not the machine's. The machine isn't conscious, and has no desires, preferences, or values—so it can't appreciate or judge what it's doing. A work of art is an expression of human experience and/or a commmunication between human beings, so machines simply don't count.

Perhaps you accept at least one of those reasons for denying creativity to computers? Very well, I won't argue with you here (but see Boden 2004: ch. 11). Let's assume, for the purpose of this discussion, that computers can't really be creative. The important point is that this *doesn't* mean that there's nothing more of interest to say.

All the objections just listed accept, for the sake of argument, that the imaginary computer's performance is indeed very like that of human beings, whether humdrum or not. What I want to focus on here is *whether it's true* that computers could, in fact, come up with ideas that at least *appear* to be creative.

COMPUTER COMBINATIONS

Well, think of combinational creativity first. In one sense, this is easy to model on a computer. For nothing is simpler than picking out two ideas (two data structures) and putting them alongside each other. This can even be done with some subtlety, using connectionist methods (outlined in Boden 2004: ch. 6). In short: a computer could merrily produce novel combinations till Kingdom come.

But would they be of any interest? We saw, above, that combining ideas creatively isn't like shaking marbles in a bag. The marbles have to come together because there is some intelligible, though previously unnoticed, link between them which we value because it is interesting—illuminating, thought-provoking, humorous...—in some way. (Think sleep and knitting, again.) We saw also that combinational creativity typically requires a very rich store of knowledge, of many different kinds, and the ability to form links of many different types. (Here, think politicians and newts again.)

And we don't only form links, we evaluate them. For instance, we can recognize that a joke is "in bad taste". In other words: yes, the links that the joker is suggesting are actually there (so it is a real joke). But there are other links there also, which connect the ideas with sorrow, humiliation, or tragedy. The joker should have noticed them, and should have refrained from reminding us of them.

For a computer to make a subtle combinational joke, never mind to assess its tastefulness, would require (1) a database with a richness comparable to ours, and (2) methods of link making (and link evaluating) comparable in subtlety with ours. In principle, this isn't impossible. After all, the human mind/brain doesn't do it by magic. But don't hold your breath!

The best example of computer-based combinational creativity so far is a program called JAPE, which makes punning jokes of a general type that's familiar to every 8-year-old (see Boden 2004: ch. 12). But making a one-off jest is usually more demanding. Ask yourself, for instance, what Jane Austen had to know in order to write the opening sentence of *Pride and Prejudice*: "It is a truth universally acknowledged that a single man in possession of a good fortune must be in want of a wife." (And why, exactly, is it funny?)

ARTIFICIAL EXPLORERS AND SELF-TRANSFORMING MACHINES

What about exploratory creativity? Several programs already exist which can explore a given space in acceptable ways.

One example is AARON, a drawing program described in Boden (2004: ch. 7). AARON can generate thousands of line drawings in a certain style, pleasing enough to be spontaneously remarked upon by unsuspecting visitors—and to be exhibited in galleries worldwide, including the Tate. (The most recent version of AARON is able to paint its drawings, too: see Boden 2004: ch. 12.)

Another is David Cope's 'Emmy', (discussed in Boden 2004: ch. 12). This composes music in many different styles, reminiscent of specific human composers such as Bach, Vivaldi, Mozart . . . and Stravinsky.

Still others include architectural programs that design Palladian villas or Prairie Houses (also mentioned in Boden 2004: ch. 12), and programs that can analyse experimental data and find new ways of expressing scientific laws (Boden 2004: ch. 8).

A few AI-programs can even transform their conceptual space, by altering their own rules, so that interesting ideas result. Some of these ideas were already known to human beings, though not specifically prefigured within the program. (See the discussion of the automatic mathematician, AM, in Boden 2004: ch. 8.) But others are first-time-fresh. "Evolutionary" programs, for instance, can make random changes in their current rules so that new forms of structure result. At each generation, the "best" structures are selected, and used to breed the next generation.

Two examples that evolve coloured images (some of which, like AARON's, are exhibited in galleries worldwide) are described in Boden (2004: ch. 12). In each case, the selection of the "fittest" at each generation is done by a human being, who picks out the most aesthetically pleasing patterns. In short, these are interactive graphics environments, in which human and computer can cooperate in generating otherwise unimaginable images. These computer-generated images often cause the third, deepest, form of surprise—almost as if a coin being tossed repeatedly were suddenly to show a wholly unexpected design. In such cases, one can't see the relation between the daughter image and its parent. The one appears to be a radical transformation of the other, or even something entirely different.

Anyone who has watched TV regularly over the past few years, or who has visited museums of contemporary art, will already know that many novel graphic images have been produced by self-transforming AI-programs of this kind. The problem is not to make the transformations: that is relatively easy. What's difficult is to state our aesthetic values clearly enough to enable the program itself to make the evaluation at each generation. At present, the "natural selection" is done by a human being (for example, the gallery visitor).

In more well-regulated domains, however, the value criteria can often be stated clearly enough to allow the evolutionary program to apply them automatically. An early example, a program for locating leaks in oil pipelines, is mentioned in Boden (2004: ch. 8). Now, scientists are starting to use these techniques to enhance their own creativity. Biochemical laboratories in universities and pharmaceutical companies are using evolutionary programs to help design new molecules for use in basic research and/or medicine. Even the "brains" and "bodies" of robots can now be evolved, instead of being designed (see Boden 2004: ch. 12).

VALUES AND CREATIVITY

One huge problem here has no special relevance to computers, but bedevils discussion of human creativity too.

I said earlier that "new" has two meanings, and that "surprising" has three. I didn't say how many meanings "valuable" has—and nobody could. Our aesthetic values are difficult to recognize, more difficult to put into words, and even more difficult to state really clearly. (For a computer model, of course, they have to be stated really, *really* clearly.)

Moreover, they change: who will proudly admit, today, to having worn a beehive hairdo or flared trousers in the 1960s? They vary across cultures. And even within a given "culture", they are often disputed: different subcultures or peer groups value different types of dress, jewellery, or music. And where transformational creativity is concerned, the shock of the new may be so great that even fellow artists find it difficult to see value in the novel idea.

Even in science, values are often elusive and sometimes changeable. Just what "simplicity" or "elegance" mean, as applied to scientific theories, is something that philosophers of science have long tried—and failed—to pin down precisely. And whether a scientific finding or hypothesis is "interesting" depends on the other theories current at the time, and on social questions too (might it have some medical value, for instance?).

Because creativity *by definition* involves not only novelty but value, and because values are highly variable, it follows that many arguments about creativity are rooted in disagreements about value. This applies to human activities no less than to computer performance. So *even if* we could identify and program our aesthetic values, so as to enable the computer to inform and monitor its own activities accordingly, there would still be disagreement about whether the computer even *appeared* to be creative.

The answer to our opening question, then, is that there are many intriguing relations between creativity and computers. Computers can come up with new ideas, and help people to do so. Both their failures and their successes help us think more clearly about our own creative powers.

FURTHER READING:

Boden, M. A. (2004), *The Creative Mind: Myths and Mechanisms* (2nd edn., revised/expanded, London: Routledge).

3
Are Autodidacts Creative?

How nice it would be to be able to answer the question "Are autodidacts creative?" with a simple "Yes" or "No"—or even a judicious "Some are, some aren't." We could all go home happy, and concentrate on other things.

But it's not so straightforward. The reason is that both crucial terms cover significantly different cases. In principle, one could compose a many-dimensional "matrix" of all the combinations, wherein each one was marked "Yes" or "No" (or more likely, "Probably" or "Probably not"). But without somehow distinguishing the various subclasses of both concepts, one simply cannot answer the question.

Or rather, one can—but not in an especially informative way. One might answer "Yes", on the grounds that all normal human adults are creative, therefore all autodidacts are creative. In other words, creativity is not a special talent possessed only by a fortunate elite. On the contrary, it is an unavoidable aspect of normal intelligence, and rests on psychological processes—such as perception, reminding, recognition, and associative memory—that are the essential basis of our everyday thinking (Perkins 1981). This answer is certainly worth giving if any reader thinks that creativity is a special faculty (a Romantic belief that has horrendous educational implications). But otherwise, it doesn't get us very far.

First, then, let's consider the different types of creativity. There are three, the last two of which are closely related: "combinational", "exploratory", and "transformational" creativity (Boden 1990, 1994). In general, a creative idea or artefact is one that is novel, surprising, and valuable. The three types of creativity differ in the psychological processes involved in generating the novel ideas—and, for that matter, in understanding or appreciating them once they have arisen.

"Novelty", here, may be understood psychologically or historically—defining P-creativity and H-creativity respectively. (Each of these exists in all three forms: combinational, exploratory, and transformational.) P-creativity is the ability to generate ideas that are new *with respect to the mind of the individual concerned.* H-creativity is the ability to generate ideas that are, so far as is known, novel *with respect to the whole of human history.* Clearly, H-creativity is a special case of P-creativity. People sometimes restrict the term "creative" to the historical sense. But that's not helpful here, for we want to know *both* whether autodidacts are likely to be more P-creative than other people *and*, if so, whether they are also likely to be more H-creative. (As we'll see, high P-creativity needn't go along with high H-creativity.)

Combinational creativity involves making unfamiliar connections between familiar ideas. Comparing one's lover to a summer's day is one example, comparing the atom to a solar system is another. (And putting an unmade bed into an art exhibition is yet another.) Most psychologists who study creativity focus on this type. But there are two more, which are related in that they both arise out of some accepted style of thinking, or structured conceptual space. These conceptual spaces include styles of dance, painting, cookery, chemistry, mathematics, carving... in short, any culturally recognized way of doing things in a particular domain of activity.

In exploratory creativity, the space is explored: the person (artist, scientist, cook, choreographer...) asks what ideas/artefacts can and cannot be reached within the space, what are the limits of the space—and maybe how the space could be expanded by being superficially "tweaked". For example, the basic ingredient of ice cream can be altered: will water, or yoghourt, do as well as cream? Or one can tweak by addition: perhaps putting nuts on top of the finished ice cream, or adding them while it's being made. The first nutty ice cream (in both senses) was a pleasant surprise, even a lasting contribution to the gaiety of nations. It may have made a good living for the inventor. But it wasn't a radical change, for either intellect or eaters.

It's important to realize that exploratory creativity can generate surprising and valuable novelties even *without* tweaking. The reason is that we're typically unaware of all the possibilities within a reasonably complex conceptual space. It took over a century to exhaust the space of aromatic molecules in chemistry, and the space of possible sonatas—even if restricted to a particular composer's style—is infinite. The possible chess games are finite, but the number is so astronomical that for all practial purposes it's infinite. This is why chess will always offer surprises. (Noughts and crosses, no: the space is so tiny that only beginners can be surprised.)

Most artists, musicians, and scientists earn their living by relying on exploratory creativity. Many of their new ideas are novel to everyone, not only to themselves. (No one would employ a workaday research chemist to tell them textbook facts, nor pay a dress designer or songwriter who never came up with anything new.) That is, ideas produced by exploratory creativity can be *historically* new; when they are, they are (by definition) examples of H-creativity. But immediately the H-novel idea is generated, people familiar with the style can see that, in a sense, it was there all along. The relevant rules of thinking had already defined a place for it in the conceptual space concerned. It just so happened that Jo Bloggs was the first person ever to reach that particular point. Good for Jo Bloggs! But although this form of H-creativity may earn him a living wage, it won't earn him a place in the history books.

Transformational creativity, on the other hand, might. For most examples of creativity recorded in the history books are transformational ones. (Most, but not all: poets, in particular, are remembered largely because of their exceptional ability to generate H-novel ideas by combinational creativity.) Here, the "tweaking" of one or more boundaries (rules) of the space is more radical, more daring—and more surprising.

Specifically, transformational creativity enables ideas to be generated which, with respect to the previously accepted style of thinking, simply *could not* have arisen before. (Compare exploratory creativity: Jo Bloggs discovered the new idea on Tuesday, but John Doe might well have discovered it on Monday; after all, it was already potentially "there".) Some dimension of the pre-existing space is not just slightly tweaked, but radically transformed—inverted, for example. So for a chef to try freezing milk instead of heating it is to do something radically different—and histories of cooking celebrate the people who did this first.

Cooking is a relatively easy case, not in the sense that it's any easier to have a "new" idea, but in the sense that it's relatively easy to evaluate the previously impossible result once it's there. Admittedly, different cultures have different culinary tastes. But within a certain culture, and given our shared human physiology, it's fairly easy to be sure that a goodly number of people will—or won't—savour the new concoction. It's more difficult to evaluate a new theory in chemistry or palaeontology: it took years of argument and experiment—not to mention personal and nationalist rivalries—to replace phlogiston by oxygen, and to decide who "discovered" dinosaurs (Schaffer 1994). And it's even more difficult to be sure of one's ground in art. Even within one country, the accepted styles and criteria of art can shift with the century, or even the decade. But, difficult or not, evaluation is crucial: creative ideas were defined (above) as being not only novel, but *valuable*.

It's all very well for someone to come up with new ideas, but these must be recognized as valuable if they are to be called creative. We all know of famous cases where virtually no one but the individual concerned found the novelty valuable at the time. There are even cases where the creator himself didn't do so (Kepler, on first thinking that planetary orbits might be non-circular, dismissed this idea as "a cartload of dung" (Koestler 1975)). But such cases are necessarily rare, because someone who was virtually incapable of judging the worth (or worthlessness) of their own new ideas *wouldn't normally be regarded as creative*. To be sure, they might be a useful member of a creative team, where the evaluative judgements were made by other team members. Even so, they'd probably lead their colleagues to waste a lot of time.

What has all this got to do with autodidacts? Well, it shows us that there can be no straightforward "Yes or No" answer to the question whether autodidacts are creative. For we must ask whether *this* type of creativity, or *that* one, is more likely in autodidacts.

What's more, if there are several different types of autodidact, then the very same queries must be raised about each of them. It might turn out that a certain kind of self-taught person was likely to show a relatively high—or low—degree of one kind of creativity, but not of the others. In general, this will depend on two things: (1) whether any of the three relevant kinds of psychological process is more likely in (some type of) autodidacts than in other people, and (2) whether the necessary mental resources (scattered ideas and/or structured conceptual spaces) are more likely to be available.

As for the types of autodidact, the discussions in Solomon 2003 indicate how many, and various, these are. For instance, one can distinguish what I'll call the "unschooled" and "defiant" groups.

Unschooled autodidacts never had the opportunity of formal education. Maybe their society simply didn't provide it, except perhaps to a favoured few. Or maybe their place—class, caste, gender, income, urban/rural location... —in that society made it unavailable *to them*. Or maybe ill health (their own and/or their parents') prevented them from getting the education that they'd have had otherwise. Probably, these different reasons for their lack of schooling tend to have different psychological effects. And certainly, there will be variations in the extent to which their elders made an effort to educate them *informally*, in a more or less diverse range of skills. Strictly, one should bear these differences carefully in mind when considering individual life histories. For present purposes, however, I'll (crudely) ignore them, and speak of unschooled autodidacts as though they were a single group.

These people may have a relatively high degree of self-confidence and determination, which they will need to educate themselves without the support (*pace* Ivan Illich 1971) or stimulus of school. Otherwise, because their lack of education was independent of their wishes, they will be a normal cross-section of their community, in terms of intelligence and adventurousness.

Defiant autodidacts, by contrast, have (for varying psychological reasons) a distrust of and resistance to authority of any sort. They may undergo many years of formal education, but they respond to it in highly non-receptive ways. At the extreme, they switch off, opt out, and turn their attention to unrelated pursuits—in which case, they may come close to being "unschooled" in the sense defined above. But if they stay in school, and pay attention at least sometimes (perhaps to only one subject), they are likely to use their intelligence so as deliberately to transgress accepted ways of thinking. Similarly, in later life they will challenge or ignore the accepted canons and conventions of their chosen occupation.

A subclass of these (let's call them "diverse defiants") will deliberately foster interests in non-school, unfashionable, and perhaps even disreputable subject domains—such as (in twenty-first-century Britain) pigeon-fancying, archery, computer games, or internet pornography. They may put just as much effort and self-discipline, and even reading time, into studying their chosen area(s) as the most demanding schoolteacher could wish. By all the usual standards of the accepted academic curriculum, however, their schoolwork may be a disaster.

Because combinational creativity is the least constrained of the three types, lack of education is no great barrier. To be sure, a person who has encountered relatively more and/or diverse ideas is in a better position to come up with unfamiliar combinations. So one might infer that an unschooled autodidact will be less capable of combinational creativity. But this doesn't follow. If their out-of-school experience has been comparably rich, then they can freely combine ideas just as everyone else can. The results will differ in content (someone with no education simply couldn't write the multiply allusive poem *The Waste Land*). But they need not be inferior in creativity—or in value, unless one values classical allusion above every other aspect of poetry. Indeed, one could say that the unschooled autodidact has an advantage, precisely because their novel combinations are likely to be relatively unexpected, so valued more highly.

Diverse defiants, too, are in a good position here. Since they have made themselves expert in one or more unusual areas, their experience is wider than—or anyway, different from—that of their peers. Someone who knows about the practice and history of archery is equipped to generate certain unfamilar combinations that just aren't possible for the rest of us. The more deviant, and the more diverse, their interests, the more this is so. Educated people may be just as adventurous in their combinational processing, but they use more conventional idea banks as their resources.

Exploratory creativity is more problematic for autodidacts. Specifically, it depends on how easy it is, given the person's life situation, to pick up the relevant styles of thinking. This involves both accessibility and motivation. Even Mozart (who was not an autodidact, but assiduously taught by his father) took a good twelve years of unrelenting effort to master the music of the day well enough to do something creative with it, as opposed to something merely competent. In general, it takes self-discipline to master a discipline. And some disciplines are accessible only through certain routes, which may be all but inaccessible outside the usual educational institutions. Modern chemistry, for instance, can't be done creatively with a chemistry set in one's back bedroom. Whereas William Perkin could discover the first aniline dyes in his study, using a few chemical crocks he'd brought home from his university laboratory (Garfield 2000), the next breakthrough in chemical dyes is most unlikely to be made by exploring chemical space in that way.

Moreover, the space of chemistry changes, and changes fast. A friend of mine, a potter, had an unschooled father. Having heard her mention chemistry as being important for glazes, he bought a textbook of chemistry on a market stall, and put hours of effort into reading it. On her next visit "home", he proudly said he'd like to discuss chemistry with her—only to regale her with talk about phlogiston. This is a true story, as well as a sad one. Her father not only didn't know that phlogiston was passé, but he also didn't know that any chemistry textbook published long ago was likely to be unreliable.

Today, a few such changes in chemical space hit the headlines, occasionally even featuring in the tabloids. Buckyballs, for instance, were so strange—and, in essence, so readily intelligible—that they were widely featured in the media. But other changes are reported only in the specialist journals and, sometimes, magazines of popular science. The autodidact, by definition, is not part of the commonly accepted scientific network. If he manages to break into the network, he'll very likely be ignored or disparaged. (Yet more likely, if he is a she.) Even highly educated professional people may experience this sort of rejection, if they try to discuss ("meddle with"?) issues relating to a different discipline. In short, autodidacts of any sort will find it very difficult, even impossible, to access the conceptual spaces of modern science, and to learn their way around them.

If someone cannot access or explore these culturally given spaces, then they cannot fruitfully transform them either. For this requires both appreciating the limits of the old space and evaluating the (still unexplored) potential of the new one. These are subtle judgements, requiring years of work (and, usually, of discussion with one's peers) behind them. Nor can the "novice" rely on the cognoscenti to make these evaluations on their behalf. For suppose that an imaginative autodidact had said "Perhaps carbon atoms can join up into hollow balls?" The only people who might have listened to him would have been those (few) experts with the confidence and imagination to consider such an idea seriously—which is to say, exceptionally creative individuals highly educated in chemistry, like Sir Harry Kroto himself.

The reference to confidence, here, raises a further way in which distinct types of autodidact are differently placed. The deviant autodidact is, by definition, rebellious. Such people have the self-assurance and the courage (two different things), not to mention the motivation, required to swim against the cultural stream. They are relatively unlikely to be discouraged by others' disapproval, for they meet it—maybe even savour it—every day. If they come up with a novel idea, which they think is valuable, they will be less put off by indifference, or even criticism, from the accepted experts. By contrast, unschooled autodidacts may retain a lifelong sense of inferiority and diffidence, especially if they have internalized any negative cultural expectations of their entire class, caste, or gender. It will be much easier for critics to take the wind out of their creative sails.

I've made two potentially misleading simplifications so far. First, I've mentioned only two broad types of autodidact, even though I've also hinted at further psychological diversities that should not be ignored. And second, I've tacitly implied that the different types of creativity are never conjoined.

In defining the three forms of creativity, I was making analytical distinctions between psychological processes that are different in principle. In practice, something normally regarded as a "single" case of creativity may involve more than one of these types. T. S. Eliot's *The Waste Land*, for example, is not only a glorious profusion of combinational creativity, full of unexpected mythical and literary allusions, including private jokes accessible only to those who share his own classical education. It also explores [sic] a new poetic form, Eliot having transformed [sic] some of the existing conventions of poetry to make a new poem possible which simply could not have been written in the pre-transformational days. So one shouldn't assume that every example of "creativity", "originality", or "imagination" can be neatly slotted into one, and only one, of the three categories. Human thinking, whether in autodidacts or anyone else, is often much richer than that. That is just one of many reasons why one shouldn't ask "Is this idea creative, *Yes* or *No*?," but rather "Is it creative in any respect(s)—and if so, *which* and *how*?"

In sum, one may be able to decide whether the fresh thinking and originality of a particular self-educated person is *relatively* strong (or weak) in one type of creativity rather than another. One may be able to do this for psychologically distinct groups of autodidact. And one may even be able to explain why one such group comes up trumps, or falls down, on one sort of creativity rather than another. But to claim that autodidacts in general are—or are not—more "creative" than the rest of us is to be guilty of sloppy thinking. We need to look at things much more closely.

REFERENCES

Boden, M. A. (1990) *The Creative Mind: Myths and Mechanisms* (London: Abacus).

—— (1994) "What Is Creativity?", in M. A. Boden (ed.), *Dimensions of Creativity* (Cambridge, Mass.: MIT Press), 75–119.

Garfield, S. (2000) *Mauve: How One Man Invented a Colour that Changed the World* (London: Faber & Faber).

Illich, I. (1971) *Deschooling Society* (New York: Harper & Row).

References

Koestler, A. (1975) *The Act of Creation* (London: Picador). (1st pub., 1964).
Perkins, D. N. (1981) *The Mind's Best Work* (Cambridge, Mass.: Harvard University Press).
Schaffer, S. (1994) "Making Up Discovery", in M. A. Boden (ed.), *Dimensions of Creativity* (Cambridge, Mass.: MIT Press), 13–52.

4

Crafts, Perception, and the Possibilities of the Body

I. INTRODUCTION

The distinction between "art" and "craft" carries a huge accumulation of intellectual baggage, and a long history of philosophical controversy. It also bears, at least in our culture, a number of sociological differences. Practitioners of art and of craft tend to belong to distinct professional groups, and many journals firmly associate themselves with only one of these activities (there are some exceptions, such as the magazine *Art and Craft*). Moreover, their activities differ appreciably in terms of social status and economic reward. Various types of snobbery, rivalry, and defensiveness attend the ascription of these terms, accordingly.

Among the distinguishing criteria that have been suggested—and contested—are: That craftworks must be functional, whereas fine art need not, even should not, have any practical use. That craftworkers should employ the "right" methods of making, often understood as traditional skills, and produce the "right" sort of artefact (a perfect pot, or spoon), whereas artists should set their own aesthetic standards. That craftsmen produce "the same piece of work, made over and over again" (this, from Diderot's *Encyclopédie*), whereas art thrives on novelty and surprise. That craftsmen focus on the execution and perfection of their skills, while artists stress the celebration or exploration of their ideas. And that craftworkers are (or anyway should be) content with anonymous, if respected, mastery rather than—like artists—aiming for the individual limelight. (The heroic notion of the artist has its roots

---

This paper is based on a shorter version given at a meeting on "The Body Politic: The Role of the Body in Contemporary Crafts" at the University of Northumbria, September 1999. The meeting was sponsored by the Crafts Council and by Northern Arts. I am grateful to Terry Diffey and Michael Wheeler for helpful comments on the draft.

in humanism and, especially, Romanticism; it would not have occurred to a medieval icon painter, for instance. One might say that, prior to humanism, there were no artists, only craftsmen.) In addition, many people—following Ruskin and Morris—insist that craftworks must be made by hand and not by machine, and a fortiori that they must not be mass-produced.

These historical references remind us that the notion of craftwork is not static, but evolving. The Arts and Crafts movement of the late nineteenth century was a pivotal moment in this continual sequence of definitions, especially in Britain. But it has been followed by many others. Indeed, a recent historian of British craft refuses to offer a definition of the term. Instead, she refers to its "shifting identity", and points out that this depends largely on craftsmen's wish to situate their activities in relation to a wide (and ever-changing) range of cultural movements (Harrod 1999: 10).

Cultural changes can also affect the interpretation of individual criteria. Consider the notion of the "handmade", for instance. Ruskin and Morris approved the handmade as part of their protest against the rise of industrialism and factory technology. A hundred years later, the handmade is lauded by some computer technologists, on the grounds that "the hands are the best source of tacit personal knowledge because of all extensions of the body, they are the most subtle, the most sensitive, the most probing, the most differentiated, and the most closely connected to the mind" (McCullough 1998: 7). Thus far, the Brotherhood would presumably agree. But this enthusiast for "digital craft" (the ambiguity is deliberate) speaks of "the seeming paradox of intangible craft" (p. 22), situating craft in virtual worlds as well as the real one. Far from rejecting technology, he stresses the creative potential of a partnership between the skilled human and the computer. Whereas a sewing machine (for example) enables one to do things more effectively than could in principle be done with mere needle and thread, a computer often enables one to do things that would be inconceivable without it. Such considerations, among others, remind us that the meaning of "handmade" is problematic.

Quite apart from such ambiguities in defining the various criteria, none of the suggested definitions gives us a clear-cut distinction. Consider functionality, for instance. Some objects classed as artworks are functional: think of a Bernini fountain (which serves a highly practical function), or a portrait in miniature prepared for a potential suitor, or an "archival" painting that records some ceremonial occasion. More wide-ranging purposes are served by paintings and dramas that offer a political critique (*Guernica, The Crucible*), or a cultural affirmation (Madonnas and Nativities, *In Which We Serve*). Some craft artefacts, by contrast, are highly impractical: a ceramic vase made by a skilled potter will be useless if it has a pinhole hollow, or even no hollow at all.

Similarly, the criterion of traditional form versus novelty and creative exploration is not clear-cut. A glassblower may eschew the "perfect" goblet, deliberately making one whose stem is not vertical, but highly oblique. (The goblet may nevertheless be functional.) And a ceramicist may systematically explore new stylistic possibilities for forming a set of plates, bowls, and jugs (perhaps also making them so large that they are practically useless): see Section VI.

My purpose here is not to argue for a particular way of drawing this distinction. The terminology of "art" and "craft" does reflect some interesting differences, such as those listed above, but that's not to say that one can draw a hard and fast line between the two. Indeed, in Section VI I shall offer a principled reason why borderline (or better: mixed) cases are only to be expected. Accordingly, I shall rely on an intuitive, and confessedly vague, sense of the difference between art and craft.

Paradigm cases of craft, I take it, include ceramics; textiles; embroidery; jewellery; cutlery and hand weaponry; carpentry and furniture making; dressmaking and millinery; bookbinding; block printing and silkscreen printing; calligraphy; toymaking . . . and so on. And the central aim of craftwork, I take it, is to produce something that is not only aesthetically satisfying but also potentially useful.

The "usefulness" is typically related to a comfortable domesticity, or even to the necessities of human life as such. That's not to deny that a craftsman may produce useless objects—such as a goblet with a rim that prevents any liquid from escaping, or a bottle made of icing sugar that allows the liquid to escape all too soon. But, as we shall see in Section V, the aesthetic interest of such craft objects lies largely in their relation to the exemplary (but unfulfillable) function concerned. In general, then, to appreciate a craftwork is in large part to use it, or at least to be drawn to use it.

Paradigm cases of art, I take it, include painting and sculpture—and also music, poetry, and choreography (among others). There is room for some semantic quibbling here, for the term "fine art" normally marks only the first two of these activities, and one prominent critic has even declared that "art is by its very nature visual" (Lucie-Smith 1984: 7).

However, the slogan "Art for art's sake" was coined not by a painter but by a poet (Baudelaire). And although almost every example of "art" mentioned in this paper is a painting, the aims typical of art can be satisfied in all these genres.

In art, I take it, the aim is not to meet a practical need but to remind, to affirm, to question, to stimulate—even to challenge. The challenge may be directed at people's everyday assumptions and worldly behaviour (think of *Guernica* again, or of Bosch's minatory devils). Or it may reflexively address the artistic activity concerned. Often, the artist explores the potential of particular art styles in a disciplined fashion, sometimes transforming them so as to generate items that were previously unthinkable (Boden 1990). (A well-documented musical example is the exploration of the harmonic space of tonality, culminating in atonality (Boden 1990: 59–61; Rosen 1976).)

The artist's audience may recognize and appreciate these stylistic explorations. In addition, they are often led to respond—to remember, enjoy, grieve, understand, question . . . —in ways that relate to specific aspects of their personal lives. But they are not enabled to fulfil an everyday functional need. In short, they are drawn to think and to emote—but not, or not primarily, to engage in some bodily act.

Given this outline characterization of the two aesthetic attitudes, the rest of this paper contrasts the way in which their artefacts impinge on the observer. The contrast I shall draw is not new. But I shall relate it to specific psychological theories of perception.

My argument implies that the crafts are more "primitive", more "fundamental", than fine art in a sense not usually appreciated. In a word, art and craft engage our minds in significantly different ways. And because these two types of mental process can be elicited by a single object, often simultaneously, and sometimes even in roughly equal measure, problematic cases of art/craft will inevitably occur.

II. INDICATIVE THEORIES OF PERCEPTION

Many psychological theories of perception—and most accounts of the role of vision in the appreciation of the visual arts—treat our senses as sources of "facts" (e.g. Gombrich 1977; Gregory 1998; Goodman 1976; Hyman 1989; Zeki 1999). The scare quotes make the point that we are speaking here of information rather than truth, since the beliefs, depictions, and representations induced by our senses may not be veridical. They may be illusory, fictional, or just plain false.

On this view, then, the function of our sense organs is to give us information about some real or imagined state of the world. This information may be more or less complete, coherent, and reliable. Nevertheless, it lies in the "factual" realm, in the sense that it is expressible in indicative sentences such as "A tiger is approaching", "That is a Cubist painting", or "The unicorn has rested his head in the virgin's lap". Because they see the prime outcome of perception as facts in this sense, these accounts can be called "indicative" theories of perception.

Indicative theories can explain much of what goes on in the fine arts. For such theories don't have to claim that the senses are mere passive recording instruments. They can allow, for example, that the eye-brain isn't a camera, but an intelligent system that actively interprets the two-dimensional (and usually "imperfect") retinal image as depicting some—real or imaginary—three-dimensional scene.

These interpretations sometimes depend on basic, and universal, visual processes. Bridget Riley's "illusory" paintings, for instance, evoke some psychological mechanisms that are shared by all human beings (and also by "seeing" machines (Gregory, 1967)). Often, however, they depend on culturally acquired knowledge.

For example, some of Riley's illusions "work" only on viewers accustomed to perceiving straight lines and right angles from a distance. They would not have the same effect on forest-dwellers whose huts are rounded and who rarely see the horizon. Renaissance perspective is especially well suited to interpretation by people accustomed to seeing straight-sided buildings and long vistas. And Cubist paintings of apples, tables, and violins assume that the viewer knows what these three-dimensional things normally look like. In all these cases, the art audience perceives the art object with an active eye (more accurately, with an active visual cortex).

Indicative theories can allow, also, that the image may remind us of other "factual information" by arousing memory associations of various kinds. (Not just the visual cortex, but the rest of the cerebral cortex too.)

Sometimes, these associations are based on culturally specific beliefs. Many official portraits, for instance, evoke highly culture-specific knowledge about the social significance of military uniforms, or courtly or religious costumes. Some associations lie largely "within" the art world, being stylistic conventions that the viewer is expected to interpret appropriately. One has to learn (or perhaps infer, from the biblical passage saying that the the Holy Ghost "descended upon" the Disciples) that the dove is used in Renaissance paintings as a visual symbol representing the Holy Ghost. And to recognize an artefact as falling within one or another artistic genre—such as Cubism, or pre-Columbian art—clearly requires familiarity with the styles concerned.

Other memory associations depend rather on the viewer's general knowledge of the world. So Bosch's painted monsters affect us because we know, for instance, that no real man has a bird's head. And Dalí's drooping watch can surprise and intrigue someone only if they've already learnt that watches can't normally be draped over a branch like a piece of fabric.

As the last example shows, an indicative account of perception can allow that the artist's image may deliberately challenge fundamental assumptions about what is "normal". To be committed to the indicative approach is not necessarily to be boring.

Indicative accounts of perception are neutral as between "postbox" and hermeneutic accounts of art. A postbox view sees art appreciation as the transmission of information from the mind of the artist to the mind of the viewer. That may be a plausible description of what is going on in some cases, if there is reason to believe that artist and viewer share the same "codes" for interpreting certain representations, and are primarily interested in the same aspects of the case. (Possibly, this may apply to some part of our response to Renaissance perspective.) But a theory of perception that stresses active interpretation, and the role of memory in the viewer's mind, can allow also that art appreciation is hermeneutic. As explained above, the viewer's response may involve cultural, idiosyncratic, and imaginative associations. So "facts" here need not be facts: there is room for fantasy, too. Nor need there be a single interpretation that is "correct", or even "most appropriate": the individual freedom stressed by hermeneutic accounts is thus respected.

The indicative theorist, then, sees the appreciation of visual art as a matter of the (conscious and unconscious) manipulation of information. This approach can account for much of what goes on in the interpretation of fine art, as we have seen. And it also covers much of what goes on, for instance, when we recognize a Bernard Leach pot, a Charles Rennie Mackintosh chair, or a Gerda Flockinger brooch as being works by the hands of those particular makers, or as having stylistic qualities recalling particular cultures (think of Leach's Japanese influences, for example). But it doesn't capture the essence of craftworks. Nor does it capture the psychological essence—and the evolutionary significance—of vision, and the other senses, as such.

III. THE IMPULSE TO ACTION

The reason why indicative theories fail to give an adequate account of perception, or of craft, is the same in both cases. Our senses evolved not only to guide bodily action, but to prompt it.

Vision, for instance, leads not only to the information that "A tiger is approaching" but also to the imperative "Flee the tiger!" As for seeing a unicorn, or even a visual depiction of a unicorn, this could prompt the imperative "Stroke the unicorn" or at least the permissive "You might want to stroke the unicorn". Similarly, an observer seeing someone confronted by a tiger would naturally expect them to run away; and someone observing the virgin would naturally expect her to have some impulse to stroke the unicorn.

This "impulse to action" is unusual in the fine arts, and (when it occurs) is ancillary rather than essential. Douanier Rousseau's tiger may cause some gallery viewers to feel a frisson of fear, but only very rarely (if ever) would anyone experience an impulse to try to escape. And it's highly doubtful whether Rousseau, or anyone else, would judge this fearful reaction to be a criterion of the aesthetic value of the painting. The director of a horror movie, of course, would specifically aim for such reactions. And presumably Bosch, in depicting Hell, was doing this too. But even for Bosch, the horror was not the prime object of the exercise: the associations with religious teachings on the nature of the good life, and the consequences of rejecting it, were more to the point.

Occasionally, an artwork's value may be judged partly by its success in arousing impulses to bodily actions of certain kinds. Some of Lord Leighton's canvasses, for example, depict silks and satins of such a rich and lustrous texture that one can—and often does—imagine reaching out and touching them, to feel their sensuous folds with one's fingertips or to lay them gently against one's face. But painting only rarely produces this sort of response.

Sculpture (normally regarded as fine art) more often invites one to touch the surface, especially if the piece represents or recalls bodily contours. This is one indication of the fact that the distinction between "art" and "craft" can be unclear. For it is typical of craftwork in general that, since it is potentially functional, it engages one on a bodily level.

Fine textiles, for instance, from silken gossamers to rough-woven hessians, prompt one to feel their texture against one's skin. Moreover, this bodily engagement can involve not just touching and stroking the surface, but also other purposive actions—such as hugging, draping, stabbing, and drinking.

A well-crafted teddy bear naturally cries out to be hugged, and a good textile to be draped across our bodies or furniture. Similarly, a well-made cup or goblet naturally invites one not only to touch its surface but to pick it up and hold it in the attitude fit for drinking (think of the aesthetic inappropriateness of holding a goblet upside down in "appreciating" it). And a well-made bowl naturally asks to be filled—with food, or with other objects of appropriate size.

It's no accident that the crafts are more universal, and more ancient, than anything one might term "fine art". Craft artefacts are a part of daily life (eating, sitting, walking, dressing, courting, ordering, obeying, fighting...), and are integrated with a wide range of bodily actions. Such actions are ultimately grounded both in our specifically human embodiment (two eyes, two hands, flexible fingers, etc.) and in our human sociality. And these two aspects—embodiment and sociality—are closely interrelated.

For instance, a teddy bear with shiny plastic in place of fur, and with no eyes or (worse) with three, would not naturally elicit a hug. It might not even attract, or anyway hold, the attention of the baby into whose cot it had been placed. Very young mammals (and even chicks) have an innate neurophysiological mechanism that causes them to "lock" their gaze onto things with two dark round blobs in a certain position and orientation (Johnson and Morton 1990). Newborn babies, only 7 minutes old, show an interest in such facelike stimuli. Their continued visual attention to human faces (most often, the mother's) leads to the learning of other facial features, and eventually to the discrimination of individual faces. In short, teddy bears are appealing because they naturally encourage us to act in "loving" ways. (Besides their large eyes, they have large heads: as Walt Disney's cartoonists are well aware, large eyes, large heads, and high voices naturally elicit our sympathies.)

Swords and daggers, by contrast, naturally arouse our interest to fight—or, sometimes, to flight. They fit snugly into our hands; and they are perceptibly [sic] apt for attacking.

This enactive aspect of craftwork is not accounted for by indicative theories. The word "naturally" was appropriate in the preceding paragraphs because perception naturally, essentially, tends to lead to action. This fact is not stressed, and risks being forgotten, by psychological theories that treat vision and touch (for example) primarily as a way of gaining factual information.

Indicative theories allow, of course, that perceptual information is used to guide action. But the tacit implication is that perception is carried out first (in a psychological vacuum, so to speak), and action may take place afterwards. If the action can benefit from the earlier perception, being guided by the information thus acquired, all well and good. But the two are theoretically distinct. To be sure, no "indicative" psychologist would deny that perception has evolved in the context of action. The theoretical focus, however, is on the collection of perceptual information—almost (to oversimplify) "for its own sake".

IV. ENACTIVE THEORIES OF PERCEPTION

In fact, perception evolved so as to prompt appropriate action, as well as to guide it. The psychologist James Gibson (1966, 1979) made this point by speaking of perceptual "affordances". According to Gibson's "ecological" psychology, perception does not inform us of bare facts, but rather affords possibilities for action.

A gap between the trees, for instance, will be perceived (by means of eyes, sonar, and/or whiskers) not as a mere gap but as a potential pathway. If the action—crawling, flying, or running through the gap—is likely to aid the creature's survival, then there will be a tendency for the relevant perception-action mechanism to evolve. In other words, the perception of a gap will tend to prompt the creature to travel through the gap, thus treating it as a pathway. A creature that has just perceived a tiger, so has already been urged to move to a different place, will be especially likely to follow the impulse to treat the perceived gap as a pathway. But the central point is that perceiving a gap always affords the possibility of travelling through it.

Similarly, certain bodily contours, and furriness, are naturally perceived by human beings as comforting, cuddly, or huggable—which is to say that they will tend to be actively stroked, cuddled, or hugged. The unicorn in the tapestry, like the teddy bear, is soft and apparently furry—with two large eyes into the bargain. Small wonder, then, that we are prompted to stroke it. But we'd be even more likely to stroke a real horse, or a stuffed "unicorn" made out of a horse. The reason is not that we are intellectually (indicatively) aware that the unicorn is merely a tapestry, but that we are bodily (enactively) aware that it lacks the inviting [sic] three-dimensional contours and silky sleekness of the horse.

Affordances concern possibilities not only for physical actions, such as jumping or walking, but also for social actions—such as mating, grooming, and offering food. The nestling's open mouth does not provide the mother bird with action-neutral information that it is hungry but actively, even irresistibly, invites her to feed it. Analogously, bodily expressions of emotion in humans and other mammals are not thought of by Gibson as providing neutral information about the creature's emotional state. Rather, they are part of some integrated perception-action cycle that prompts, or at the very least invites, the other animal to approach, to comfort, to mate, to submit, to flee, or to attack.

In human beings, basic inherited mechanisms (such as smiling, frowning, or pupillary dilation) are overlain by culturally acquired behaviours. A wink, after all, is not just a wink: in our society, it may be an expression of friendship or complicity, or a sexual invitation. And it is effortlessly perceived in these ways: no conscious reasoning is needed. (This may not be true if the wink is a prearranged one-off signal between conspirators, for then one may actually wonder "Just what was I supposed to do when she winked at me?") Still less is reasoning required to see that someone is happy. We rely for this "information" (which is, among other things, a licence to approach) partly on our innate response to smiles, and partly on our learnt discriminations between different types of smile—even on this particular person's repertoire of smiles, grins, sneers, and lip-twitchings. (Hence the enigmatic nature of the Mona Lisa's expression: without knowing her as an individual, we can't be sure that she is smiling, nor what response her "smile" is inviting.)

(Gibson himself spoke of the "direct" perception of affordances, claiming that the psychological processing involved goes on without involving the higher levels of the brain. This aspect of his theory is highly controversial, even for cases where cultural learning is not involved (Gyr 1972; Gibson 1973). If conscious deliberation is not required, it does not follow that no unconscious inference is needed. However, we may ignore this controversy here. The important point is that we perceive possibilities for action—never mind whether such perception is "direct".)

Not all affordances concern positive possibilities of action. For Gibson speaks also of "negative" affordances. A thicket of trees, for example, can be seen as an obstruction, as the absence of potential pathways. Similarly, a flimsy or top-heavy structure can be seen as unstable and/or incapable of offering firm support—in a word, as unsafe. What is unsafe is, in general, actively avoided.

Negative affordances are evolutionarily important. A fox must be able to recognize both obstacles and pathways if it is to escape the hounds. And a gibbon or squirrel, leaping from branch to branch, has to avoid thin branches or twigs unsuitable for holding the animal's weight. Some of these affordances are innate. Extremely young babies, for instance, will refuse to move over a "visual cliff" (a sudden steep decline in the floor, covered by strong transparent glass).

In general, then, perception affords a (more or less limited) range of possibilities for bodily action. Clearly, a bat—to choose an example by no means at random (Nagel 1974)—equipped with sonar and the power of flight enjoys affordances somewhat different from ours. But even bats respond to faces. And, crucially, the point here is not that bats can fly, but that bats are prompted to fly by certain types of stimulus.

Being prompted to do something, of course, is not the same as doing it. I don't know to just what extent the bat can inhibit its impulses to fly. Certainly, it can do so less efficiently than we (if we wish) can inhibit our own natural impulses to action. A grown man in our culture may hug a teddy bear only, if at all, in the presence of the child whose teddy bear it is. If he does inhibit his natural tendencies in this way, because of social conditioning, he will not fully appreciate the aesthetics of the teddy bear. Analogously, someone prevented by museum regulations from touching a seductive statue, or a beautifully rounded pot, will not fully appreciate its beauty either.

Gibson's theory of perception has steadily gained ground in academic circles since it was suggested over thirty years ago. It affords a rationale to certain sorts of enquiry in comparative psychology, since different species have evolved to recognize and respond to different affordances. And some neurophysiological evidence has encouraged this approach.

For example, forty years ago (before Gibson had developed his theory) the first "bug-detectors" were discovered in the frog's retina (Lettvin et al. 1959). These are cells which respond specifically to the visual stimulus of a moving dark-light boundary of high convexity. Such a stimulus is likely to be produced by, and so "interpreted as", a living fly or other small insect. (A frog surrounded by dead flies is not able to see them, and will starve to death.) Indicative psychologists described these cells as registering the information that a living bug was present. The implication seemed to be that if the frog were hungry and "decided" to eat, it would use these visual feature-detectors to locate its food.

Later neurophysiological work, however, showed that the visual bug-detectors are nicely connected to brain cells governing movements of the frog's tongue. Accordingly, the long sticky tongue automatically flashes out to the very point in three-dimensional space which corresponds to the point in the retina that is registering the "buggy" stimulus (Arbib 1982). In other words, the frog, considered as a whole organism, is naturally wired to generate the perception-action cycle of seeing and capturing edible objects. It doesn't have to "decide" to catch a fly, still less to make this decision and then gather—or recall—perceptual information as to the fly's location. The perception just naturally instigates the flycatching action.

In recent years, Gibson's approach has also influenced aspects of artificial intelligence and artificial life—especially certain types of robotics (Boden 1996; Wheeler 1999). Traditional robots are indicative to their very core. They use their camera-eyes and reasoning power both to locate objects and to decide whether, and how, to move them. Only then do they actually attempt to move them. This is all very well if the object is rigidly clamped to an industrial workbench, or lying passively on the floor. But if it moves, even slightly, while the robot is working out its location and deciding what to do, then the robot's claw will miss it when it does attempt to act. In that case, the perception-reasoning-execution sequence must be started all over again. (Clearly, not a good evolutionary strategy in the presence of a prowling tiger.)

The newer ("situated") robots are more like the frog, in the sense that appropriate actions are automatically prompted by the appropriate environmental cues (Brooks 1991). Their positive and inhibitory "reflexes" are engineered, not programmed: no reasoning is involved. Beetle-like robots are being developed, for instance, to be sent in squads to clean sewer pipes. They can climb over (many) obstructions, and in general can be left to "do their own thing" without being monitored, still less instructed, by a human being.

(That's not to say that today's situated robots are as successful, for industrial engineering purposes, as traditional robots are. Indeed, it's highly controversial whether this general approach can in principle generate interestingly flexible action (Kirsh 1991). Really accomplished robots—like people—may need thought as well as perception.)

These Gibsonian robots are currently arousing interest in the art world (as installation art, for instance), and cyberspace versions are blossoming within virtual reality (Grand and Cliff 1998). In addition, they are being applied in toy design. Furry toy dogs are being developed in Japan that will not only walk but also climb over (a limited range of) obstacles, and learn a number of "tricks" such as turning their heads towards their owner's voice and obeying simple commands. The teddy bear who will "naturally" lock his eyes onto yours, while you naturally lock yours onto his, is not far away.

Irrespective of such "aesthetic" applications, however, the Gibsonian theory of perception helps us to understand what is distinctive about the crafts.

V. CRAFTS AND BODILY ACTION

The crafts are grounded in, and deliberately evoke, "enactive" (non-indicative) psychological mechanisms. Not only are their artefacts typically functional, but many of the functions concern basic aspects of life and domesticity, such as eating, drinking, cooking, mating, and keeping warm. The bodily actions associated with such functions have their roots far back in human history, and some in human biology too. The distinctive aesthetic power of craftwork cannot be understood unless this is realized.

It is this enactive aspect which explains our handling of the goblet, our touching of the textile, and our sensuous stroking of the body-contoured carving. It accounts for our urge to recline on the pile of silken cushions, to stab aggressively with the dagger, and to hold and swing the heavy jewelled sword. And it even explains our impulse to approach—or respect, or fear—the person adorned with "decorative" jewellery or body painting.

Ceramics, textiles, carvings, metalwork, jewellery, millinery... all these give us artefacts that can enter intimately into everyday human life. They arouse affordances of many different kinds, both "bodily" (such as drinking or sitting) and "social" (such as stroking, hugging, fearing, or respecting). As remarked in Section IV, Gibson's theory allows for both these classes of elicited action.

Just as facts can be learnt, so affordances can be learnt too. I've remarked (in Section II) that someone interested in fine art can learn that a dove—in a certain type of painting—represents the Holy Ghost. Correlatively, someone encountering the gold collars of the Viking chiefs, or the orbs and sceptres of the British monarchy, can learn that—in the relevant social context—these craft pieces signal status of a certain kind and demand active obedience and/or respect of a certain sort.

Such ceremonial objects are not "purely" decorative. That is, they do not merely delight the eye. Indeed, even the most inexpensive beads and bangles are not purely decorative either. Their colours, textures, and forms naturally engage the attention both of the wearer and of others—and that, at base, is the point. Cultural messages are received too, of course. That is why each of the two most popular soap operas on British TV can signal the personality and social status of a main character by getting her to wear a succession of outrageous earrings. In short, a bead or a bracelet is naturally perceived as a move in a subtle game of social interaction. This aspect of its aesthetics can be deliberately ignored, much as the huggability of the teddy bear can be suppressed by adult males. But no competent jeweller would do so.

Some craftworks even extend our sense of the possibilities of the body, by reminding us that certain familiar bodily actions could—just—be achieved in highly unusual ways. Think of a "crazy" hat, for instance, or a gondola-shaped glass perfume bottle. And the oblique-stemmed goblet mentioned in Section I, besides affording drinking, reminds the user forcefully of the care one must always take in avoiding spillage and in handling so fragile a material as glass.

Occasionally, a "useless" artefact playfully challenges our expectations by offering negative affordances as well as positive ones. A water bottle made of icing sugar, or a vase with a pinhole hollow, are of no practical use. And the drinker who relies on a flat-rimmed goblet will die of thirst. But besides (perhaps) having beautiful colours and/or contours, such objects remind us of the normal range of action afforded by the relevant types of thing.

In short, the crafts not only exploit the possibilities of the body, but often help us to see them more clearly and/or more imaginatively.

VI. THE INEVITABILITY OF BORDERLINE CASES

Since human perception is fundamentally enactive, it follows that fine art, too, is in fact produced and appreciated by basically enactive psychological mechanisms. This accounts for the (perhaps rare) occasions where someone shivers in fear at Rousseau's tiger, or recoils with disgust at Dürer's serpent or Bosch's hellish monsters. And it explains the frequent sensuous response to Leighton's painted silks.

But fine art in general (and abstract art in particular) does not specifically aim for this type of response. Accordingly, art criticism does not stress it either. This is why indicative accounts of vision (and memory) can capture a great deal of what is going on in the fine arts.

No one would regard the canvasses of Bosch or Leighton as lying on the art/craft borderline. On the contrary, they are paradigm cases of "art". For it's crystal clear that their main intent is not to prompt us to bodily action, still less to produce a functional object for daily use towards some practical end. The fact that these canvasses may actually elicit a shiver of horror, or a wish to touch the "satin", does not invalidate that insight.

The "action-filled" paintings of Pollock are an interesting case. (I owe this example to Michael Wheeler.) One might say that they "work", at least in part, by exploiting the sensitivity of our enactive perceptual mechanisms to the kinds of effects in the visual field that suggest movement. In Pollock's abstract art, this movement cannot be attributed to anything represented in the picture, such as a waterfall or a dancer. It can be attributed only to the flying (and dripping) paint and/or to the artist who threw it onto the board in the first place. For someone who happens to know something about Pollock's painting technique, the latter attribution will naturally be enforced. In short, the aesthetic effect of the work depends partly on the viewer's natural inclination to perceive movement and the active origin of movement—abilities that are emphasized more strongly in Gibson's theory than in indicative accounts. Unlike Leighton's painted silks, however, Pollock's work does not directly prompt action on the viewer's part. At most, it may (indirectly) lead viewers to imagine the artist's action, and perhaps even to imagine acting in that way themselves.

Although none of these three examples is a borderline case of art/craft, they do show that the associative (indicative) mental processes that are necessary for the appreciation of fine art can go on at the same time as (enactive) perception—or, at the very least, that both types of psychological process can be elicited by one and the same artefact. It's only to be expected, therefore, that there will be some cases where the two types are roughly equal in strength. That being so, it is in principle possible for an artefact to be deliberately made so as to prompt indicative and enactive responses in broadly equal measure. In such cases, we will find it especially difficult to pigeonhole the work as either "art" or "craft". Either classification would be largely arbitrary, because our psychological engagement satisfies criteria of both categories.

Consider, for instance, a large hand-printed and embroidered silken wall-hanging, a collage based on the themes of "music" and "Venice". The item that I have in mind affords a sensuous beauty, inviting the viewer not only to revel in the delicate colours but also to stroke the silks, trace the metallic threads, and feel the contrasting textures. It's a beautiful, and highly skilled, piece of craftwork.

However, it also leads the viewer to thoughts of Venetian music, music in general, Venice as an architectural delight, and the inevitable demise of political power. For example, one small part of the hanging bears a fragment of Shakespeare's song "If music be the food of love", another an excerpt from a biography of Vivaldi, another a depiction of a lute. Someone who doesn't recognize these, or who fails to see their relevance to mid-millennial Venice, won't realize the full aesthetic potential of the piece. They can still appreciate it as an elegant craft object, but not as a celebration of the power that music affords in human lives, nor as a reminder of the role that Venice has played in European culture but plays no longer. That is, they fail to see it as a piece of fine art.

In fact, it is both. The person who designed it (my daughter) intended to explore, to remind, to stimulate, to surprise—all characteristics of art. She also intended to make a decorative object for use in a domestic setting, which would be viewed and handled with sensuous delight—all characteristics of craft. If the human mind were not capable of appreciating one and the same object in all these ways, she could not have achieved both goals. The goals are compatible, but their psychologies—and their aesthetics—are different.

Another example of an arts/crafts enterprise that depends on a "mixed" psychology (in both maker and viewer) is the work of the ceramicist Andrew Lord. As a potter, Lord revels in the intimate relation between his own bodily actions and the clay. His pots remind viewers of this relation, and prompt them to touch as ceramics typically do.

Moreover, he bases his work on familiar traditional forms, drawn from Mycenaean, Delft, and pre-Columbian pottery. For sure, then, he is a skilled craftsman.

But he is also an artist. Despite their provenance in domesticity (jugs, bowls, plates, vases...), most of Lord's pieces are very large, even man-sized, so are not usable in practice. They're also too expensive to be used: they are exhibited in galleries of "art" rather than "craft", and fetch high prices accordingly. The reason they are regarded as art by the galleries concerned is that they satisfy the criterion mentioned in Section I: "Often, the artist explores the potential of particular art styles in a disciplined fashion, sometimes transforming them so as to generate items that were previously unthinkable."

Lord does not make individual pots: rather, he makes collections of pots. Each of these comprises at least five objects, based on a "form palette" of twenty-seven basic shapes. His work involves systematic exploration of the stylistic possibilities inherent in these shapes. Any one collection is both internally coherent and coherently related to every other collection based on the same set of underlying forms.

Sometimes, for example, Lord tries to recreate a specific art style (such as Cubism) in all the pots. This is comparable to representing the alphabet in different fonts: each font must be recognizably different from the others, while each letter token must resemble all the others within the same font. Much as the letter "I" is more difficult to vary than the letter "R", so a plate is arguably more difficult to vary than a jug. (For some intriguing ideas about the psychological processes involved in this sort of exercise, see the discussion of "Letter Spirit" in Hofstadter 1995.) Sometimes, he tries to represent, in three-dimensional form, the way the light falls at different times of day. And sometimes, he moulds each pot collection with a particular body part (fist, eyeball, chest...), emphasizing the origin of the pots in his own bodily activities.

A person may be irresistibly led to caress the surface and contours of Lord's pots, and to exult in their subtly coloured glazes. They may recognize them as versions of traditional forms, such as a Delft jug or a pre-Columbian bowl, and see that some (at least) are functional. And they may be able to decode the imprints of fist or eye, and to picture the potter's clay moulding in the process. Such a person can appreciate the craft aesthetic of Lord's work. But only if they can see "what he is up to" in his interrelated collections, and appreciate the extent to which he succeeds or fails in adapting these styles in creative ways, will they be able to appreciate his work also as art.

In this case, as in the example of the wall hanging, a particular viewer may not be able to appreciate both the aesthetics that are implicit in the one artefact. Someone catapulted into our culture from another might (enactively) appreciate all Lord's ceramic objects as craft pieces. That is, they might recognize a jug as such, and even try to pick it up by its handle, without knowing that it is Delft-based or Mycenaean. But they could not see these pieces also as art, because so many of the (indicative) associations involved would be missing.

The converse situation, in which someone could see the pieces as art but not as craft is less likely. For their craft status relies on widely (even universally) shared bodily responses to the physical aspects of the work.

VII. SUMMARY

The aesthete's "Art for art's sake" is like the psychologist's "Perception for its own sake". Both slogans sum up attitudes that civilized human beings can consciously decide to adopt. But neither is faithful to our fundamental psychology.

Indicative theories of perception (and memory) encourage fine artists to look down their noses at the crafts because—shock, horror!—even highly decorative craftworks are potentially useful. For on this view, use—and indeed action in general—is essentially distinct from information, even though it is guided by it. And information is the name of the art game.

By contrast, an enactive theory of perception helps us to understand why a prime aesthetic attraction of the crafts is their close engagement with the varied possibilities of bodily action.

However, this psychological distinction does not offer us a hard and fast line between art and craft. Since indicative and enactive processes can be elicited by one and the same object, mixed cases of art/craft are possible. Inevitably, some designer makers will choose to work in a way that deliberately exploits this fact.

REFERENCES

Arbib, M. A. (1982), 'Modelling Neural Mechanisms of Visuomotor Coordination in Frog and Toad', in S. Amari and M. A. Arbib (eds.), *Competition and*

Cooperation in Neural Nets (Lecture Notes in Biomathematics 45) Berlin: Springer-Verlag, 342–70.

Boden, M. A. (1990), *The Creative Mind: Myths and Mechanisms*. (London: Abacus).

—— (1996) "Introduction", in M. A. Boden (ed.), *The Philosophy of Artificial Life* (Oxford: Oxford University Press), 1–35.

Brooks, R. A. (1991), "Intelligence Without Representation", *Artificial Intelligence*, 47: 139–59.

Gibson, J. J. (1966), *The Senses Considered as Perceptual Systems* (Boston: Houghton Mifflin).

—— (1973), "Direct Visual Perception: A Reply to Gyr", *Psychological Bulletin*, 79: 396–97.

—— (1979), *The Ecological Approach to Visual Perception*, (Boston: Houghton Mifflin).

Gombrich, E. H. J. (1977), *Art and Illusion: A Study in the Psychology of Pictorial Representation* (5th edn., London: Phaidon).

Goodman, N. (1976), *Languages of Art: An Approach to a Theory of Symbols* (2nd edn., Indianapolis: Hackett).

Grand, S., and D. Cliff. (1998), "Creatures: Entertainment Software Agents with Artificial Life", *Autonomous Agents and Multi-Agent Systems*, 1.

Gregory, R. L. (1998), *Eye and Brain: The Psychology of Seeing* (5th edn., Oxford: Oxford University Press).

Gregory, R. L. (1967), "Will Seeing Machines Have Illusions?", in N. L. Collins and D. Michie (eds.), *Machine Intelligence 1* (Edinburgh: Edinburgh University Press), 169–80.

Gyr, J. W. (1972), "Is a Theory of Direct Visual Perception Adequate?", *Psychological Bulletin*, 77: 246–61.

Harrod, T. (1999), *The Crafts in Britain in the Twentieth Century* (London: Yale University Press).

Hofstadter, D. R. (1995), *Fluid Concepts and Creative Analogies: Computer Models of the Fundamental Mechanisms of Thought* (New York: Basic Books).

Hyman, J. (1989), *The Imitation of Nature* (Oxford: Basil Blackwell).

Johnson, M., & J. Morton (1990), *The Development of Face Recognition* (Oxford: Blackwells).

Kirsh, D. (1991), "Today the Earwig, Tomorrow Man?", *Artificial Intelligence*, 47: 161–84; repr. in M. A. Boden (ed.), *The Philosophy of Artificial Life* (Oxford: Oxford University Press, 1996), 237–61.

Lettvin, J. Y., H. R. Maturana, W. S. McCulloch, & W. H. Pitts (1959), "What the Frog's Eye Tells the Frog's Brain", repr. in W. S McCulloch, *Embodiments of Mind* (Cambridge, Mass.: MIT Press), 230–55.

Lucie-Smith, E. (1984), *The Thames and Hudson Dictionary of Art Terms* (London: Thames & Hudson).

McCullough, M. (1998), *Abstracting Craft: The Practiced Digital Hand* (Cambridge, Mass.: MIT Press).
Nagel, T. (1974), "What Is It Like To Be a Bat?", *Philosophical Review*, 83: 435–50.
Rosen, C. (1976), *Schoenberg* (Glasgow: Collins).
Wheeler, M. (1996), "From Robots to Rothko: The Bringing Forth of Worlds", in M. A. Boden (ed.), *The Philosophy of Artificial Life* (Oxford: Oxford University Press), 209–36.
Zeki, S. (1999), *Inner Vision: An Exploration of Art and the Brain* (Oxford: Oxford University Press).

5
Creativity and Conceptual Art

I. INTRODUCTION

If one has a view about the nature of creativity in general, it should apply to all forms of art (and to science too, though that isn't our concern here). In particular, if one believes that there are several different types of creativity, one must say how these map onto various examples of art—whether these are general movements, specific art forms, or individual artworks. With respect to conceptual art, do all examples of this genre spring from the same type of creativity? And if so, what is it?

My own approach to creativity does distinguish different types, as I explain in Sections II and III. In Section IV, I argue that the one which prima facie seems most appropriate isn't apposite, in fact. Section V spells out the categorization I favour. Finally, in Section VI, I relate this viewpoint to the evaluation of conceptual art.

II. WHAT IS CREATIVITY?

A creative idea is one that is *new*, *surprising*, and *valuable* (Boden 2004).

The term "idea" is a shorthand, here. In art, the new idea sometimes *is* an "idea" in the normal sense: a concept, if you prefer. But it need not be. It may be a method for producing artefacts (a new type of paintbrush, a revolutionary camera or developing technique, or a novel way of casting bronze). Or it may be a general style of painting, or sculpting. Or it may be a musical composition, or passing harmony; or a new dance step or choreography . . . and so on. In Sections IV and V, I'll mention a wide range of creative "ideas" drawn from conceptual art.

Besides the ambiguity of "idea", each of the three criteria of creativity is ambiguous. That's largely why disagreements about creativity are often carried on at cross-purposes.

There are two importantly different senses of "novel". On the one hand, an idea may be new to the person who had it: it's a first-time occurrence within their particular mental biography. Let's call this P-creativity, where the "P stands" both for "person" and for "psychological". On the other hand, an idea may be—so far as is known—new with respect to the whole of human history: that is, it's H-creative.

From the psychological point of view, which seeks to understand how creativity happens and how it's even possible, P-creativity is the more important concept. For every instance of H-creativity is a special case of P-creativity. (If it's the first ocurrence in human history, then it must also be the first occurrence in the mind of its originator.) From the historical point of view, H-creativity is the focus of special interest. But since every H-creative idea is P-creative too, we can always ask what type of P-creativity was involved. This applies to the twentieth-century emergence of conceptual art, just as it does to any other artistic movement.

The second criterion, surprise, has three meanings. One may be surprised because something is statistically unusual, so contrary to common-sense expectations—like an outsider winning the Derby. Or one may be surprised because one hadn't realized that the new idea had been a possibility all along—like discovering a beautiful village tucked away in a hollow between two spurs of the motorway. (Its location had always been marked on the map, but one hadn't examined the whole map closely.) Third, one may be surprised by something that one had previously thought impossible, and which one still sees as utterly counter-intuitive. Here, think of the events categorized by the religious as miracles, or imagine the impact on non-physicists of the introduction of wireless, or television.

The third criterion, being "valuable", has many different meanings. For various reasons, these can't be wholly pinned down. What's valuable in music isn't necessarily valuable in, or even applicable to, architecture. What's valuable in a baroque fugue may not be valuable in the blues. And what's thought valuable in the 1960s may be scorned in the 1970s. As that remark suggests, values can change (sometimes, virtually overnight) as a result of shifts in fashion—some deliberately engineered for commercial purposes, some arising from unpredictable events (such as what an admired "celebrity" chooses to wear to a party). There may be some universal or near-universal values: symmetry and shininess, perhaps? (Boden, 2006 8.iv.c). But even these can be deliberately transgressed, and their opposites admired in their stead (think of the highly asymmetrical architecture of Daniel Libeskind).

One class of values merits special mention here, namely, what ecological psychologists call "affordances" (Gibson 1966, 1979). These are naturally evolved tendencies to behave towards a perceived feature in a particular way. Some are positive: affordances suggesting opportunities for locomotion, for feeding, for stroking, for courting... and so on. Others are negative, such as affordances eliciting fear or disgust. (The latter have presumably evolved to prevent us, and other animals, from eating rotting and/or contaminated food.) The "crafts" in general depend on the elicitation of positive affordances, which is why they are universal, relatively unvarying, and—unlike "art"—capable of speaking for themselves (Boden 2000). In other words, craftworks can be appreciated without specific cultural knowledge, whereas artworks cannot. Even if an artwork does exploit inborn affordances (as many do), it's primarily interpreted as a moment situated within a particular cultural context.

The defining characteristic of a new artistic movement is that certain aspects of a wide range of artworks are now valued within a certain culture (or subculture) which weren't valued before. Usually, many—even most—of the previous values are retained. Occasionally, however, almost none is retained. As we'll see, the latter applies to the twentieth-century movement known as conceptual art.

III. THE THREE TYPES OF CREATIVITY

The three types of surprise listed above correspond to three types of creativity: combinational, exploratory, and transformational (Boden 2004: chs. 3–6). They're distinguished by the types of psychological process that are involved in generating the new idea.

The exercise and appreciation of each of these forms of creativity depends upon specific cultural knowledge. Someone from a different culture may not even be able to recognize the novelty involved, and a fortiori they may not be able to understand/appreciate it. In the context of conceptual art, it's worth pointing out that "someone from a different culture" needn't be a foreigner: they may be your next-door neighbour. If so, they'll have to undergo a learning process if they're ever to understand the novelty and to judge the aesthetic value.

Combinational creativity involves the generation of unfamiliar (and interesting) combinations of familiar ideas. In general, it gives rise to the first type of surprise mentioned above. Just as one doesn't expect the outsider to win the Derby, because that doesn't normally happen, so one doesn't expect ideas X and Y to be combined, because they seem to be mutually irrelevant. Everyday examples of combinational creativity include visual collage (in advertisements and MTV videos, for instance); much poetic imagery; all types of analogy (verbal, visual, or musical); and the unexpected juxtapositions of ideas found in political cartoons in newspapers.

Exploratory and transformational creativity are different. They're both grounded in some previously existing, and culturally accepted, structured style of thinking—what I call a "conceptual space". Of course, combinational creativity too depends on a shared conceptual base—but this is, potentially, the entire range of concepts and world knowledge in someone's mind. A conceptual space is both more limited and more tightly structured. It may be a board game, for example (chess or Go, perhaps), or a particular type of music or sculpture.

In exploratory creativity, the existing stylistic rules or conventions are used to generate novel structures (ideas), whose possibility may or may not have been realized before the exploration took place. (You may or may not have had some reasons to expect to find a village nestling between the motorways.) It can also involve the search for, and testing of, the specific stylistic limits concerned. Just which types of structure can be generated within this space, and which cannot?

Transformational creativity is what leads to "impossibilist" surprise. The reason is that some defining dimension of the style, or conceptual space, is altered—so that structures can now be generated which *could not* be generated before. Imagine altering the rule of chess which says that pawns can't jump over other pieces: they're now allowed to do this, as knights always were. The result would be that some games of chess could now be played which were literally *impossible* before. The greater the alteration, and the more fundamental the stylistic dimension concerned, the greater the shock of impossibilist surprise.

However, not every dimension will have been changed. (Otherwise, why call it a new form of *chess*?) So there will be both structural continuities and structural discontinuties between the untransformed space and its seemingly impossible successor. If some feature of the game which you enjoyed before the change is retained, you'll find something to enjoy in the transformed version. You may, however, be so averse to jumping pawns—perhaps they make you feel giddy?—that you decide to revert to old-style chess nevertheless. In art, where aesthetic judgements presuppose recognition of the relevant cultural style, there will be aesthetic continuities and discontinuities too. And the discontinuities may or may not be regarded as valuable.

After the transformation has happened, the artist may add new rules, defining *and exploring* the new style more fully. One clear example concerns the composer Arnold Schoenberg (Rosen 1976). He transformed the space of Western tonal music by dropping the fundamental home-key constraint: it was no longer the case that every composition must favour one of a finite number of sets of seven notes (the major and minor scales). Atonality was born. But besides dropping this constraint, Schoenberg experimented by adding new ones. At one point, for instance, he said that each composition should contain *every* note of the chromatic scale. Musical exploration could then ensue on this basis. But the radical transformation was the decision to drop the constraint of a home key.

The three types of creativity are analytically distinct, in that they involve different types of psychological process for generating P-novel ideas. But as we'll see when we discuss examples, a given artwork can involve more than one type. That's partly why it's generally more sensible to ask whether this or that *aspect* of an artwork is creative, and in what way. However, people often ask about the creativity responsible for *the artwork as such*, because they assume that a particular aspect is in question even if this hasn't been explicitly stated.

In general, transformational creativity is valued most highly. (That's less true of literature than of the other arts, because language offers scope for especially rich creative combinations, and the theme of human motivation offers huge exploratory potential.) However, novel transformations are relatively rare. All artists spend most of their working time engaged in combinational and/or exploratory creativity. That's abundantly clear when one visits a painter's retrospective exhibition, especially if the canvasses are displayed chronologically: one sees a certain style being adopted, and then explored, clarified, and tested. It may be superficially tweaked (a different palette adopted, for example). But it's only rarely that one sees a transformation taking place. The artists whose names are recorded in the history books are usually remembered above all for changing the accepted style. (Again, that's somewhat less true of writers.)

Typically, the stylistic change meets initial resistance. And it often takes some time to be accepted. That's no wonder. For transformational creativity *by definition* involves the breaking/ignoring of culturally sanctioned rules.

IV. IS CONCEPTUAL ART TRANSFORMATIONAL?

It may seem, given what I've just said, that conceptual art is a paradigm case of transformational creativity. After all, it's certainly shocking. One common reaction to it is "That's ridiculous! What on earth made anyone think of that?"—and that's the polite version. Another is "That's not art!" This reaction goes with outraged bewilderment at the fact that the work in question is exhibited in a gallery and/or taken seriously by what Arthur Danto (1964) called "the artworld".

Prima facie, then, it seems as though we're dealing with a case of "impossibilist" surprise.

If these artworks really do arouse impossibilist surprise in the viewers, it would follow that conceptual art is transformational. For the type of surprise and the type of generative creativity go hand in hand. But is this culture shock genuinely impossibilist?

Impossibilist surprise and transformational creativity were both defined in terms of some accepted cultural style, or conceptual space. Each style covers, or makes possible, indefinitely many individual structures—some of which are actually produced by artists. By the same token, however, that style is incapable of generating other structures. For that to happen, some change ("transformation") of the space must be made. The newly created space can then allow the generation of previously impossible structures.

Does that apply to conceptual art? What cultural style, or conceptual space, was transformed by Marcel Duchamp's *Fountain*, for instance?—Sculpture, perhaps? It was certainly shocking, considered as sculpture, since it was a mass-manufactured object bought from a warehouse, not something lovingly forged by Duchamp's individual skills. It may seem that this is an example of impossibilist surprise. But it isn't, really, for sculpture as such isn't an artistic style. Rather, it's a form of human activity conceived in highly general terms. Michelangelo or Barbara Hepworth were equally sculptors, but worked within very different styles. The problem (the shock) with *Fountain* wasn't the style of its physical form—the nature of the curves, or even the lustre of the ceramic—but its manufactured provenance.

There was another source of shock too, namely its unsavoury associations. Duchamp wasn't the first artist to exploit affordances of disgust. Jonathan Swift, for instance, had a nice (?) line in scatology, which he used to challenge our safe complacencies (just read the usually expurgated passages of *Gulliver's Travels*). As for the visual arts, Francisco Goya aroused people's disgust (and fascination) by his painting of the cannibalistic Saturn, bloodily devouring his own child. But Goya, having chosen to depict that mythical/political theme, couldn't avoid disgusting us. The same applies to satirical cartoonists such as George Rowlandson and William Hogarth: a biting visual commentary on some social habits (as in *The Rake's Progress*, for example) could hardly fail to evoke disgust.

Duchamp, by contrast, seemed to employ unsavouriness for its own sake—or, more accurately, in order to shock the viewers (as opposed to commmunicating something shocking to them). Whether or not he was the first artist to do that, he certainly wasn't the last. This strategy became fairly common within late-century conceptual art.

Using elephant dung to make a portrait of an African Virgin Mary, as Christopher Ofili did, was one example. This isn't an entirely clear case, because although elephant dung may disgust Western gallery visitors, it's routinely handled for many purposes—including painting—in some African (and other) cultures. But exhibiting piles of one's own faeces, as has sometimes been done, certainly is. So too is designing a turd-making machine, complete with peristaltic pump—as in Wim Delvoye's room-sized installation, *Cloaca*. This twentieth-century successor of Jacques de Vaucanson's famous "digesting" duck (Boden, 2006 2.iv.a) really does break down and ferment food, but it's intended more as cultural commentary than as simulated biology. (The final irony is that viewers/collectors are willing to pay $1,000 per turd.) Even the aesthetic force of Tracey Emin's unmade bed depends largely on involuntary responses of disgust on the viewer's part—a point which she herself has made in interviews. The same applies to bisected cows floating in formaldehyde: part of the power is due to the object's disgust value. (Only part of the power: Damien Hirst's oeuvre is a meditation on death, corporality, and our failure to look these in the face.)

One might argue that Duchamp wasn't challenging the notion of sculpture, so much as the notion of art. Certainly, part of what he was doing was undermining the art world's claim to confer the status of "art" on items exhibited in its galleries. That's why his readymades are sometimes categorized as *art criticism*, not *art objects* (Beardsley 1983: 25).

But others have been explicit about challenging the accepted notion of *sculpture*. Consider, for instance, Claes Oldenburg's work exhibited in New York's Central Park in 1967. This piece, officially called *Placid Civic Monument*, raised orthodox eyebrows in four ways.

First, the sculpture—though handmade—wasn't a result of the artist's own handiwork, but of a group of men temporarily employed by him. Second, it was ephemeral. Having taken two hours to create, it was deliberately destroyed only three hours later. Henceforth, it could be "exhibited" only through a brief film, some still photos, and various texts recording its creation and its brief existence. Like the mass manufacture of *Fountain*, these unorthodox aspects challenged the idea of sculpture *in general*, not any particular sculptural style.

Oldenburg's third challenge to orthodoxy concerned the stuff of which the artwork was made. Instead of moulding a physical object to be placed on a plinth, or on the ground, he (or rather, a few professional gravediggers) dug a hole in the earth of Central Park. The hole itself, he said, was the sculpture. (In his notebooks, he ignored its official title and simply called it *The Hole*.) Its stuff was *the absence of stuff*. It had 3D form, of course, before it was destroyed (not by moles, earthworms, and rainfall but by the diggers themselves, who filled it in and smoothed it over after taking their lunchbreak). But its form was defined by *what it was not*, namely, the surrounding soil.

The particular form chosen wasn't (if you'll forgive the pun) immaterial. As a 6-foot-long, 6-feet-deep, rectangular trench it could be seen by the cognoscenti as an inversion of Donald Judd's minimalist rectangular blocks, which were attracting New Yorkers' attention at the time. It was also strongly reminiscent of graves. Indeed, the art historian Suzaan Boettger points out that it was dug at a time of vociferous protest about the Vietnam war, when graves sprang more readily to mind than usual (2003: 19ff.). Only three weeks after Oldenburg's quasi-grave was dug, 100,000 people joined in an anti-war march on Washington—and in his diary he explicitly connected the hole with his concerns about the war. In addition, Oldenburg's diary, and his hand-shot film, repeatedly juxtaposed/contrasted the invaginated form of the trench with the phallic Cleopatra's Needle monument, nearby in the Park. What's more, both he and (so his diary memoir recalls) the gravediggers repeatedly referred to the earth as "virgin" ground, and remarked on its dampness and redness (Boettger 2003: 17). In short, the shape of this hole was neither random nor meaningless—a point we'll return to in Section 5.

Oldenburg's fourth challenge was invisibility: in his diary, he called the hole "a nonvisible monument". For it was debatable whether one can actually see a hole—as opposed to seeing its walls, or boundaries. Some previous sculptors, such as Henry Moore, had used holes very effectively. But theirs were "stylistic" holes as opposed to "constitutive" ones. A Moore piece was made of stone or bronze as usual, but its style was defined not only in terms of the types of physical curves and surfaces involved but also in terms of there being some curves and surfaces which were formed by gaps in the physical stuff. The artwork *had one or more holes in it*, and this was a feature (initially, a transformation) enabling stylistic exploration in the sense defined in Section III. In Oldenburg's piece, by contrast, the artwork *was* the hole. The challenge was to the very notion of sculpture, not to any particular sculptural style.

Some others took the invisibility challenge even further. For example, in 1968 Sol LeWitt made (or rather, he persuaded a metalworker to make) a stainless-steel 10-inch cubical box and buried it in the ground (Boettger 2003: 88 ff). The box contained a small work of art he'd given to the owners of the ground where it was buried, but neither that nor the box was ever seen again. Both parts of this sculpture were straightforwardly visible in principle, to be sure—but in practice, they weren't.

Similarly, consider Walter de Maria's *Vertical Earth Kilometer*, made in 1977. This was a perfect cylinder, made of highly polished solid brass, exactly 5 centimetres in diameter and 1,000 metres long (actually, 167 twenty-foot rods screwed together). So far, so orthodox. Unusual, yes. (Have you ever seen a sculpture 1,000 metres long, or weighing nearly 19 tons?) But not shocking. The shock came when de Maria buried it vertically in the earth (in Kassel, Germany), so that it was invisible. The only indication of its existence was its circular top, level with the ground and kept free of grass by its 'keepers'. (Two years later de Maria fashioned *The Broken Kilometer*; a mathematically precise layout of 500 brass cylinders with the same diameter, and the same overall length and weight. Still on display in Manhattan, this easily visible sculpture can't be properly understood except by reference to the earlier, invisible, one.)

Last, consider Michael Heizer's variously invisible sculptures (Boettger 2003: 107–15, 191–7). These included a large steel cone, buried up to its lip; an (empty) two-part plywood box some 4 feet square, sunk into the ground up to the level of its top edge; and his hugely influential *Double Negative* of 1969. The first of those three examples involved invisibility-by-burial, the last, invisibility-by-absence; and the second combined both.

The aesthetic point, in most of these cases, was to reinforce the conceptual art emphasis on ideas rather than sensory perception—what Lucy Lippard (1973) called the dematerialization of the art object. If the idea behind the artwork was more important than its nature as a physical thing, it needed to be *thought* rather than *perceived*. There might actually be a material object. And this might have been constructed with considerable skill (not "perfunctory" attention, as suggested by LeWitt—who famously defined conceptual art as being "free from the dependence on the skill of the artist as a craftsman": LeWitt 1967: 822). But it needn't be seen, so much as thought about. And since it needn't be seen, it might as well be made invisible.

There are various ways in which this could have been done. LeWitt's little steel box, Heizer's plywood container, or de Maria's 500 cylinders, could have been wrapped in blankets, for example. But burying and blanketing have different associations: in the terminology of Section III, they give rise to different combinations of ideas. A buried artefact brings to mind notions of hoarded treasure; lost valuables; unsuspected potential; long-gone civilizations; hubris and futility; plus death and graves, again—not to mention funerary gifts to comfort the deceased on their dark journey. None of those concepts would be triggered by blanketing, which would rather suggest warmth, caring, vulnerability, and perhaps the sweet promise of infancy. So the artist had to choose the causal source of the invisibility. Having done that, his verbal descriptions, with the accompanying documents if any, could encourage, or validate, some associations (combinations) rather than others. In short, the true artwork, here, was more in the burying than the making. And the shock value lay in sculpting the box, cylinder, or cone meticulously—only to conceal it, for ever, from view.

The shock value of Heizer's *Double Negative* was rather different. It consisted of empty space, as Oldenburg's Central Park project did too. But it was/is permanent, not ephemeral. And it wasn't made by a few men wielding spades, but required dynamite and bulldozers to dislodge and remove almost a quarter of a million tons of rock. For this sculpture is made up of two horizontal rectangular notches, placed opposite each other in towering cliffs separated by a chasm in the Nevadan *mesa*. These notches, and the space between them, could hold a skyscraper lying on its side: they're 50 feet high, 30 feet wide, and over a quarter of a mile long. (They can be reached only in a heavy 4-wheel-drive vehicle, and aren't easy to find: visitors are advised to inform the local airport so that a search party can be sent out if they don't check in again soon.)

Heizer himself saw it as *utterly* new: "My work is fully independent of anyone else's, and it comes directly out of myself. . . . Whatever I was doing, I was doing it first" (quoted in Boettger 2003: 109). However, doing something first doesn't necessarily mean doing it wholly independently. For one thing, Heizer was explicitly reacting against Manhattan minimalism, and scorning the New York art scene of the 1960s. For another, he and de Maria had experimented with land art together in the late 1960s—de Maria having proposed a bulldozer-dug artwork ten years earlier than that (Boettger 2003: 115 f.). And for another, he was recalling massive monuments in pre-Columbian America (which he knew a lot about, since his father was an archaeologist specializing in these things). As for the dynamite and the bulldozers, both his grandfathers had been prominent in the mining industry of the West.

These psychological sources of Heizer's creativity were also involved in the aesthetic appreciation of them. Viewers could hardly miss the contrast between the vast desert *mesas* and the decadent sophistications of the narrow streets of SoHo, nor escape thoughts of ancient temples and pyramids. And besides envisaging centuries-old rock-dragging slaves, they'd wonder at the enormous power of the modern machinery used to build *Double Negative*.

Shock value was prominent, too, in John Cage's composition *4′33″*, which consisted of just over four-and-a-half minutes of silence (Tomkins 1965: 69–144; Solomon 1998/2002). Instead of invisibility, there was inaudibility.

The performance of the composition consisted in the pianist's closing the lid of the keyboard at the beginning of the piece (and at the beginning of the three carefully timed "movements"); lifting it at the end (of the composition and of its component movements); using a stopwatch to determine just when to open or close the lid; and turning the pages of the score—which showed staves with no notes written on them. These hierarchical boundary-indicating actions were the temporal equivalent of the earthen walls of Oldenburg's invisible monument.

Someone might want to say that Cage had accepted an orthodox musical style, and then transformed it. To be sure, he had a pianist sit at a piano, and he defined three separate movements. But he'd written an instruction on the (empty) score saying that the piece was for performance by *any* instruments. And he'd chosen the timings of the movements at random, constrained only by the overall period of four minutes thirty-three seconds. *Everything* else, including sound, was dropped. So whether there really were any instruments, or any movements, was highly problematic. Given these considerations, it's not at all clear that he "accepted" the familiar style, nor that he "transformed" it. Rather, he gestured towards it.

Perhaps he was providing a new conceptual space, a new style for others to explore? That description, too, suggests the existence of more structural constraints than were in fact involved. Rather, Cage was alerting other musicians to the nature and power of "silence", and reminding them of the possibility of using chance to make certain compositional choices. Those ideas could, in principle, be applied to many different styles, perhaps transforming them in the process. But providing an idea which others can follow isn't necessarily the same thing as creating a newly structured space. Not all influence is exploration. (Similarly, Heizer's and de Maria's revolutionary sculptures led to an explosion in what's now called land art, or earthworks: Boettger 2003. But this is less an artistic *style* than an entire art *form*, which can be instantiated by following many different styles.)

Cage's main aim in composing *4'33"* was to challenge the orthodox view of music as such. He'd already done that for many years, by making (percussive) music out of what would normally be termed "noises". (In the 1930s, he'd also predicted the rise of electronic music.) Now, in 1952, he wanted to show that music (as he understood the term) is in fact continuous, that what's discontinuous is our voluntary attention to it. In other words, music is made by the listeners as much as by the performers or composer.

The trench in Central Park may not have been absolutely empty: there were probably insects flying around in it, and a few leaves may have been blown into it. But Oldenburg wasn't interested in that fact. Cage, by contrast, was very interested in the fact that there wasn't absolute silence during the performance of *4'33"*. The movements of the piano lid and the page turnings were audible. So were the rain on the roof, and the birds in the rustling trees. Indeed, the first performance, in Woodstock, was held in a room—aptly named "The Maverick Concert

Hall"—that was open to a forest at the back. Also clearly audible were the moment-by-moment reactions of the audience. These reactions altered over the years. The Woodstock listeners, despite being a group devoted to avant-garde music, were outraged: their initial bemusement gave way to steadily mounting fury, and there was uproar when the pianist got up at the end. Twenty years later, people had got the point: at least one audience exulted in the piece while it was being performed, and gave a standing ovation when it was over.

A superficially similar idea, though one originated with a very different aim, had been expressed over half a century earlier by the French composer Alphonse Allais (Solomon 1998/2002). His funeral march for the last rites of a deaf man (*Marche Funèbre, composée pour les Funérailles d'un Grand Homme Sourd*) consisted of twenty-four measures or bars of silence. It was defined by a score consisting of twenty-four blank staves of equal length, with a note saying that the performance must consist entirely of measurements, not of sounds—plus the teasing instruction that it be played *"lento rigolando."*

The similarities to Cage are intriguing. But they don't negate Cage's claim to H-creativity. For the blank score and the measurements were being proffered in a very different spirit in the two cases. Allais had been intending to be funny (he was, in fact, a regular cabaret performer); and he thought of his Funeral March as being genuinely silent ("for a deaf man"). Cage, on the other hand, was denying the possibility of utter silence. And, even more important, he was being absolutely serious. In later life he often referred to *4'33"* as his most important work, and confessed to an interviewer "I always think of it before I write the next piece" (Solomon 1998/2002: 3). Indeed, he'd already wanted to write this piece as early as 1947, but he'd feared that it wouldn't be taken seriously. It was the blank white canvasses of his friend Robert Rauschenberg, seen in 1951, which finally gave him the courage to proceed (Revill 1992: 164). In short, whereas Allais had hoped to make people laugh, Cage had feared becoming a laughing stock.

Rauschenberg's H-creativity, too, had apparently been compromised by the same Parisian joker. For in the mid-1880s, an exhibition of *Les Arts Incohérents* had included a completely white painting by Allais, wittily named *Anaemic Young Girls Going to Their First Communion Through a Blizzard*. What's more, a black canvas of the same period depicted, or so he said, *Negroes Fighting in a Cave at Night*. But again, Allais was merely trying to be funny, whereas Rauschenberg wasn't.

As for predecessors casting doubt on the notion of silence, Cage mentioned in a talk given in 1948 (when he was still weighing the risks of composing *4'33"*) that he'd been greatly impressed by a book on *The Art of Noises*, published by an Italian Futurist in 1916. Although Cage didn't mention this at the time, the book contained a whole chapter pointing out that the so-called "silence" of the countryside was no such thing—and that the country noises were probably a key contribution to our perception of nature's "beauty". But even that avant garde author hadn't gone so far as to define *music* in terms of silence. There, Cage was being genuinely original.

Music, of course, is conventionally regarded as "a performance art". But following someone glimpsed on a bus isn't. Vito Acconci's journeys in his *Following Piece* of 1969 were not only ephemeral (as all performances are, in the absence of recording technology), but unwatched: invisibility again. Also, and unlike the carefully planned hole and cylinder, they were largely outside the artist's control. The targeted subject was chosen by Acconci at random, and then diligently followed by him until he/she entered a private place, such as a home or office. This might take only five minutes, or it might take all day. Any possible biographical interest was compromised by the fact that there was no guarantee that the "home" or "office" in question was that of the person concerned: they could have been visiting a friend, or following up a business contact.

Scrappily recorded on the hoof, by snatched photographs and by jottings in notebooks, these followings were "exhibited" post hoc by these evidentiary documents being shown in galleries. Sometimes, Acconci's photographs and video clips seemed to be selected by orthodox aesthetic criteria; but that wasn't always so (Davies 2004: 208). In brief, his activities fitted our usual notions of "art" even less well than performances such as juggling or fire-eating do. A fortiori, there was no accepted style being structurally transformed.

One challenging 'performance artist' even dispensed with the performance itself. In a 1969 exhibition called *Art in the Mind*, Bruce Naumann took this title literally. His exhibit was a verbal snippet giving instructions for a possible performance: "Drill a hole into the heart of a large tree and insert a microphone. Mount the amplifier and speaker in an empty room and adjust the volume to make audible any sound that might come from the tree" (quoted in Davies 2004: 209). But there was, and had been, no tree, no drill, no microphone... in a word, no performance. Even if, following Cage, one prefers to regard Naumann's piece as a description of possible or intended music, in fact there was no music (i.e. no sound). Normally, one would regard *imagining* an artwork and *experiencing* it as very different phenomena. Here, they were—shockingly—one and the same.

As a final example, consider Robert Barry's canvas called *All the things I know but of which I am not at the moment thinking—1.36 P.M., 15 June 1969, New York*. There were various aspects of culture-shock involved here (see Binkley 1976). These included the irrelevance of the perceptible aspects of the piece; the logical paradox concerning things "of which I am *not* at the moment thinking"; and the fact that 1.36 p.m. on that June day wasn't an iconic moment in any sense—such as the time when John Kennedy was assassinated, or when the artist's mother died. The moment wasn't special, and the things listed were so unimportant that they *weren't* being thought about... yet this piece was mounted for serious inspection on a gallery wall.

In all the cases I've mentioned, the artist's aim was to challenge orthodox notions of art (sculpture, music, painting, collage, performance...) by playing down what's perceptible and trying instead—as LeWitt put it (1967: 822)—"to make his work mentally interesting to the spectator". And in most cases, though not all, the emphasis was on apparently unimportant, even randomly chosen, ideas as opposed to significant aspects of life.

Cage was a partial exception, for *4'33"* was supposed to make one concentrate very hard on what's perceptible; however, this wasn't what was *usually* perceptible in a musical performance, and it certainly wasn't what's usually regarded as important. Oldenburg was a partial exception too, for graves—and, in that context, ephemerality—are among the most significant things of all.

In sum, the only sense in which conceptual art can be called transformative is in the challenge it poses to the accepted concept of "art" itself. Various *changes* are evident, to be sure. We pass from handmade to readymade; from skill to artlessness; from physical object to temporal happening; from musical instruments to rustlings and mutterings; from tonality and atonality to continuous noise; from stuff to the absence of stuff; from visible material to the mere idea thereof... and so on. But none of these changes counts as a stylistic transformation in the sense defined above. Accordingly, conceptual art doesn't qualify as transformational creativity on my analysis.

V. COMBINATIONS AND CONCEPTUAL ART

If conceptual art isn't transformational creativity, what sort of creativity is it? Well, it's not grounded in exploratory creativity, either, for that's defined as the exploration of an accepted artistic space. Conceptual artists reject previously accepted styles. Indeed, that's what lies behind the common feeling that this endeavour simply isn't art: in other words, that something fundamentally different is going on from what went on before (what Davies calls the "radical discontinuity" thesis—2004: 2). (Before *what*, exactly? Perhaps *Fountain*, or perhaps mid-century New York.)

In saying that conceptual art isn't *grounded in* exploratory creativity, I don't mean to say that it doesn't ever *involve* exploratory creativity. For it does sometimes produce a new conceptual space that's explored by the originating artist and/or by others.

Think of LeWitt again, here. He exhibited various series of canvasses exploring a similar compositional idea. This might be (for example) a square grid, or an arrangement of coloured pyramid-like triangles painted on neighbouring gallery walls. Also, he constructed a 3D enamel-on-aluminium sculpture of open cubes and closed bars of increasing/decreasing size, arranged on a rectilinear grid. Sometimes, he even specified the conceptual space, providing a list of abstract instructions about how such pieces might/should be executed. In those cases, he might leave the execution to others—as Oldenburg allowed his hole to be dug by cemetery workers.

Moreover, in defining conceptual art as such, LeWitt (1967) said that the crucial idea in each case "becomes a machine that makes the art". In other words, "all of the planning and decisions are made beforehand and the execution is a perfunctory affair". In addition, he said, to use the chosen idea was "to work with a plan that is pre-set", and to avoid "the necessity of designing each work in turn" (1967: 824). This art, he said, was not "subjective": on the contrary, "The artist's will is secondary to the process he initiates from idea to completion." And, perhaps most telling of all, "For each work of art that becomes physical there are many variations that do not" (1969: items, 7 and 12). In short, in his practical work he defined and explored various conceptual spaces; and in his writing he claimed that this, at base, is what art is all about.

Much the same applies to some of the other artists I've mentioned. Heizer, for instance, built many massive and "part-invisible" structures in wild landscapes. Similarly, Acconci did other followings, embarked on other journeys, and exhibited evidence of them later. Indeed, David Davies (2004: 233 f.) has argued that Acconci's work should be seen as similar in spirit to Naumann's. Although Acconic actually did something, whereas Naumann merely gave a list of instructions, his photographs (according to Davies) illustrate *a general type* of performance rather than being records of some specific perfomance event.

LeWitt also said that "The conventions of art are altered by works of art" (1969: item 19). Out of context, one might interpret that as a reference to transformational creativity. But we saw in Section IV that this isn't what conceptual art is concerned with. In other words, his phrase "the conventions of art" doesn't refer to artistic styles, but rather to our ideas about what art, as such, *is*. Similarly, we've seen that Oldenburg, de Maria, Heizer, Cage, and Barry challenged our ideas about what sculpture, music, or collage-on-canvas *is*.

In each case, the challenge consisted in juxtaposing the familiar notion of art, sculpture, music... etc. with other familiar notions that are normally regarded as irrelevant, or even antithetical to it. The artworks mentioned in Section IV exemplified many conceptual alterations in "the conventions of art". Here are some of them:

- Instead of personal making, execution by the hands of others.
- Instead of chisels, bulldozers.
- Instead of unique handicraft, mass production.
- Instead of skill, perfunctoriness.
- Instead of the artist's subjective choice, a machine's inexorable following of a preset plan.
- Instead of perceptible beauty, conceptual interestingness.
- Instead of emotional expression, intellectual engagement.
- Instead of physicality, absence.
- Instead of visibility, burial.
- Instead of sophistication, nature in the (almost) raw.
- Instead of sound, silence.
- Instead of musical intentions, the noises of the natural and built environments.

- Instead of painting, scraps of text.
- Instead of artefact, performance.
- Instead of contemporary witness, documentary records.
- Instead of performance, an idea for a (non-actualized) performance.
- Instead of experiencing an artwork, imagining it.
- Instead of coherence, paradox.
- And instead of mental focus, mental absence (what I'm not bothering to think about).

In short, what we have here are cases of *combinational* creativity. We're invited to consider the mutual relevance of ideas normally held to be irrelevant, contrasting, or oppositional. We're even invited to go further, strengthening juxtaposition into definition. These unfamiliar combinations of familiar ideas are elevated from cabaret jokes into intriguing insights, and from insights into a new understanding of "art" and its various forms. (Forms, not styles: e.g. sculpture and music as such.)

Once a new combination of ideas—that is, "art" plus X—has been accepted by conceptual artists as interesting, the concept of X may be experimented with (in a sense, "explored") by several different people. For example, Cage and his followers used silence and randomness as key musical concepts for many years after *4′33″* was first performed. Similarly, consider the examples of art burial described in Section IV. These artworks, and the many inspired by them, were exploring the implications of a particular idea—namely, invisibility-caused-by-burial. But that idea was "interesting" only in the (combinational) context of the idea of *art*. Invisibility as such, burial as such, weren't the point. (By contrast, when Schoenberg introduced his rule that every chromatic note should be used, he was specifically opposing styles based on the major and minor scales.)

Other unfamiliar combinations, or reversals, may be introduced not as defining criteria of "art", but as ideas intended to shock us out of our former complacencies about what art is. Duchamp's *Fountain* is a prime case in point: instead of something satisfying the good taste and sophistication of the aesthete, we're faced with the unsavoury quotidian earthiness of the urinal. Several other, even more unsavoury, examples were mentioned early in Section IV.

One unfamiliar combination can be conjoined with others. So Oldenburg, at the very same time as he's upsetting our ideas about sculptural physicality, turns our minds to thoughts of graves, death, war, and the archetypal female. We saw in Section III that it's characteristic of combinational creativity that *many* ideas may be co-relevant. The surprise is in the realization of relevance, and in the further associations that this realization brings to mind.

VI. VALUES AND CONCEPTUAL ART

Those remarks about the realization of relevance are germane to the final aspect of my definition of creativity—namely, that the surprising novelty be valuable. Whether a particular artwork (or artistic genre) is produced by combinational, exploratory, or transformational *processes* is a psychological question. Whether it's an example of combinational, exploratory, or transformational *creativity* is a partly aesthetic question, because of the implicit reference to value.

Someone who regards conceptual art as entirely lacking in aesthetic (as opposed to historical or sociological) interest might agree that it's due to combinational thinking. But they'd deny that it exemplifies combinational creativity, because—for them—it wouldn't count as "creativity" at all. Novelty, yes: but novelty alone isn't enough.

In saying that the artworks I've mentioned are examples of combinational creativity, I've implicitly suggested that they're aesthetically valuable. But I haven't explicitly said *why*. Nor have I made any evaluative comparisons, such as saying (what in fact I believe) that de Maria's invisible sculpture, or Heizer's massive earthworks, or Cage's silent music, or even Barry's paradoxically titled collages, are more aesthetically valuable than Acconci's random stalking. What are the criteria by which such judgements can be made?

In general, the richer the associations, and the deeper the relevance, the greater the aesthetic value of the novel combinations. Combinational creativity in general depends on intellectual interest and emotional resonance, as opposed to the appreciation of structured artistic styles. And intellectual interest, above all, is what conceptual art is aiming for.

To be sure, different types of creativity can exist within the same artwork. So we've seen (with respect to LeWitt and Acconci, for example) that exploratory and combinational creativity can go hand-in-hand in conceptual art. But it's clear from Lewitt's explicit comments on his work (as from Cage's, too), that the challenging conceptual combination was considered more important than the stylistic exploration.

To evaluate conceptual combinations, the observers (or art critics) need to be able to do a number of things. They must recognize *which* ideas are being combined. This is relatively straightforward when several ideas are presented together (in a Barry collage, for instance), but less so when some of the relevant ideas are left unstated (as the concepts of "art" or "sculpture" are, in Duchamp's *Fountain*). Sometimes, specialist knowledge is needed to see the relevance (as in de Maria's New York exhibit, which gestures towards his earlier work in Germany). At other times, general knowledge and human empathy are the prime motors of the viewer's aesthetic response (remember the comparison of *burial* with *blankets*, in relation to invisibility). And always, the individual resources of the viewer's mind can add depth to their appreciation.

People's judgements of the interest—and the attractiveness—of the ideas evoked matter too. Urine, elephant dung, and turds may sometimes be relevant, even in a sense interesting: nevertheless, they won't be judged by everyone to be valuable. (Do *all* shocks carry "shock value"?) An artist who doesn't merely want to shock the viewer, but hopes to attract their interest and appreciation too, must somehow persuade them—or hope that a sympathetic art critic will persuade them—that the piece is genuinely *worthy* of their attention: at least for a moment, and perhaps for much longer than that.

All these aesthetic questions arise in appreciating combinational creativity in general. (Think of poetic imagery, for example.) Conceptual art is just a special case.

Partly because there's no accepted *style* involved (at least in 'pure' cases of combinational creativity), and partly because the mental associations aroused differ so much between individuals, it's inevitable that agreement on the aesthetics will be difficult.

You may not share my own preference for de Maria over Acconci, for instance. You might never come to do so, even if we were to sit down and talk about it. You might not be persuaded (one can hardly say "convinced") by my pointing out that the randomness in selecting Acconci's unknowing prey will only rarely lead to an engaging, still less a gripping, human story. And you might never resonate with my appreciation of the delectable absurdity in crafting a flawless metal cylinder only to hide it from view. Such difficulties aren't unfamiliar.

For as remarked in Section II, aesthetic values in general are varied, changing, and often elusive.

Certainly, people who value the sensuous qualities of traditional painting, sculpture, or textiles will feel bereft at their absence from conceptual art. Likewise, admirers of skilled craftsmanship will be cast adrift when no art object has been crafted, or when it has been carelessly thrown together or lifted off a warehouse shelf. And those who take joy in stylistic exploration will feel short-changed by "one-offs" that may be ephemeral, and which in any case don't lead to a series of artworks developing the same style. The shock of a new thought, or the amusement caused by a daring conceptual juxtaposition, may be scant recompense.

However, these are matters more of individual preference than of aesthetic principle. That's why combinational creativity is usually more difficult to justify than its exploratory cousin. Transformational creativity is a halfway house, since stylistic rules are (by definition) broken. Here, justification of the transgressive art object will involve both showing its affinity to the previous style and indicating its potential for the development of a new one.

In sum, and despite its startling difference from previous artistic practice, conceptual art *isn't* the result of transformational creativity. The huge shock that it carries results, rather, from highly unexpected combinations of familiar ideas—including, in particular, our culturally cherished notions about art and artistry as such.

REFERENCES

Beardsley, M. C. (1983), 'An Aesthetic Definition of Art', in H. Curtler (ed.), *What is Art?* (New York: Haven), 15–29.

Binkley, T. (1976), "Deciding About Art", in L. Aagaard-Mogensen (ed.), *Culture and Art: An Anthology* (Atlantic Highlands, NJ: Humanities Press), 90–109.

Boden, M. A. (2000), 'Crafts, Perception, and the Possibilities of the Body', *British Journal of Aesthetics*, 40: 289–301.

—— (2004), *The Creative Mind: Myths and Mechanisms* (2nd edn., expanded/revised, London: Routledge).

—— (2006), *Mind as Machine: A History of Cognitive Science* (Oxford: Clarendon Press).

Boettger, S. (2003), *Earthworks: Art and the Landscape of the Sixties* (Berkeley and Los Angeles: University of California Press).

References

Danto, A. (1964), "The Artworld", *Journal of Philosophy*, 61: 571–84.
Davies, D. (2004), *Art as Performance* (Oxford: Blackwell).
Gibson, J. J. (1966), *The Senses Considered as Perceptual Systems* (Boston: Houghton Mifflin).
—— (1979), *The Ecological Approach to Visual Perception* (Boston: Houghton Mifflin).
LeWitt, S. (1967), "Paragraphs on Conceptual Art", *Artforum*, 5/10 (June), 79–83; repr. in K. Stiles and P. Selz (eds.), *Theories and Documents of Contemporary Art: A Sourcebook of Artists' Writings* (Berkeley and Los Angeles: University of California Press), 822–6.
—— (1969), "Sentences on Conceptual Art", *Art-Language*, 1: 11–13; repr. in K. Stiles and P. Selz (eds.), *Theories and Documents of Contemporary Art: A Sourcebook of Artists' Writings* (Berkeley and Los Angeles: University of California Press), 826–7.
Lippard, L. (1973), *Six Years: The Dematerialization of the Art Object 1966–1972* (New York: Praeger).
Revill, D. (1992), *The Roaring Silence: John Cage: A Life* (New York: Arcade).
Rosen, C. (1976), *Schoenberg* (Glasgow: Collins).
Solomon, L. J. (1998/2002), 'The Sounds of Silence, John Cage and 4'33",' available only on the Web, at <http://music.research.home.att.net/4min33se.htm>.
Tomkins, C. (1965), *The Bride and the Bachelors: Five Masters of the Avant-Garde* (New York: Viking).

6

Personal Signatures in Art

I. INTRODUCTION

An individual artist's personal signature is some (typically involuntary) aspect of their works which enables observers to recognize their authorship. The personal signature is a familiar phenomenon in the visual arts, and in other forms of art too. It is a special case of the "semiotic" (Ginzburg 1992), or "idiographic" (Allport 1942), approach of the humanities, wherein superficial and seemingly trivial clues act as signs affording some deeper knowledge of the individual human being concerned. This approach also characterizes diagnostic medicine—and psychoanalyis, too. So Freud remarked in *The Moses of Michelangelo* that "[the art connoisseur's] method of enquiry is closely related to the technique of psycho-analysis, [being] accustomed to divine secret and concealed things from unconsidered or unnoticed details, from the rubbish heap, as it were, of our observations" (quoted in Ginzburg 1992: 99).

Freud's remark, here, was a specific reference to Giovanni Morelli, the man who was primarily responsible for the burst of interest in the personal signature that took place in the nineteenth century. As we'll see in Section II, heated public discussion—not to mention national embarrassment—ensued when he sought to attribute paintings and sculpture to one artist or another.

The connoisseurs steeped themselves in the observation of works of art so that they could learn to recognize each artist's personal signature. Having recognized it, they tried to describe it—but they didn't try to explain it. Reasons for the existence of the personal signature, for the relative ease of recognizing it, and for the difficulty of describing it in explicit terms, are given in Section III. Those reasons also explain why the personal signature is so hard to eliminate.

Helpful information was provided by Nigel Llewellyn, Paul Brown, Jonathan Bird, and Willard McCarty.

The early twentieth century saw a recoil from aesthetic concern with, and celebration of, the personal (Section IV). In that cultural context, some artists of the second half-century turned with relief to the impersonality of computers, and occasionally even tried to annihilate their own individual 'mark' (Section V). Nevertheless, and despite the abstract nature of the computer itself, it persisted.

That's not to say that it persisted always, and entirely. For example, the computer artist Harold Cohen, on seeing an image produced by his recent colouring program, confessed "I'd never have had the courage to choose *those* colours" (p.c.). His personal mark qua colourist, then, had not been faithfully retained. To be sure, many of the program's images did employ a colour mix that connoisseurs of Cohen's previous work would recognize. Nevertheless, there had been a change: in his words, "a world-class colourist" (the program) had surpassed "a first-rate colourist"—namely, Cohen himself. Moreover, this had happened despite the fact that Cohen *had not* aimed to escape from his characteristic palette.

Unlike Cohen, the computer artist Paul Brown (whose work has been publicly exhibited since 1967) has been trying for many years—as yet, unsuccessfully—to eliminate his personal signature. Brown (with the author of this paper, among others) is now engaged in a project, described in Section VI, whose aim is to generate computer art, produced by line-drawing robots, that is guided by his aesthetic sensitivities but *does not* display his authorial hand.

But is that outcome in principle possible? Could robots developed (more specifically: evolved) under Brown's aesthetic guidance shake off his idiosyncratic style? Might they, perhaps, develop individual signatures of their own (and if so, how)? Finally, if they were to escape Brown's style, could he properly take the credit for creating the artworks/products that ensue? Or should the robots be credited instead?

II. THE PHENOMENON OF THE PERSONAL SIGNATURE

The existence of the artist's personal signature was already recognized, and being written about, almost four centuries ago. Giulio Mancini (1558–1630), an art collector and highly skilled diagnostic physician (to Pope Urban VIII), alerted people to it at a time when annual exhibitions of paintings were being held in Rome—and causing disagreement about the attribution of specific items (Ginzburg 1992: 207). Handwritten copies of his art-historical manuscript *Considerazioni sulla Pittura* were widely circulated, and he is now seen as an early "connoisseur" (Mahon 1947: 279 ff.). But interest waned over the following years, and the topic fell into abeyance.

It made its comeback in the late nineteenth century. At that time, the provenance of countless pictures and sculptures in both private and public collections was uncertain, or even unknown (Llewellyn 1997: 297 f.). This was due to the many unrecorded sales and movements of artefacts since the fifteenth century, and especially to the unnumbered thefts and transportations that had taken place in Europe's wars—not least, the relatively recent Napoleonic wars. To make matters worse, many of the long-dead artists were themselves obscure, and some of the *written* signatures on the paintings were forgeries. Even those documentary archives of the great houses which still survived were often unreliable.

So the recently founded national collections—such as the Louvre, stuffed with artworks gathered from the four corners of war-torn Europe, or even Prince Albert's Manchester exhibition of *Art Treasures of the United Kingdom* (1857)—were comprised of largely anonymous treasures. Given the curators' desire to educate the general public about these artefacts, so as to laud European and/or national civilization in general, this was doubly embarrassing. (It became triply embarrassing when the experts mentioned below repeatedly claimed to have discovered misattributions in the major national galleries of Italy, France, Germany, and Great Britain.)

The attribution of art, in these circumstances, was a pressing need. And it was undertaken by a new class of person: the connoisseurs. Men such as the physician (again!) Giovanni Morelli (1816–91), and his disciple Bernard Berenson (1865–1959), mistrusted the labels—both names and dates—on the works displayed in the public collections. A signature, in the usual sense of the term, was unconvincing. So was an iconic sign (such as Albrecht Dürer's initials). Indeed, they scorned all the written sources, from Giorgio Vasari's anecdotal *Lives of the Most Excellent Painters, Sculptors, and Architects* (1550/1568) to the weightier volumes written by later scholars of art. "Most of them", they felt, "blunt and paralyze our taste for a true living knowledge of art, rather than quicken and refine it" (Morelli 1877/1883: vi).

Instead, they insisted on direct confrontation with the artwork itself (the "true living knowledge") as the only way to appreciate art—or to attribute it reliably. And isolated episodes of confrontation were not enough: the art appreciator must become familiar with the artist's whole oeuvre, and that of his stylistic brothers. Accordingly, the early connoisseurs travelled indefatigably all over Europe, seeking to identify regional schools and artists, and to attribute specific artefacts to one name or another.

They learnt from this experience that individual artists—lying within a given style or school—could be recognized by tiny clues in their work. The first to point this out was Morelli. In artists' finished works (paintings, sculpture, and architecture), and especially in their drawings, he said, we can see the distinguishing marks—"the family features, both intellectual and material"—of the various regional schools of Italy, and of the individual masters within them (Morelli 1877/1883: 7). "For instance," he added, "their manner of arranging drapery, the way they indicate light and shadow, the preference they give to pen and ink, or to black and red chalk, etc."

Using these clues, Morelli suggested attributions for paintings whose artists were unknown. And he offered many revised attributions, too. For example, with respect to two easily confused masters of Ferrara, Cosimo Tura (*c*.1430–95) and his pupil Lorenzo Costa (*c*.1460–1535), Morelli noticed systematic differences between the shapes of hands or of ear lobes in their work (see the sketches in Morelli 1877/1883: 237 f.). As a result, he argued that the attribution (to Costa) of a painting of St Sebastian held in Venice was wrong: it was "an unmistakable work of Cosme [i.e. Tura]"—*even though* it bore Costa's name. Similarly, he said, another famous painting thought to be by Costa was in fact done by his pupil Ercole Grandi—although he admitted that "[possibly], the composition of the picture comes from Costa, and only the execution belongs to Grandi" (p. 237). (His attributions were often complicated by the fact that the less important parts of the painting would have been assigned to apprentices: often, only the faces would have been painted by the master.) A third Ferraran canvas was ascribed by Morelli to Francesco Bianchi (1460–1510), *despite* the picture's 'posthumous' date of 1516, "which might have been stuck on at any later time, and which therefore I regard as apocryphal" (p. 240). The grounds for ascribing it to Bianchi were that "my eyes... clearly recognise the master in the forms of the hands and ears, and the attitudes and movements of the figures" (ibid.).

Berenson, too, stressed the personal signature in discovering the artist responsible for an artwork—especially those features which were painted/sculpted unwittingly and/or were difficult to imitate (Llewellyn 1997: 315 f.). The most easily attributable features, he said, are ears, hands, drapery, and landscape. Next, come hair, eyes, nose, and mouth. And the least reliable—though still helpful up to a point—are the shape of skull and chin, human figures in movement, architecture, colour, and chiaroscuro. (Assuming that this is true, one might ask *Why?* Why are ears and drapery more 'personal' than chins and colour? A tentative answer is given in the next section.)

Berenson went beyond Morelli, however. The art historian Nigel Llewellyn credits him with a remarkable aptitude for finding memorable phrases for expressing the particular aesthetic qualities of different artists. Commenting on Benozzo Gozzoli's work in the Louvre, for example, Berenson ranked him as a "mediocre" artist but an admirable "anecdotal illustrator", whose "rare facility of execution, but also of invention" awakens our childishness and our love of fairy tales (quoted in Llewellyn 1997: 313). This, one might say, is the personal signature at one remove: not the actual marks on the canvas, but the spontaneous psychological response that they evoke in the viewer.

Indeed, Berenson made a point of distinguishing the material form, or "morphology", of the artwork (Morelli's prime focus) from its "spirit", or "quality". And only a few, he believed, are capable of fully appreciating that: Berenson specifically rejected the rational-scientific leanings of Morelli, insisting rather on the connoisseur's aesthetic subjectivity, his personal taste and judgement. Clearly, that opened the way for lengthy—sometimes interminable—discussions, and highly subjective biases, concerning disputed attributions.

These discussions were rarely good-tempered. Despite his avowal that "To bickering and strife I am a declared enemy", Morelli rarely bit his tongue when criticizing his opponents (1877/1883: vi–vii); and Berenson's waspish arrogance is legendary. Connoisseurs in general regarded (regard) themselves as a cut above the rest of us—not to say a neo-Romantic elite. To praise an artist was, in effect, to praise themselves. But our interest here is not in the often vituperative disputes over this or that attribution, where the reputations of the competing connoisseurs, and those of the public and private collections, were at stake. Rather, it is in the notion of the personal signature (the set of "family features") itself.

As a way of bolstering art appreciation, as well as aiding attribution, the concept rapidly gained ground toward the close of the nineteenth century. One reason was that it fitted well with the philosophy of

Romanticism. Artistic creativity, on this view, is a special faculty gifted to an elite, possessed only by a few individuals. Indeed, their very individuality (like the individuality of languages and of entire cultures, recently argued persuasively by Wilhelm von Humboldt—1836; cf. Boden 2006: ch. 9.iv), was itself a focus of celebration for the late nineteenth-century art lover—and, of course, for the artists themselves. To recognize, and value, someone's personal signature was to engage in such a celebration.

A second reason for the rapid acceptance was that the new concept appeared to be grounded in good empirical evidence. Morelli himself compared the "dreary dilettantism" of most art critics with his own careful connoisseurship, which sought to "attain a real Science of Art" (1877/1883: vii). Sir Henry Layard agreed, declaring that Morelli's work was "the most important contribution ever made to the history of art, . . . which has succeeded for the first time in resting research on the authenticity of Italian paintings on solid scientific grounds" (quoted in Llewellyn 1997: 309, my trans.). And despite the embarrassment involved, the owners of art collections were usually persuaded by his meticulous comparisons and well-informed arguments. Of the fifty reattributions which Morelli proposed for items in the Dresden gallery/museum, for instance, fully forty-eight were accepted by the director (Llewellyn 1997: 308).

As these discussions proliferated, and not least because of Berenson's influence, interest spread from distinctive marks (such as ear lobes) to overall stylistic features that could be recognized, but not necessarily itemized. One painting would have the 'feel' of one artist, another the 'feel' of another. Careful visual comparisons might be highly persuasive, of course—but no definitive stylistic checklist was available.

The concept of the personal signature eventually spread into literary criticism (and musicology) too. Indeed, Dr Johnson (1781) had already mocked two of the family features of John Donne's poetry, its linking of hugely heterogeneous concepts and its display of erudition: who but Donne, he had asked scornfully, would have thought a good man is a telescope? In the twentieth century, detailed accounts of the rhetorical styles of different authors were fairly common. For instance, Christopher Ricks (1963) defended the subtleties of John Milton's Latinate syntax and epic similes against T. S. Eliot's complaint that Milton's poetry was dry, clumsy, over-erudite, and "an influence for the worse, on any poet whatever . . . an influence against which we have to struggle".

Nevertheless, the emphasis in literary studies was rather different from that in the visual arts. The attribution of (published) poems, prose, and drama is typically straightforward, so that the 'need' for the new concept was less pressing. Accordingly, discussions of the individual characteristics of the texts were often enmeshed with discussions of the authors as individuals: the personal signature became confused with the personality signature. This was driven by two assumptions: that to understand a written text properly one should know about the personality (and biography) of the author, and that paying close attention to the texts would provide clues to the author's personal psychology.

Both those assumptions would be questioned in the early twentieth century. For example, C. S. Lewis specifically rebutted them (Tillyard and Lewis 1939). One does not have to understand the poet, he said, in order to understand the poetry. Nor does one need to rely on the commentaries of the literary critics (shades of Morelli, here). All one needs to do is to focus closely on the text itself. Lewis was not alone. This period saw a modernist reaction against Romanticism in literary criticism, leading eventually to the postmodernist declaration of "the death of the author" (Barthes 1968/1977) and Jacques Derrida's claim for the supremacy of the text alone: "*il n'y a pas dehors texte*". On this view, not only are the author's biography and personality irrelevant (as Lewis had intimated), but so is his/her intention in writing the text concerned.

The anti-Romantic revolution affected the arts in general. If poetry and prose were being depersonalized, painting and architecture were depersonalized too—a point to which we'll return in Section IV.

However, if the postmodernists weren't interested in the fact that the work of individual artists carries their own 'mark', they didn't actually deny it. How could they? By then, it had been established beyond doubt. The personal signature is a real phenomenon—but why?

III. THE PSYCHOLOGICAL SOURCES OF THE PERSONAL SIGNATURE

If we want to understand the nature of artistic creativity, we must ask why personal signatures exist. Is it merely because of egoism and self-advertisement? Consider, for instance, Alfred Hitchcock's artistic conceit—the pun's intended (but see below)—of playing micro-parts in his own films. But Hitchcock's films are recognizable to film buffs even without his fleeting appearances in them. So perhaps there are deeper reasons why artists are not stylistically anonymous?

We don't need to succumb to the Romantic myth of the individual genius in answering such questions. For creativity is a feature of intelligence in general, possessed by every normal human adult (Perkins 1981; Boden 2004: ch. 10). Possibly, the Shakespeares, Mozarts, and Picassos of this world have some extra capacities that are denied to the rest of us. But if so, these might be rather 'boring' to those of a Romantic cast of mind. A larger short-term memory, for instance, might underlie Mozart's capacity to hear a symphony 'as a whole', or Charlie Parker's ability to improvise jazz combining unusual complexity with unusually long-sustained simplicity (Boden 2004: 274 f.). It's more likely that the artists remembered in the history books have the same cognitive skills as ordinary mortals, but employ them better—and are driven by much more pressing motivations.

The personal signature, as we have seen, is a concept developed by critics largely in order to distinguish individual artists *within one and the same school*. In other words, it is focused on exploratory creativity (Boden 2004: 1–5, ch. 4). In exploratory creativity, the artist (or, for that matter, the scientist) adopts a culturally accepted style, or conceptual space, and works within its rules/constraints to generate new structures. Creativity in general is the production of novel *and valuable* ideas, and since the style in question is culturally valued the individual structures generated within it will very likely be valued too. Only if the rules are broken, or if the artist's idiosyncracies outweigh the stylistic virtues, will the new artwork be dismissed as worthless.

(Sometimes, of course, the rule-breaking art is valued precisely because it is stylistically different. And sometimes, an initial judgement of 'worthlessness' is only temporary. Even Picasso's artist-friends dismissed *Les Demoiselles d'Avignon* when they first saw it, leading him to keep it hidden in his studio for several years; but today, it is widely seen as one of the most important paintings of the century.)

That last suggestion may seem paradoxical: if exploratory creativity is grounded in a predetermined style, where do "the artist's idiosyncracies" come in? In other words, how can the artist both remain true to the style and put his/her own personal mark on it?

The answer lies in the fact that although the style is predetermined, its individual instances are not. A style is merely a general schema. It's a set of—largely tacit—rules, guidelines, or constraints that actively shapes the artist's work, and which therefore informs each example of it. But no artistic style lays down *exactly* what is to be done. If it did, the execution of individual works of art would be determined in every particular by the style itself. (Morelli pointed out that the personal signature resisted even the one-to-one stylistic tuition given by the masters running the Renaissance studios—Llewellyn 1997: 308.)

(One could say much the same about a musical score, or the script for a play. To be sure, these are specific works of art, not general artistic styles. But the similarity, here, lies in the fact that neither the score nor the script determines precisely how the piece is to be interpreted or performed. The instrumentalists or actors, the conductor or director, must make countless decisions that are not prefigured in the text. It follows that different performances of one and the same work may vary hugely. Indeed, it is not only the original authors who have their own personal signatures: the performers do, too—think of Glenn Gould and Rosalyn Tureck playing Bach. Moreover, these signatures arise for comparable psychological reasons: see below.)

The indeterminacy in style, *any* style, is one of the reasons why creative thinking is unpredictable. (Others are explored in Boden 2004: ch. 9). For, no matter how austere and strict the artistic style may be, there are always choice points at which *either x or y or z* must be done. In addition, there will be choice points at which x can be done in one of many (unspecified) ways. In other words, stylistic artistry is guided by both menus and constraints—neither of which are fully determinate. Perhaps the style allows for relatively few alternatives at a certain stage: that is, perhaps the choice point concerned has relatively few degrees of freedom. Even so, it is up to the individual artist to decide which one is selected.

Occasionally, the artist makes the style so simple, and so highly explicit, that the room for individual variations at the choice points is severely limited. Perhaps the best example of this is the American artist Sol LeWitt. Not only did he write down formulaic rules for composing his wall drawings, which usually consisted of many straight lines (sometimes, as many as 10,000) positioned at specified distances from each other and/or drawn for a specified number of minutes), but he trained his assistants to execute these instructions in a particular way. He even halted the construction of one of 'his' pieces at the Tate gallery because he felt that the execution of his faxed instructions by the Tate's staff (which they had assumed was utterly straightforward) was unacceptable. He sent out two of his own staff from New York to do the job instead.

This example shows, however, that even "severely limited" stylistic choice is not the same thing as *zero* choice within that style. Indeed, LeWitt (1971) himself acknowledged this. He recognized that "The artist must allow various interpretations of his plan", and that "There are decisions which the draftsman makes [in interpreting the artist's plan], within the plan, as part of the plan. . . . The draftsman's contributions are unforeseen by the artist, even if he, the artist, is the draftsman." In short, even the most rigorous style requires a host of detailed decisions to be made, for each of which there is more than one acceptable outcome.

In principle, every such decision could be made randomly. In practice, very few—if any—are entirely random. Consider Mozart's and Haydn's dice music (O'Bierne 1968), for instance, or Bryan Johnson's (1969) novel *The Unfortunates*. (This was published as twenty-seven separate sections in a box, to be shuffled before being read: only the opening and closing sections were fixed.) In all these cases, random decisions are made (by the performer or reader), either by shuffling or by throwing a die. However, the personal signature of the artist-creator informs most or all of the candidate components. (So if Johnson was attempting to kill the author even before the author's death had been officially announced by Roland Barthes, he failed.) Similarly, the two alternative endings provided by John Fowles for his novel *The French Lieutenant's Woman* were equally written in his idiosyncratic style, even though it was left to the reader to choose which one to prioritize.

The prime reason for the existence of the personal signature is not that authors consciously wish to stamp their own mark on their work. Admittedly, they may do this up to a point—and were especially prone to do so during the Renaissance and Romantic periods. But even then, they did not adopt every tiny personal mannerism deliberately. Moreover, the personal signature of the various masters is recognizable even in mediaeval art, whose aim—despite the occasional cheekily idiosyncratic gargoyle—was to glorify God in a culturally accepted way rather than to draw attention to the originality of the human artist/craftsman.

In other words, the personal signature is not primarily a matter of the author's intention. So Hitchcock's self-conscious little cameos are not true exemplars of the class. (In fact, they were inserted partly to encourage filmgoers to pay attention to the *visual* structure of the film, something which was not typically done in those days.) Rather, the signature is a consequence of the fact that the human mind is finite.

We employ the same types of choice, whether 'stylistic' or idiosyncratic, in comparable cases because *it is more economical to do so*, in terms of the information processing involved. Once a certain choice has been made—the shape of an ear lobe, for instance—it can be employed as a mini-schema: that is, as a conceptual constraint and/or a motor habit. As such, it can be followed automatically, precluding further deliberations.

That phrase "further deliberations" may be misleading, since even the initial choice may be made unwittingly. For example, in first deciding how to depict an ear lobe (where highly mimetic portraiture is not in question) a painter may simply sketch a plausible form and leave it at that. Admittedly, they will probably have had training in how to draw human heads; but the evidence of individual variation reported by Morelli suggests that the masters (the trainers) did not lay down precise rules for ear lobes. In other words, ample stylistic space was left for a strong personal signature to emerge there.

By contrast, some thought would normally be given—by both master and pupil—to choosing the shape of the eyes or mouth. For these facial features are naturally [*sic*] interpreted by us in terms of the personal characteristics of the man or woman whose face it is. (Borrowing Berenson's vocabulary, one might say that this has to do with the spirit of the work as well as its morphology.) We are not interested in what shape the Virgin Mary's ears were, nor in how they are represented in a painting. But we would dearly like to know what her eyes and mouth looked like, and we care quite a bit about how they are depicted, because they carry visual communications about the sort of person she was and about her emotional state at a given time—in a Nativity or a Pietà, for example. Even in a style (such as Renaissance religious painting) wherein the depicted person's individual psychology is not the main point at issue, inappropriate messages from the eyes and mouth would be troubling.

This may explain Berenson's discovery that the best clues for attributing a painting to a particular artist are the (personally insignificant) ears, hands, drapery, and landscape, while the (personally meaningful) hair, eyes, nose, and mouth are less helpful. As for the least helpful of all (namely the shape of skull and chin, human figures in movement, architecture, colour, and chiaroscuro), these may have been regarded by the leading master of the school/s concerned as sufficiently significant, in aesthetic (not personal) terms, to be included *within the style*, so allowing only a few degrees of freedom for individual choice.

Economy of information processing, which explains the repeated use of schemas (both cultural-stylistic and idiosyncratic), also influences the occurrence of one particular thought rather than another—for instance, a particular poetic image, or a visual detail in a painting. Jerry Fodor's (1983: 104 ff.) pessimistic claim that creative thinking cannot be scientifically explained, because *any* concept can be inferentially linked to *any* other, is true only in the most tortured sense. Given time, one can indeed find an associative pathway between any two ideas. (Many answers have been suggested, for instance, to the Mad Hatter's unanswered riddle, "Why is a raven like a writing desk?") But life's too short, and most situations are too pressing, to do so in every case. Accordingly, one's thoughts are guided by assessments of *relevance*. This is clearest in the case of linguistic communication, but it applies also to the visual arts.

In a nutshell, "relevance" can be defined in terms of a cost-benefit analysis, weighing effort against effect (Sperber and Wilson 1986). The more information-processing effort it would take to bear x in mind in the context of y, the more costly this would be: and high cost gives low relevance. The more implications, regarding things of interest to the individual concerned (such as Mary's mood and personality), that would follow from considering x, the more effective it would be: and high effectiveness gives high relevance.

The suggestion is not (paradoxically) that we pre-compute just what effort and effect would be involved in considering this or that concept/belief before picking the most economical one. Rather, it is that psychological mechanisms—exceptionless, involuntary, and unconscious—have evolved which have much the same result (Sperber and Wilson 1986: 155–71). For example, our attention is naturally [*sic*] caught by movement, because moving things are often of interest. (Think tigers!) Similarly, even the newborn baby's attention is preferentially caught by human speech sounds. In general, current sensory input indicates relevance—and is used, *without* conscious inference, to interpret potentially ambiguous sentences (such as "Put the blue pyramid on the block in the box").

But besides being built into our sensory systems, relevance recognition is built into our memories. Similar and/or frequently co-occurring memories are easily accessible (that is, highly relevant), because evolution has seen to it that they are 'stored' together in general schemas. Such schemas include artistic styles, and artists' personal signatures too. If relevance were not so important in our mental economy, Morelli's connoisseurship could not have arisen: there would have been no stylistic or personal regularities for him to study.

That is not to say that every school of art, or every artist, seeks relevance in the same degree. Different schools, and different individuals within them, adopt cognitive strategies that vary in the measure of cost or benefit—that is, of relevance—they attach to a given conceptual 'distance'. A conjunction of images that is acceptable in a surrealist painting would not have been acceptable in fifteenth-century Ferrara. Representational art in general demands greater relevance (i.e. requires less effort in computing meaningful associations) than surrealism, Dada, or fully abstract art.

Indeed, surrealism and Dada, and caricature too—which all use recognizable imagery/objects in unrealistic or culturally unfamiliar ways—require more than one level of interpretation. The first ('literal') interpretation of the artwork is implausible and/or incoherent: a second-order interpretation, often involving assumptions about the artist's knowledge and intentions, is needed. In short, many decisions are required, from both artist and audience, about what is—what possibly could be—relevant. That is why such genres are more psychologically taxing than paintings of smiling cherubs or fluffy kittens.

(Someone whose culture was innocent of art depicting cherubs and kittens, although familiar with babies and cats, would be able to interpret our chocolate-box pictures of them—though perhaps without recognizing their sentimentality. But certain artistic juxtapositions that would strike us as puzzlingly surrealistic might be immediately intelligible cultural commonplaces for them. Indeed, such "puzzles" can sometimes be solved by art-historical research. Scholars regularly point out that certain images, in certain contexts—a dove in a Renaissance religious painting, for example, or a bridge depicted on a Japanese ceramic—have some specific symbolic meaning, which the artist in question may have expected the viewer to understand.)

Similarly, different literary styles involve different levels of effort and/or different types of information processing in both author and reader. The remarks about non-representational painting, above, are reminiscent of computational analyses of the use of irony, hyperbole, and metaphor in literature (Sperber and Wilson 1986: 237–43). As for personal signatures, some of these are taxing, too. Milton's epic similes in *Paradise Lost*, and (ironically, given Eliot's scorn for Milton) the literary allusions in *The Waste Land*, make huge cognitive demands even on the classically educated reader. And, according to Dr Johnson, only Donne would see a connection between a good man and a telescope.

In general, it is very difficult to say just what a given artist's signature consists in. Morelli tried his best, but was forced to supplement verbal concepts (such as 'ear lobe') with visual images drawn from the painter's oeuvre. Berenson had to rely on vague remarks about the "spirit" of the work. Dr Johnson had to trust his readers' (tacit) ability to interpret his scornful remark about Donne and the telescope in the light of other, unspecified, aspects of the poet's verse. Indeed, as remarked above, the artist's personal style may be recognizable, but experienced more as a 'feeling' than as an itemized checklist. Even the artist himself may not be able to say what his signature is (this applies to Brown, as we'll see).

That is not surprising. Recognition in general rests on some form of parallel distributed processing (Boden 2004: ch. 6; 2006: ch. 12). The need to encounter a large set of different examples is as pressing for human beings as it is for artificial neural networks—hence Morelli's indefatigable travels all over Europe to see as many pictures as possible with his own eyes. But the recognition may be based more on 'feel' than on itemized features, because the nature of the class may be very difficult to capture in words.

On the one hand, there is usually no set of necessary and sufficient conditions that apply to every example within a given category: a Rembrandt, for instance. Rather, there are what Wittgenstein called family resemblances—and Morelli, family features. (Artificial concepts that do have cut-and-dried conditions have been studied, but they are very different from concepts in everyday life: Bruner et al. 1956.) On the other hand, many of the perceptible features that contribute to the successful classification are not consciously identifiable. Even if (which is not always the case) one can visually pick out 'the Churchill nose', one cannot necessarily say just what sort of nose that is.

The same is true of recognizing a dear friend's face. Indeed, to recognize a personal signature can be to experience a very 'human' form of aesthetic satisfaction. For the shock of recognition on encountering an unfamiliar picture by a much-loved painter, or an unfamiliar poem by a revered poet, can be comparable to encountering the artist himself. Morelli again, describing a portrait in the Borghese gallery painted—but not signed—by Giorgione: 'The master's spirit met mine, and the truth suddenly appeared to me. "Giorgione, it's you," I exclaimed with emotion. And the picture replied "Yes, it's me."' (quoted in Llewellyn

1997: 295; my trans.). Insofar as art involves communication between one human being and another—sometimes said to be the very essence of art (O'Hear 1995)—this recognition of the hand of an individual person has *aesthetic* value, as well as being rewarding in a more general way.

But as we have seen, the personal signature does not exist in order to prompt rewarding responses such as these. On the contrary, it satisfies the artist's psychological need to preserve his/her mental energy. Someone who paints a picture for the very first time will not yet have established a pattern; and someone who daubs oils on canvas on only half-a-dozen occasions in their lifetime may not do so either. But a committed artist, whether professional or amateur, with a body of work already accomplished will inevitably have developed an idiosyncratic style. (So a young artist may be praised for having "found your own voice".) This personal style may reflect their historical context, but it will be idiosyncratic nevertheless. It can cover both distinctive choices at specific choice points (ear lobes, for instance), and a characteristic manner of making the many different choices allowed for by the overall style.

That does not mean that the personal signature is utterly rigid. Even the most telltale aspects of an artist's work will not be *precisely* the same on every occasion. As LeWitt (1971) put it, when discussing how his plans were actually executed, whether by himself or by others: "Each individual, being unique, given the same instructions would carry them out differently.... Even if the same draftsman followed the same plan twice, there would be two different works of art. No one can do the same thing twice." His comment prior to my ellipsis allows room for the existence of a personal signature, whereas his comments after the ellipsis imply that *even this* is variable to some extent. Hence, again, the need for perceptual recognition to be achieved despite the existence of partially conflicting evidence (or what connectionist AI terms 'weak constraints').

Possibly, the personal signature may change to some extent over the years. Despite some remarks about how the young Raphael's style differed from the mature version, Morelli seemed to think that it does not. He normally implied that the personal signature, once established, is unchangeable (1877/1883: 310 f.; cf. Llewellyn 1997: 308 f.). Whether that is true is an empirical question, answerable only by detailed art-historical study. In the (relatively rare) cases of *transformational* creativity, it must change to some extent, and may perhaps be exchanged for a radically different one. Are there any 'personal' aspects of Picasso's painting which survive despite the several transformational changes during his career? Or are there any 'personal' commonalities between Gauguin's Impressionist and post-Impressionist canvasses? If not, does stylistic transformation *always* involve abandoning an earlier pattern of idiosyncracies for a different one?

Let's agree, for the sake of argument, that—even within exploratory creativity—the personal signature may *change* to some extent. But, given the psychological need for informational economy, can it ever *disappear*? Can it, for instance, be shaken off deliberately? If artists wanted to avoid a personal signature, could they do so? And could they use computers to help them to do so?

Those questions are explored in later sections. First, we must ask whether artists ever have wanted to do this—and why.

IV. THE FLIGHT FROM THE PERSONAL

In the visual arts of the early–mid-twentieth century, certain movements consciously rejected the individualistic and expressive traditions of Romanticism. But instead of returning to a previous Classicism (as had happened in the seventeenth and eighteenth centuries), they produced new styles wherein the personal was subdued.

That's not to say that the personal signature disappeared. To be sure, explicit self-reference (like Hitchcock's) and transparently autobiographical detail were now avoided. But these new artists didn't attempt to lose their individual mark. They were just as happy—not to say eager—as their predecessors to produce work that was recognizably *theirs*. Without this broadly depersonalizing movement, however, the artistic goal of entirely eliminating any telltale signature would not have arisen. Even now, that goal is rare—and perhaps in principle impossible to achieve (see Section VI).

The modernists' flight from the personal was not merely a swing of the intellectual pendulum, wherein an older artistic style and/or philosophy is overturned largely because it has become boring. Nor was it simply a matter of artists coming to believe that Romanticism is essentially trivial, 'mere' self-expression being unworthy of their efforts. Besides those two reasons for change, there was a third: the new art was associated with a positive fascination for technology in general, and for its industrial (mass-produced) uses in particular. In other words, fine art was reflecting broad cultural changes that were decidedly impersonal in nature.

The excitement aroused by industrial materials and processes of production began early in the century, with the constructivists (such as Naum Gabo, Vladimir Tatlin, and Alexander Rodchenko). Most of them were based in Russia, or at the newly founded (1919) Bauhaus school of design in Germany. Some worked in both places: Gabo, for example, left Russia in 1922 to live in Berlin, and lectured at the Bauhaus. In the 1920s, the architect Le Corbusier (1923) famously described houses as "machines for living": the notion that they might be cosy nests idiosyncratically furnished for individual people was seen as self-indulgent sentimentality. By the 1930s, consructivism was spreading throughout Europe. (Gabo switched countries again, moving from Germany to England in 1935.)

These artists were adamant that art had a greater purpose than personal expression. For some of them, it played a dynamic role in the emergence of the Soviet socialist state. For many, it contributed to broadly egalitarian public projects: agitprop, housing, the design of industrial clothing, and so on. Others, such as Kasimir Malevich and Wassily Kandinsky, saw art as having a transcendental or spiritual function, echoed (they believed) in the pure geometry of their abstract forms. The Dutch architecture-and-art group De Stijl, at much the same time, also favoured an explicit geometrical purism. In general, then, the personal was being deserted in favour of the public and/or the impersonally abstract.

Besides their suspicion of personal expression, many visual artists of the time reacted positively to manufactured artefacts. Among the earliest to do this was the Dadaist Marcel Duchamp, who introduced his industrial "readymades" with *Roue de Bicyclette*, [*Bicycle wheel*], in 1913. His most famous readymade, sometimes described as the most influential work of art of the twentieth century, appeared in 1917: this was *Fountain*, a smoothly shining white-porcelain urinal submitted to—but rejected from—an exhibition in New York. In the 1920s, Duchamp supplemented readymades by pieces 'manufactured' by his own hands. He worked on a number of motorized artefacts called "Rotoreliefs" (featured in his film *Anaemic Cinema*), which could be seen either as *machines* or as *works of art*.

Similarly, in 1930, Laszlo Moholy-Nagy, who had worked alongside many of the expatriate Russian constructivists at the Bauhaus, completed his electro-mechanical *Light-Space Modulator*. Described by the artist as an "apparatus for the demonstration of the effects of light and movement", this was clearly an 'industrial' production. It mirrored the widespread interest in the clean, error-free—and, of course, impersonal—finishes that manufacture could enable. Many other artists of the period engaged with industrial methods to a greater or lesser extent. (Further examples included Fernand Leger, Hans Richter, Alexander Calder, and Viking Eggeling.)

These pre-Second World War artists directly influenced post-war developments such as the pan-European 'systems art' movement—and the transition within the arts from *object* to *process*. That transition occurred in the late 1960s, most evidently in the movement known as conceptual art (see Chapter 5 of this volume). Indeed, one contemporary artist/critic argued that it happened over a mere six years, from 1966 to 1972 (Lippard 1973).

Before that time, the artwork was typically perceived—and evaluated—as an object: a self-contained artefact, whose significance might be self-contained but need not be. That is, the object would often point to something, and/or to someone (such as the person who had created it), outside it. Now, it was replaced by the process from conception to actualization, where the object that may—or may not—result was evaluatively demoted to the status of mere end product. ("Or may not", because some artworks consisted merely in a list of instructions describing a process that had not taken place, and probably never would. In other words, the art-making process was sometimes omitted, or anyway identified with the thought processes in the artist's mind.)

In many cases, there was also an implication that the process can be repeated (this was especially clear whenever the artist provided a list of art-making instructions). That further undermined the uniqueness of the object—and, by implication, the personal contribution of the artist who produced it.

This depersonalizing trend was epitomized by the work of LeWitt. He is well known for his statement that "the idea becomes a machine that makes the art", where "all of the planning and decisions are made beforehand and the execution is a perfunctory affair" (1967: 824). Once the plan has been chosen, he said, "The artist's will is secondary to the [artmaking] process he initiates from idea to completion" (1969: item 7). Indeed, he produced many 'remote' artworks, where he faxed instructions intended to be followed by anonymous people who, by following these instructions, would make the work using standard off-the-shelf materials such as 2-inch by 2-inch wooden strips. Despite his admission (cited in Section III) that every "unique" individual will carry out the plan in a slightly different way, Romanticism had clearly been abandoned.

In short, the object was no longer celebrated as a unique artefact, and the artist as an individual person had faded into the background. Earlier in the century, the abandoning of the personal had simply been implied, by artists' adoption of 'industrial' processes and materials. By contrast, LeWitt and like-minded artists now made this anti-personal aspect explicit.

(Various puzzles resulted. If someone copies the instructions, buys some timber, and makes an artwork accordingly, have they created a *genuine* LeWitt? Or would it be a fake? If the artistic interest is in the idea that drives the process, there's no fundamental aesthetic distinction between original and copy. Nevertheless, in the commercial artworld the object made by the artist in his/her atelier still retains its status. Someone's 'copy' of the LeWitt is financially worthless, whereas the 'original' work has monetary—and aesthetic?—value, as do the instructions themselves. Indeed, LeWitt himself sometimes 'trumped' the conceptual integrity of his procedures, sending his assistants to the Tate to ensure the quality of the artwork as object: see Section III.)

The depersonalization that was happening in this period wasn't confined to conceptual art, although that's where it was most evident. Artists in the more traditional world of painting were using the then-new acrylic paints that enabled smooth, flat, areas of plain colour. They used straight-edge and masking tape to achieve 'industrial' finishes. And many painted the edges of their stretched canvasses instead of framing them, in order to emphasize the abstract autonomy of the object—which self-referentially documented its own construction and *did not* stand in some semiological relationship to anything outside of itself. Moreover, the manner in which the paint was applied was supposed to be free of any individual mark of the artist.

(Again, however, puzzles resulted. The French artist Yves Klein provided an interesting—and possibly apocryphal!—comment on the relation between process, signature, and object. He painted many canvasses in his trademark *International Klein Blue*. When he first exhibited some of them, he noticed that people simply scanned the show as a whole. So at his next show he put different prices on each canvas, to encourage the audience to examine them individually.)

V. THE COMPATIBILITY OF COMPUTERS

Given the cultural background described in Section IV, it is hardly surprising that modernist artists were a sympathetic audience—and that some were soon enthusiastic players, too—when computers arrived on the scene. Computers, after all, execute processes [*sic*] that are driven by abstract, formal rules, with—usually—not a person in sight. Indeed, computer art as a whole is sometimes termed *generative* art, meaning art that is generated by some impersonal and/or abstract process (see Chapter 7 of this volume).

Computers are mind-guided, to be sure—but at one remove. So they are only indirectly affected by factors concerning the economy of information processing in human minds. And, of course, they are immune to the motor habits of the programmer, and normally cannot develop any motor habits of their own. (As we'll see, certain sorts of robot may be exceptions to that.) The psychological basis for the personal signature, outlined in Section III, therefore disappears. Or, more accurately, it is pushed into the background. The aims and imagination (and programming skills) of the computer artist will always have idiosyncratic features, which may or may not be reflected in the computer output. But for those mid-century artists who already wished to obscure, or even escape from, their human individuality, it seemed that the very *impersonality* of computers might help.

(Today, that is still a very natural assumption. So much so, that three leading computer artists have recently felt the need to reassure newcomers to the genre that *if* they want to set their individual stamp on the computer's behaviour, then they can. As they put it:

> As a designer working with generative processes [i.e. computer art/design] one may still wish to leave a recognizable mark on a creation. This may be achieved statically using fixed components with a trademark style [Hitchcock's cameos, again!]. *A more interesting way to achieve this is to ensure either that the organization of the artefact bears the stamp of its designer, or that its behaviour falls within the gamut of work typically produced by the designer.* Of course the designer may not be interested in producing a recognizable style, however the utilization of generative techniques does not preclude this option. In this sense, generative design still requires the skill and artistry that encompasses any mode of design. (McCormack et al. 2004: 6.1, italics added)

We'll return to the issue of "the organization of the artefact [bearing] the stamp of its designer" in Section VII.)

Computer art began in the 1950s, although there was no public exhibition of it until 1965 (in Stuttgart), and no international exhibition until 1968 (Brown, in press). Most of the earliest works weren't static computer-produced images or 'canvasses', but machines with moving parts controlled by computers. In short, Duchamp's mechanical Rotoreliefs, and Moholy-Nagy's part-electrical *Light-Space Modulator*, were now upstaged by the more flexible kinetic art made possible by electronic technology.

In 1956, for instance, Nicolas Schoffer created CYSP 1—named for CYbernetic SPatiodynamism 1. An 'electronic brain' built by the Dutch electronics company Philips controlled the system and, in addition to its internal movement, CYSP 1 was mounted on a mobile base that contained actuators and a control system. Photosensitive cells and a microphone sampled variations in colour, light, and sound, so that (said Schoffer) it "is excited by the colour blue, which means that it moves forward, retreats or makes a quick turn, and makes its plates turn fast; it becomes calm with red, but at the same time it is excited by silence and calmed by noise. It is also excited in the dark and becomes calm in intense light" (quoted from <http://www.olats.org/schoffer/cyspe.htm>, referenced 15/08/06).

Furthermore, Schoffer claimed that "Spatiodynamic sculpture, for the first time, makes it possible *to replace man* with a work of abstract art, acting on its own initiative, which introduces into the show world a new being whose behaviour and career are capable of ample developments" (italics added). If the human artist is indeed "replaced" by some abstract, electronic, art, then surely the personal signature *must* disappear? (And, given the cultural attitudes sketched in the previous section, perhaps all the better for that?)—Well, maybe. But maybe not: see below.

CYSP 1 wasn't the only electronically controlled mobile sculpture of the late-1950s. Others included Edward Ihnatowizx's *SAM* and the *Senster*. These impersonal, 'autonomous', artefacts were soon joined by others, such as Gordon Pask's *Colloquy of Mobiles*, and—in 1968—shown in the *Cybernetic Serendipity* exhibition at London's Institute of Contemporary Arts (Reichardt 1968). That exhibition, curated by Jasia Reichardt (at the suggestion of Max Bense, who had organized the Stuttgart show), was hugely influential in this nascent corner of the art world. And general-purpose digital computers, as opposed to specially built devices like CYSP 1 and the *Senster*, were now arriving on the scene. In consequence, computer art became increasingly visible, with the Computer Arts Society being founded in 1969.

That's not to say that it was accepted by mainstream artists and critics, for it was not. Indeed, in 1967 the editor of *ArtForum* rejected an art historian's article on the genre, saying: "I can't imagine ARTFORUM ever doing a special issue on electronics or computers in art, but one never knows" (Brown 2005: 3). Even in the 1970s, London's Slade School was most unusual, as a high-prestige 'traditional' institution, in offering postgraduate courses in this area (Brown, forthcoming). Today, the area is still seen by orthodox critics as maverick, if not worse. (However, some of the early hostility has been replaced by welcome in postmodernist circles, due to the use by some computer artists of methods and metaphors drawn from artificial life—Boden 2006: 1.iii.b–d. One example is described in Section VI.)

Some of the first computer artists became involved partly because of their fascination with the then-new machines as such: "toys for boys", one might say. Others were drawn in by their interest in specific applications: the Slade "Systems" group, for instance, were especially intrigued by Martin Gardner's (1970) report of John Conway's mathematical "Game of Life". Yet others, such as Cohen, saw computer art as a way of helping them to understand their own creative processes.

But some turned to computer art precisely because, already influenced by modernism, they favoured impersonality. Ernest Edmonds, then a young painter fascinated by abstract structures, was a case in point (see Chapter 7 of this volume). So was Paul Brown.

Brown's desire to flee the personal was especially strong. As a 20-year-old art student, he was enthused by *Cybernetic Serendipity*. For besides the intrinsic interest of the various pieces on show, the exhibition suggested to him that computers might be used to do something which, thanks to the modernist influences described in Section IV, he already wanted to do. Namely, not merely to create 'impersonal' works, but *to lose his personal signature* in doing so.

It turned out that this was easier said than done. One reason is that Brown himself, after forty years as a professional artist, still cannot say just what his personal signature is. As remarked in Section III, recognizing it and describing it are two very different things. Whatever it is, in Brown's case, it certainly is not a matter of a specific mark (such as a particular form of ear lobe) recurring in his work. It is more a matter of an overall stylistic 'feel' that he cannot pin down in words.

(More Berenson than Morelli, one might say.) Nor is it something which only Brown himself can recognize. Others too, who are familiar with his oeuvre, can often recognize a previously unseen 'Brown' just as instantly, and just as confidently, as Morelli was able to recognize an unfamiliar Giorgione in the Borghese (see Section III). Even his very earliest pieces (Brown 1977) have an evident visual kinship with his recent/current work.

He had hoped as a young man that the clarity with which art-making has to be defined if computers are involved might help him both to identify his signature and (by changing the generative rules) to lose it. Reasonable enough hopes, one might think. But no: even though all his art has been computer-generated since the 1970s, it still betrays its human author's individual hand. And this, even though he has deliberately aimed for authorial anonymity.

It appears, then, that if one wishes to use computers so as to lose one's personal signature, deliberate self-effacement in the hands-on practice of one's art is not the way to do it. Can some other way be found?

VI. EVOLVING ANONYMITY

Today, Brown is using computers in a new way in trying to achieve his long-standing artistic goal. An interdisciplinary team, with Brown as a leading member, aims to evolve line-drawing robots whose products are of some aesthetic interest (no more than that!), but which do not carry the telltale traces of a work by Brown himself.

The first obvious question to ask about this project, named *Drawbots*, is "Why evolve line-drawing gizmos, as opposed to simply designing (programming/building) them?" The second is "Why use robots, as opposed to computer graphics (i.e. programs for drawing images on paper or virtual images in cyberspace)?"

The answer to the first question is that if the line-drawing computer system has been evolved then, thanks to the many random mutations that will have taken place, it has *not* been prespecified in detail by the artist-programmer. Accordingly, there may [sic] be a chance of avoiding that individual's personal signature. Whether that "may" can, in practice or even in principle, be replaced by a "will" is the key point at issue.

As for the second question, the answer is that a robot, being a material object functioning in the physical world, can be affected not only by its program and/or internal design but also by unexpected—and perhaps serendipitous—events in the physical environment. Again, this offers a means by which the programmer's personal signature may be bypassed, or anyway diluted. (An early example of this sort of thing occurred in the 1970s, when the moving 'legs' of a kinetic sculpture—alias a robot—happened to scratch the wooden floor of London's Royal Academy. Although the RA was doubtless incensed, the sculptor, Darrell Viner, was intrigued. He was so "fascinated by the structure of the repetitive scratches and their relationship to cross-hatching" that he went on to make artworks produced by comparable, though simulated, means—Brown, forthcoming: 5.)

The "serendipity" in the physical events involved can even include cases where a radically new feature appears in the robot's behaviour. In a previous experiment done by a member of the *Drawbots* team, a population of robots evolved a new sensory capacity—not merely an improved sensory capacity—as a result of contingent, and previously unremarked, facts about the physical environment (Bird and Layzell 2002). That suggests the possibility that a fundamentally transformative change in the Drawbots' drawing style might occur. If so, then presumably the new style would not bear Brown's individual mark, even if the previous style had done so.

There is a third obvious question also, namely, "What can it possibly mean to talk of *evolving* robots?" Very briefly (for more detail see Boden 2006: 15.vi–vii), designs for robots—both their 'bodily anatomy' and the detailed structure of their controller, or 'brain'—can be randomly mutated by a computer program, and the results compared for their success in achieving the task that the programmers have in mind. As in biological evolution, the most successful designs at each generation are selected for further breeding. (The testing/comparison is done in simulation; but every so often, the current best design is implemented in a real robot, to ensure that it does behave as the simulation suggests.)

The selection is sometimes done interactively, by a human being making the comparisons. At other times, it is done automatically by the program itself. This requires that a 'fitness function' be specified by the programmer, which the program can use to make the selection at each generation. (The fitness function itself may evolve, again either interactively or automatically.) As we'll see in Section VII, this fact is the Achilles' heel of the *Drawbots* research.

The Drawbots themselves are small wheeled vehicles carrying a retractable pen. And the task in the team's minds is line drawing. By that is meant not drawing pictures that represent real things (as both stick-men and Renaissance cartoons do), nor even drawing geometrical designs, but simply drawing *lines*... which can curve, cross, stop, and approach each other in myriad ways—and which may sometimes change in thickness too. Brown's hope is that robots can be evolved which will draw aesthetically acceptable lines *that do not exhibit his personal signature*. In other words, the fitness function/s to be followed by the robot should guarantee aesthetic acceptability but should not be so 'rich' as to express his personal style.

In principle, that would not preclude there being a telltale identifier, or quasi-signature (one can hardly say a "personal" signature), *produced by an evolved robot itself*. This would be a pattern that distinguishes its drawings from those of its siblings and close cousins. The evolution of such patterns is in principle possible because new performance details will follow from random mutations, and these details can be perpetuated provided that they do not compromise fitness.

Such details could include drawn patterns or line features discriminated by the gizmo's visual sensors. Indeed, a robot might even develop particular motor habits, driven by motor circuits conserved in its 'brain' (see Section III). Suppose that a sudden movement, caused by a recently mutated motor circuit, led to a mark that was then selected (along with the rest of the drawing) by Brown. This might lead the motor circuit to endure, forming the basis of a future motor habit. That habit could be involved either in many different stylistic choices, or only in one (think of an overall stylistic 'feel' and of ear lobes, respectively). In short, the general style that is selected via the fitness function could allow for idiosyncratic expression (alias signatures) by different robots within the same generation or lineage.

If the fitness function were to include measures of computational economy, the different robots might even develop quasi-signatures for much the same (psychological) reasons that human beings do. However, it is hardly likely that such patterns would arise as a matter of course, as they do in the work of human artists. For the root of the personal signature, as we saw in Section III, is the need for economy in information processing within a highly complex system—a criterion that does not apply in robots as simple as those being considered here.

Whether it is possible for the Drawbots to lose the stamp of Brown's individual artistry depends on a number of things. One is the extent to which Brown, or anyone else, can say just what his personal signature consists in. If he knew that, he would be in a much better position to try to avoid it. However, for the reasons given in Section III, he does not.

Possibly, the research may help him towards a better—if still incomplete—understanding of this. For in examining the various drawings made by the Drawbots, he will have to ask himself two questions: *Is it aesthetically acceptable?* and *Is it evidently a 'Brown'?* In answering that second question over and over again, as the drawing style mutates across the generations, and in posing it to colleagues with an appropriately practised critical eye, he may achieve a more explicit understanding of just what his own style is. (Then again, he may not.) But that could happen without his ever answering *No* to the second question. In that case, he still would not have 'lost' his signature, despite understanding it more deeply. Whether the increased understanding would enable him to dilute it, if not to shed it, in his (non-evolutionary) future work is an interesting question.

Another factor that will affect the likelihood of success in the project is the extent to which aesthetic acceptability can rest on relatively primitive visual features. "Primitive", here, means both *simple* and *naturally salient*. For example, shininess (of satin, silver, polished ivory, lurex, chromium . . .) is relatively simple to discriminate, and naturally salient too. That's so for good evolutionary reasons, involving the fitness-enhancing nature of reflective expanses of water (Boden 2006: 8.iv.a). In other words, it's no accident that shininess is aesthetically appealing to a very wide range of individuals and cultures. Are there any features of line drawings such as those the Drawbots could produce which are naturally attractive (and easily discriminable) in a comparable way?

For example, if the Drawbots were able to change pens, might they evolve a preference for the shiny lines left by a silver pen? They could do so, if their visual apparatus could discriminate shininess. To be sure, the robotics team would have to build reflectance into the fitness function: no robot 'naturally' prefers it. But reflectance is such an easily discriminable property, and so near-universally liked by human beings, that the team could not be accused of cheating were they to do that. (Some cultural groups positively avoid shininess, regarding it as vulgar; but that is irrelevant here, since this critical attitude has developed *precisely because* the liking for shininess is so very common.) Nor would putting silveriness into the fitness function result in drawings that display Brown's personal signature, for that (whatever it is) is not a matter of shininess.

It's easy to see that Brown's authorial mark does not involve shininess. What it *does* involve is less clear. Suppose it were to turn out that all the perceptible features favoured (via the fitness function) by 'aesthetically competent' Drawbots were relatively high-level and/or complex, with no 'natural' attractiveness for human beings in general. In that case, their drawings would probably be more specific to Brown's personal style. His project would have failed. However, "success" and "failure" here admit of several levels. In the language used above, Brown's signature may become more or less *diluted*, even if it cannot be entirely lost.

Among the naturally discriminable features that are already being considered by the *Drawbots* team are holes, line crossings, and fractals (of varying complexity or depth). But why should one expect any of these things to be 'naturally' attractive?

Well, consider fractals, for instance. These are ubiquitous in Nature, both in living things and in environmental features such as rocks and coastlines. According to the 'biophilia' hypothesis (Wilson 1984), *Homo sapiens* has evolved to respond favourably not only to conspecifics and other aspects of our original ecological niche (the African Savannah) but also to living things and natural environments in general. If that's so, then fractals might well have some natural attraction for us.

That's merely an argument for plausibility. But there is also some evidence that fractals of a certain kind are spontaneously favoured in art as in nature—and even, as William Congreve said of music, that they can soothe the savage breast. Richard Taylor claimed, in the late 1990s, that Jackson Pollock's canvases, far from being random splashes of paint, have specific fractal properties to which most viewers respond in a positive way, and by which his paintings can be distinguished from fakes (Taylor et al. 1999a and b). Specifically, people prefer those Pollock paintings which have a fractal dimension of 1.5 (his later paintings reach 1.8+). By comparison, people asked to choose between natural images (or between simulated coastlines) prefer a fractal dimension of 1.3. Taylor's claim aroused huge interest (e.g. Spehar et al. 2003), and was later followed by experiments showing that viewing Pollock's images can actually reduce stress (Taylor et al. 2005).

Taylor's early remarks about how to discriminate genuine Pollocks from fakes, have recently been challenged (Jones-Smith and Mathur 2006). One aspect of that challenge is especially intriguing here: Katherine Jones-Smith reported that a careless doodle done by her showed the same fractal properties as those found in Pollock's work. She didn't ask whether the doodle had any aesthetic value. To the contrary, she implied that, being a thoughtless scribble, it did not. But if she had asked people whether they "liked" it, or whether they preferred it to some other mark (maybe one produced accidentally), she might have found that people ascribed some—albeit small—degree of aesthetic merit to it. If that were so, it suggests that a suitably fractal-favouring Drawbot might make aesthetically acceptable ('natural') drawings that don't show anyone's individual mark: not hers, not Pollock's, and not Brown's either.

VII. THE LIKELIHOOD OF SUCCESS—AND WHAT IT WOULD MEAN

The best way of estimating the result of the *Drawbots* project is simply to wait and see. Meanwhile, are there any specific reasons to suspect that it will succeed, or fail? And if it succeeds, would it follow that the creativity exhibited in the drawings of the newly evolved Drawbots must be attributed to the Drawbots themselves, rather than to Brown? *'No signature, no creative authorship'*, perhaps?

As remarked above, the Achilles' heel of the project lies in the fitness function. This is true in two related senses, one philosophical and one psychological.

First, if it is Brown who is continually deciding on the fitness function as the research proceeds then perhaps it is *his* aesthetic judgement, and also *his* artistic creativity, which is really responsible for the final drawings? (For shorthand purposes, let's ignore the creative role of the other human beings on the team.) Many philosophers would say that there is no "perhaps" about it, that *of course* Brown's creativity lies behind whatever aesthetic interest the Drawbots' drawings happen to have. For they believe that it is in principle absurd to ascribe creativity, or aesthetic judgement, to any computer system—no matter how superficially impressive its performance may be.

Their belief typically rests on assumptions about one or more of four highly controversial issues, including intentionality and consciousness (Boden 2004: ch. 11). Accordingly, it can be challenged—though not definitively refuted. However, even if one were happy to reject their claim as a general philosophical position, that would not settle the question at issue here. For in the specific case of the *Drawbots* research, the human source of the fitness function is a distinct embarrassment for anyone wanting to grant all the creative credit to the computer.

This embarrassment would persist whether or not the project succeeded in its own terms—that is, irrespective of whether Brown's signature had been lost. For if the final fitness function were to exploit only what in Section VI were called "primitive" aesthetic properties, so that Brown as an individual artist had become invisible in the final-stage drawings, it would still be true that the aesthetic decisions involved in developing the fitness function were *such as are naturally made by human beings*. Brown's hand (judgement) would still be there—but functioning as the hand of a generic human being, not of a particular individual. (In terms of the distinction made in Section III, the fitness function would describe the general style, without imposing his detailed 'authorial' implementation.)

That argument would apply even if the robots' drawing style had shown a truly fundamental change: a new style (presumably, a 'non-Brown' style), as opposed to an improved style. We saw in Section VI that the physical 'embodiment' of the Drawbots makes it in principle possible for such serendipitous change to occur. By definition, the stylistic change would have been caused by some unconsidered and/or contingent feature of the robots' physical environment. So Brown couldn't be credited with initiating it. But he could, perhaps, be credited with 'causing' it, since the incipient change will be maintained (and perhaps developed) only if it is approved/selected by his personal decision or by the fitness function already evolved under his direction. In such a case, Brown might be regarded as the creative spirit behind the final drawings *even though* he never foresaw them, and *even though* they are free of his personal mark.

What of the psychological question? Are there any psychological reasons to expect that Brown *will not* be able to decide on a fitness function that entirely avoids his personal signature?

One psychological consideration discussed in Section III was relevance. This issue is less obviously crucial here than it would be if Brown were trying to evolve robots capable of realistic representational drawings. If the Drawbots were intended to draw human faces, for instance, they had better include depictions of eyes, mouth, and even the (relatively less relevant) ear lobes. And they had better *not* add horns, or wings. But if a tinge of surrealism were to be favoured (by Brown), then a horn-like protuberance appearing in generation 1,000 might be selected and 'shaped' so that recognizable devilish/goatlike horns were visible at generation 9,000. The same might occur if Brown felt that familiar myths about the Devil were relevant to the 'topic' of the drawings. In either case, Brown's own judgements about relevance would be reflected in the robots' behaviour, and—to the extent that these are idiosyncratic—so would his personal mark.

In fact, Brown has always been an abstract artist, so is not aiming to evolve 'representational' robots. Even so, issues of relevance—or rather, issues of what he deems to be relevant—may arise. Aesthetic acceptability depends in part on intelligibility. To be sure (and as already remarked), intelligibility may be more or less easy to achieve in differing artistic styles. But utter chaos will satisfy nobody. In other words, one factor underlying judgements of aesthetic acceptability is the computational effort that is involved in comprehension. A 'messy' line drawing (or doodle), for instance, may be unacceptable largely because its components *do not* appear to be mutually relevant. That is, they do not appear to be 'coherent', or to 'make sense'. (Perhaps there are no closed curves, suggesting bounded physical objects? And/or perhaps there are no T-junctions where one line stops as it meets another, suggesting occlusion of a line/edge by some other physical thing?) These judgements, as we've seen, are not usually conscious—and it may not be possible to make them conscious. It follows that it may not be possible for Brown to avoid them deliberately.

A closely related issue is the extent to which Brown can banish his own preferred schemas from the fitness function. (Compare: evolving robots to draw faces *without* eyes.) If he cannot, because these schemas are so deeply entrenched in his mind and experience, they will inevitably be reflected in the fitness function and therefore in the final drawings.

At that point, we come full circle to the issue discussed above in terms of "simplicity" and "naturalness". The more that the features favoured in the fitness function are complex, culture-based, and idiosyncratic to Brown, the less will the final-generation Drawbots be free of his personal stamp. If the Brown signature is preserved, despite all his efforts, that will be because he has found it necessary to build relatively 'rich' criteria into the fitness function. As we've seen, it is still an open question as to how rich the final criteria of aesthetic fitness will need to be. If they are all relatively simple, then Brown's creative inspiration may seem less important. At most, the fact that he is a human being will be relevant, not the fact that he is Paul Brown. (Any idiosyncratic 'signature' visible in the drawings might be attributable to the evolutionary vicissitudes of the robots themselves, as explained in Section VI.)

What if, contrary to all his hopes, Brown's personal signature *remains* still visible to experts (dare we say connoisseurs?) looking at the robots' drawings? In such a case, and *even if* one were willing in principle to grant creativity to some computer systems, it would seem bizarre to attribute creativity to the Drawbot. For we saw in Section II that the concept of the personal signature arose specifically in order to attribute a given work of art to one creative source (normally, one human individual) rather than another. The signature, in short, points to the person. This was recognized by the computer artists (quoted in Section V) who spoke of "the organization of the artefact [bearing] the stamp of its designer". Whether that telltale organization were deliberately designed, as they were assuming, or gradually evolved, as in the *Drawbots* project ('failure' here being supposed), it would point to one person: Brown.

REFERENCES

Allport, G. W. (1942), *The Use of Personal Documents in Psychological Science* (Social Science Research Council Bulletin, 49 New York).

Barthes, R. (1968/77), 'The Death of the Author', in S. Heath (ed., trans.), *Image, Music, Text* (New York: Hill and Wang), 142–8 (this essay was written in May 1968, during the Paris *événements*).

Bird, J., and Layzell, P. (2002), 'The Evolved Radio and Its Implications to Modelling the Evolution of Novel Sensors', *Proceedings of Congress on Evolutionary Computation*, CEC-2002, 1836–41.

Boden, M. A. (2004), *The Creative Mind: Myths and Mechanisms* (2nd edn., expanded/revised London: Routledge).

—— (2006), *Mind as Machine: A History of Cognitive Science* (Oxford: Oxford University Press).

—— (2007), 'Stillness as Autonomy', *CADE-2007*, (Computers in Art and Design Education), Perth, Sept. 2007.

Brown, P. (1977), 'The CBI North West Export Award', 1st pub. in *Page Sixty Two—Special Terminate CACHe Issue: Bulletin of the Computer Arts Society, Northern Hemisphere* (Autumn 2005), 12–13.

—— (2005), 'Editorial', *Page Sixty Two—Special Terminate CACHe Issue: Bulletin of the Computer Arts Society, Northern Hemisphere* (Autumn 2005), 1–3.

—— (in press), 'The Mechanization of Art', in M. Wheeler, P. Husbands, and O. Holland (eds.), *The Mechanisation of Mind in History* (Cambridge, Mass.: MIT Press).

—— (forthcoming), 'From Systems Art to Artificial Life: Early Generative Art at the Slade School of Fine Art', in C. Gere, P. Brown, N. Lambert, and C. Mason (eds.), *White Heat and Cold Logic: British Computer Arts 1960–1980, An Historical and Critical Analysis* (Cambridge, Mass.: MIT Press).

Bruner, J. S., Goodnow, J., and Austin, G. (1956), *A Study of Thinking* (New York: Wiley).
Fodor, J. A. (1983), *The Modularity of Mind: An Essay in Faculty Psychology* (Cambridge, Mass.: MIT Press).
Gardner, M. (1970), 'The Fantastic Combinations of John Conway's New Solitaire Game "Life" ', *Scientific American*, 223/4: 120–3.
Ginzburg, C. (1992), 'Clues: Roots of an Evidential Paradigm', in C. Ginzburg, *Clues, Myths, and the Historical Method* (Baltimore, Md.: Johns Hopkins University Press), 96–125 and 200–14, trans. J. and A. C. Tedeschi (Italian edn. 1986).
Humboldt, W. von. (1836), *On Language: The Diversity of Human Language-Structure and Its Influence on the Mental Development of Mankind*, trans. P. Heath (Cambridge: Cambridge University Press, 1988).
Johnson, B. S. (1969), *The Unfortunates* (London: Panther).
Johnson, S. (1781), *The Lives of the Most Eminent English Poets; With Critical Observations on Their Works*, ed. R. Lonsdale (Oxford: Clarendon Press, 2006).
Jones-Smith, K., and Mathur, H. (2006), 'Revisiting Pollock's Drip Paintings', *Nature*, 444 (Nov. 30), E9–10 (published online 29 Nov.).
Le Corbusier [pseud.; i.e. C.-E. Jeanneret] (1923), *Vers une Architecture* (Paris), English trans. by F. Etchells of 13th French edn., *Towards a New Architecture* (London: John Rodker, 1927).
LeWitt, S. (1967), 'Paragraphs on Conceptual Art', *Artforum*, 5/10: 79–83; repr. in K. Stiles and P. Selz (eds.), *Theories and Documents of Contemporary Art: A Sourcebook of Artists' Writings* (Berkeley and Los Angeles: University of California Press), 822–6.
—— (1969), 'Sentences on Conceptual Art', *Art-Language*, 1: 11–13; repr. in K. Stiles and P. Selz (eds.), *Theories and Documents of Contemporary Art: A Sourcebook of Artists' Writings* (Berkeley and Los Angeles: University of California Press), 826–7.
—— (1971), 'Doing Wall Drawings', *Art Now*, 3/2; excerpts in Lippard (1973: 200 f.).
Lippard, L. R. (1973), *Six Years: The Dematerialization of the Art Object from 1966 to 1972* (New York: Praeger).
Llewellyn, N. (1997), 'Une science du regard: Les Connaisseurs', in E. Pommier (ed.), *Histoire de l'Histoire de l'Art*, 2. *xviii et xix siècles* (Paris: Louvre), 293–325.
McCormack, J., Dorin, A., and Innocent, T. (2004), 'Generative Design: A Paradigm for Design Research', in J. Redmond, D. Durling, and A. de Bono (eds.), *Futureground*, vol. 1 (Melbourne: Design Research Society), available as a pdf-file from McCormack's home page.
Mahon, D. (1947), *Studies in Seicento Art and Theory* (London: Warburg Institute).

Morelli, G. (1877/1883), *Italian Masters in German Galleries: A Critical Essay on the Italian Pictures in the Galleries of Munich-Dresden-Berlin* (London: George Bell and Sons), trans. from German by L. M. Richter.

O'Bierne, T. H. (1968), 'Dice-Music Trios', *Musical Times*, 109 (1508), 911–13.

O'Hear, A. (1995), 'Art and Technology: An Old Tension', in R. Fellows (ed.), *Philosophy and Technology* (Cambridge: Cambridge University Press), 143–58.

Perkins, D. N. (1981), *The Mind's Best Work* (Cambridge, Mass.: Harvard University Press).

Reichardt, J. (ed.) (1968), *Cybernetic Serendipity: The Computer and the Arts*, special issue of *Studio International*, published to coincide with an exhibition held at the Institute of Contemporary Arts, 2 Aug.–20 Oct. 1968 (London: Studio International).

Ricks, C. (1963), *Milton's Grand Style* (Oxford: Clarendon Press).

Spehar, B., Clifford, C., Newell, B., and Taylor, R. (2003), 'Universal Aesthetic of Fractals', *Computers and Graphics*, 27: 813–20.

Sperber, D., and Wilson, D. (1986), *Relevance: Communication and Cognition* (Oxford: Blackwell).

Taylor, R., Micolich, A. P., and Jonas, D. (1999a), 'Fractal Analysis of Pollock's Dripped Paintings', *Nature*, 399: 422 (one page only).

—————(1999b), 'Fractal Expressionism', *Physics World* (Oct.).

Taylor, R. P., Spehar, B., Wise, J. A., Clifford, C. W. G., Newell, B. R., Hagerhall, C. M., Purcell, T., and Martin, T. P. (2005), 'Perceptual and Physiological Responses to the Visual Complexity of Pollock's Dripped Fractal Patterns', *Journal of Non-Linear Dynamics, Psychology and Life Sciences*, 9: 89–114.

Tillyard, E. M. W., and Lewis, C. S. (1939), *The Personal Heresy: A Controversy* (London: Oxford University Press).

Wilson, E. O. (1984), *Biophilia* (London: Harvard University Press).

7

What Is Generative Art?*

I. INTRODUCTION

Since the late 1950s, an ever-diversifying set of novel art practices has arisen which are still little known or discussed in aesthetics and art theory. (For a wide variety of examples, see Krueger 1991; Wilson 2002; Candy and Edmonds 2002; Whitelaw 2004; Woolf 2004; Popper 2007.) As Jon McCormack, one of the artists concerned, has put it, "[M]uch of the innovation today is not achieved within the precious bubble of fine art, but by those who work in the industries of popular culture—computer graphics, film, music videos, games, robotics and the Internet" (McCormack 2003: 5). The "bubble of fine art" refers to a shifting socially accepted norm. Artists often work outside the norm of their day, as famously illustrated by Marcel Duchamp and his readymades or John Cage and silence. The novel approaches that McCormack mentions are closely related, both theoretically and methodologically—so much so, that they are often all lumped together under one label: "computer art", "electronic art", or "generative art". One aim of this paper is to clarify how they can be distinguished.

Theoretically, this new art originated in cybernetics and general systems theory. The young painter Roy Ascott, later to be highly influential in the field, identified the novel activity as "a cybernetic vision" (1966/7). And the exceptionally creative cybernetician Gordon Pask was a key influence. For besides producing and/or imagining some of the first artworks of this general type (in the 1950s), he provided

---

* This chapter is co-authored with Ernest A. Edmonds (Creativity & Cognition Studios, Australasian CRC for Interaction Design, University of Technology, Sydney, Australia).
We are grateful for helpful comments given to us by Dustin Stokes, of the Centre for Cognitive Science at the University of Sussex.

much of the theoretical impetus that inspired the more philosophically minded artists in the field (Boden 2006: 4.v.e).

Very soon, the "cybernetic vision" was bolstered by ideas about structure and process drawn from computer science. This paper's co-author Ernest Edmonds, for instance, turned from paintbrush and easel to the computer in the 1960s: he thought he could produce more interesting art in that way (see Section III). At much the same time, music and visual art was produced which reflected AI's computational theories of mind. Indeed, Harold Cohen, a renowned abstract painter in 1960s London, deserted his previous working practices largely because he felt that doing computer art would help him to understand his own creative processes (McCorduck 1991; Boden 2004: 150–66, 314 f.).

Over the past twenty years, this artistic field has been inspired also by ideas about emergence, evolution, embodiment, and self-organization. These concepts are borrowed from various areas of cognitive science, and in particular from artificial life (A-Life). However, the theoretical roots of A-Life reach back to mid-century cybernetics and automata theory (Boden 2006: 4.v.e, 15.iv–v). In short, the theoretical wheel has turned full circle.

The methodological wheel, meanwhile, has climbed an ascending spiral. For the art practices outside the bubble are grounded in technologies for communication and information processing whose power and variety have burgeoned over the last half-century. (Often, this means that the customary lone artist is replaced by a team, some of whose members may be computer scientists and/or tele-engineers.)

Most of them rely heavily on digital computing, and in particular on methods drawn from AI/A-Life. Specifically, they have employed both symbolic and connectionist computation, and—more recently—cellular automata, L-systems, and evolutionary programming too. This is an ascending spiral, not a linear ascent, because two of those "recent" methods were foreseen (by John von Neumann) in 1950s cybernetics, and all three had been mathematically defined by the 1960s—but none could be fruitfully explored, by artists or scientists, until powerful computers became available much later (Boden 2006: 15.v–vi).

The resulting artworks are highly diverse. They include music, sonics, the visual arts, video art, multimedia installations, virtual reality, kinetic sculpture, robotics, performance art, and text. And whereas some of these outside-the-bubble activities place ink or paint onto a surface, others involve desktop VDUs or room-scale video projection. Yet others eschew the virtuality of cyberspace, constructing moving physical machines instead.

The labels attached to these new art forms vary, and have not yet settled down into a generally accepted taxonomy. The names preferred by the artists involved include: generative art, computer art, digital art, computational art, process-based art, electronic art, software art, technological art, and telematics. All of those terms are commonly used to denote the entire field—and (although distinctions are sometimes drawn) they are often treated as synonyms. In addition, there are names for subfields: interactive art, evolutionary art, video art, media (and new-media and multimedia) art, holographic art, laser art, virtual art, cyborg art, robotic art, telerobotics, net art . . . and more. Again, the extension of these labels is not always clear.

It's partly for that reason that "a satisfactory critical framework of new forms in art technology has yet to be developed" (Candy and Edmonds 2002: 266). We hope that the distinctions made in this paper may help towards such a framework. Mainly, however, we aim to outline some philosophical problems that arise with respect to the art that lies outside McCormack's "precious bubble".

In Section II, we sketch the history and current usage of some of the new labels within the artistic community concerned. Then, in Section III, Edmonds gives a brief autobiographical account of why he chose—and now chooses—one name rather than another for his own art.

Section IV distinguishes various categories, focusing especially on computer art, generative art, evolutionary art, robotic art, and interactive art. The terms we define here use words that are already being used by the artists in question. Indeed, we hope that our analysis may help readers to interpret these artists' discussions of their work. But we are not aiming to offer a report of common usage because, as already remarked, such usage is not consistent. Rather, our account is intended as a theoretical tool with which to highlight certain distinctions that have philosophical and/or aesthetic interest.

The philosophical issues concerned are indicated in Section V. We'll see that judgements concerning creativity, authorial responsibility, agency, autonomy, authenticity, and (sometimes) ontology are even more problematic outside the precious bubble than inside it. To explore these matters fully would be beyond the scope of this paper. But we identify some pertinent questions, and some possible responses to them.

II. A TERMINOLOGICAL HISTORY

The terms "generative art" and "computer art" have been used in tandem, and more or less interchangeably, since the very earliest days. For the first exhibition of computer art was called *Generative Computer-graphik* (see the description of the event in Nake 2005). It was held in Stuttgart in February 1965 and showed the work of Georg Nees. Four years later he produced the first PhD thesis on computer art, giving it the same title as the exhibition (Nees 1969). That thesis was soon widely consulted by the small but growing community, harnessing the words *generative* and *computer* together in its readers' minds.

In November 1965 Nees showed again in Stuttgart. On this occasion, the exhibition also included the computer graphics work of Frieder Nake. Both artists used the term "Generative". The word was used here to identify art that was produced from a computer program and, hence, was at least in part produced automatically. In that sense, the work of the graphic artist Michael Noll that was exhibited in New York between the two German shows was also generative.

Others pioneering the activities outside McCormack's bubble also adopted the term. For example, when Manfred Mohr, who knew Nake, started producing drawings with a computer program in 1968 he termed it "generative art". (Mohr still uses that description of his work and uses it in the same sense.) And the philosopher Max Bense—who had composed the manifesto for the original Stuttgart exhibiton of 1965—was writing about what he called "generative aesthetics" (Nake 1998). Alternative tags were already being offered, however: an influential discussion by the art historian Jack Burnham (1968), for instance, identified the new work as "process art".

In music, the use of computer systems to produce work started very early on. By 1957 Lejaren Hiller and Leonard Isaacson had created the *Illiac Suite for String Quartet* (Hiller and Isaacson 1958) and in 1962 Iannis Xenakis completed the *Stochastic Music Program*. Xenakis published essays on formalized music in the following year (Xenakis 1963; English trans. Xenakis 1971) and was a key figure in the development of computer-generated music. Probably as a result of this early start, the development of computer-generative music preceded that of computer-generative visual art.

Not all generative visual art involves computers. Pre-computer examples include such clear cases as Kenneth Martin, whose 1949

What Is Generative Art? 129

abstract painting used basic geometrical figures (squares, circles, diagrams) and rules of proportion (Martin 1951/1954). Later, his *Chance and Order* and *Chance, Order, Change* series combined rule-driven generation with random choice. Whilst chance events—such as selecting a number out of a hat—determined the course of the work, everything else was determined by the rules that Martin had devised. Other non-computer generative artists are identified in Section IV, where we'll see that the generative processes involved vary widely in type.

Today, the term "Generative Art" is still current within the relevant artistic community. Since 1998 a series of conferences have been held in Milan with that title (Generativeart.com), and Brian Eno has been influential in promoting and using generative art methods (Eno 1996). Both in music and in visual art, the use of the term has now converged on work that has been produced by the activation of a set of rules *and* where the artist lets a computer system take over at least some of the decision making (although, of course, the artist determines the rules).

Rules are at the heart of this type of art. But what computer scientists call rule-based programming (e.g. Kowalski and Levy 1996) is not necessarily implied. The computer-art community regards it as important that the artwork is generated from a set of specified rules, or constraints, rather than from a step-by-step algorithm. But the detailed implementation method (i.e. the specific computer system that's being used) is not normally seen to be significant.

To understand this point, consider an oversimplified illustration of the programming concepts just mentioned. When a program is written in a step-by-step (algorithmic) way, the programmer instructs the computer to "do A", then "do B", then under certain conditions "do C", otherwise "do D", and so on. When a programmer writes rules (constraints), however, they tell the computer that (for example) "Z should always be bigger than Y", 'X must never equal W', and so on—but they leave it to the computer system to work out how to apply those rules.

So in the step-by-step approach, the programmer is explicitly directing the actions of the computer. In the rule-based approach, by contrast, the translation from the specified rules to computer actions is not immediately clear. To know just how the specification of a rule determines computer behaviour we need to be aware of the details of the computer system that interprets the rules—which even a professional computer scientist may not know. Another way of putting this is to say that the artist leaves the computer to do its own thing without knowing *just what it is* which the computer will be doing.

One could argue that the art community's objection to a step-by-step algorithm is more a matter of taste than anything else. For even when a programmer has written explicit step-by-step code, he or she does not necessarily—or even usually—know the outcome. If they did, there would be no bugs (except those due to typing mistakes and punctuation errors). After all, the earliest programming was often done in order to calculate numerical values that were almost impossible to obtain otherwise. Those early efforts were relatively simple: most programs today are hugely more complex. So despite the differences between the two programming approaches described above, there is no distinction at the most fundamental level. Both types of program are unpredictable by their programmer.

However, computer artists—and computer scientists, too—know from their own experience that when writing algorithmic code there is a 'feel' of fully controlling the computer. This 'feel' does not carry over to systems where they are specifying sets of rules, or constraints.

In other words, rule-driven systems appear to have a greater degree of autonomy, relative to the conscious decisions of the human artist. That phenomenological fact is significant because autonomy is a concept that's closely connected with art-making (see Section V). This explains why computer artists are more comfortable in speaking of "generative art" where the system is rule-driven, not algorithmic—and why they usually avoid step-by-step programming.

The concepts of generative art and (programmed) computer art were assimilated right from the start. With the recent appearance of art using methods drawn from A-Life (for examples, see Whitelaw 2004; Tofts 2003; 2005: 80-103; Popper 2007: 118-29), the label "generative art", as used in the community concerned, has acquired biological overtones. In biology, the key word is common in discussions of morphological development and growth in plants and animals, and in references to reproduction. One or both of those meanings is/are sometimes explicitly stressed by self-styled generative artists whose work focuses on emergence, self-organization, and/or evolution. McCormack himself is one such example (e.g. Dorin and McCormack 2001; McCormack et al. 2004). Even so, the formal-mathematical sense remains a core aspect of the label's meaning.

III. A TERMINOLOGICAL AUTOBIOGRAPHY

[Addendum by M.A.B.: *The core of Edmonds's artistic oeuvre is an exploration of the possibilities inherent in colour as such. (As for his computer-science oeuvre, that includes one of the first logic-programming languages.) The subtlety of his colours, and the sequence of their changes, cannot be conveyed here, and nor can their audio aspects—but they are indicated on his website (www.ernestedmonds.com). It's worth noting that the curators of a major Washington DC festival in 2007 celebrating the fiftieth anniversary of the "ColorField" painters—Mark Rothko, Clyfford Still, Kenneth Noland, and the like—have chosen to include live showings of some of his recent work in the Experimental Media series at the Corcoran Gallery and the Ellipse Arts Center.*]

I (that is, Ernest Edmonds) had been committed to painting since my early teenage years, strongly influenced by the constructivists. I started to use a computer in my artwork in 1968, when I wrote a program that searched for an arrangement, a layout, of a given set of picture elements.

At the time, I was working on some problems in logic that involved finding sets of numbers that displayed, or revealed, certain conditions. The problem was to show that various axioms were independent by demonstrating that values existed that showed that no one of them could be derived from the others. The details of what this means do not matter here. Suffice it to say that I realized that I could write a computer program that would search for such numbers, and I did so. This resulted in the publication of my first research paper, which was in the *Journal of Symbolic Logic* (Edmonds 1969).

An interesting thing to notice is that the paper makes no mention of computers or computer programs. The program had enabled me to find the required set of numbers. All I had to do in the proof was to provide them. Whilst the computer was used to help me solve a problem in a non-computing domain, the computer itself was not part of the solution.

This is exactly how it was to turn out in my first use of the computer in art. I wrote a program to search for a visual layout which satisfied a set of conditions that I was able to specify. As with the logic, the computer could be dispensed with once the problem was solved, and the work itself neither used nor referred to a computer program at all. It is just that I could not have made the piece, called *Nineteen*, without the use of the computer.

With respect to a more specific concern for generative art, a crucial step was actually made conceptually in 1980. I realized that my long-standing interest in time could lead to a new kind of art, with the use of computers. Music, particularly serial music, had been very influential on my visual work; and I was fascinated by film. During the 1970s, I made some abstract films the hard way, by filming static abstract images and splicing the film together from very many such still clips. I started working on what I came to call video constructs. These are time-based, generative, abstract works (Edmonds 1988). The generative rules at the core of these works were, and are, based on the rules that I started to formulate when making *Nineteen* and which I used in my painting through the 1970s and on.

I did not show such a work publicly until 1985, but in many ways that showing was the culmination of much of the work of the 1970s. *Fragments* was the generative work shown at Exhibiting Space, London, as part of my exhibition *Duality and Co-Existence*, in 1985. In 2004, a restored version of *Fragments* was issued as a limited edition DVD and shown in the exhibition *Australian Concrete Constructive Art* (at the Conny Dietzschold Gallery, Sydney).

Why were generative processes interesting in my art? Well, there are many answers to that question, but I will start with the most pragmatic of them.

Making art is an iterative process. One makes a mark, for example, looks at it and then makes another (or not, of course). Art-making is a continual process of conception, action, and perception followed by reconceptualization—and so on. An important issue is that of matching the time and effort of the making (the laying down of a mark, for example) with its appropriate place in the cycle. Time-based work is very hard to make if each step has to be explicitly constructed. Using the computer as a generative engine magically removes this major problem. So, from a pragmatic point of view, I constructed a generative engine to make my time-based work so that the cycle of making, evaluating, and refining the work was faster and tighter.

My pragmatic answer to the question begs many points, of course. The key underlying issue is that of the order and use of rules in the works in the first place. That makes the generative solution possible. My motivations are not ideological or political. I understand and am sympathetic with many computer-artist colleagues who use rules and generative methods in order to distance themselves from the art-making, and who do this for ideological reasons (see Chapter 6 of this volume).

For me, however, it is simply a matter of reducing the enormous decision space of art-making to something manageable.

Ever since *Nineteen* my work has involved rules. Often, they were constraint sets, as described in Section II. But, with the advent of the time-based work, they became generative. The distinction here is important.

The use of rules in art-making does not necessarily imply that the art is generative in the sense that I have used the word in the past. (Note that we define G-art in a different way in Section IV.) The function of the rules in the process is a crucial issue. Where the rules are constraint sets, the art-making on the part of the human artist is as free, or almost as free, as ever. It is just that conditions are placed upon what is successful, whose results lie beyond the artist's intuition. A satisfactory work must not violate the constraints. As in mathematics or computer science, the fact that the problem space (of making the artwork) is bounded by clear constraints does not necessarily lead to any method or process for designing or making art.

In what I count as generative art, by contrast, the rules must be constructive. There are parallels here with mathematical logic (Goodstein 1951). That is to say, they must provide or imply a specific process that can lead to the desired outcome. That is the defining feature of generative art as I came to see it. Only if the rules are constructive does the artist hand over to the computer a significant element of the decision making that is at the core of the art-making.

There is no doubt that I am interested in the rules themselves, not merely in what they might generate. Early on, I saw that they were more than just a convenience. The rules define the form. Think of a fugue, or of serial music. Think of perspective, or the golden section. This is the second answer to the question of why I found generative processes artistically interesting. Generative art enables the artist to concentrate on the underlying rules themselves: the structures that define the artwork, as against the surface. (This is a position clearly associated with distaste for decoration and ornament.)

It is all a little more complicated than this, however. In generative art that follows the evolutionary A-Life approach (see Section IV), for example, sometimes the 'fitness function' is not automated. Sometimes a human operator, whether audience or artist, makes the fitness decision on the basis of who knows what: their intuitive judgement, one might as well say. In such cases, the rules are not fully constructive, because their deployment requires the intervention of a human agent.

This compromise to the core concept of generativity is normally accepted by computer artists, and I accept it also. It applies more widely than in A-Life evolution. In general, it is a matter of enabling *interaction* to come into the picture without dropping the term "generative art".

I was interested in interaction from the beginning of my concern for the role of computers in my art. Indeed, I made interactive work as early as 1970. However, when I started to use logic to generate time-based works in the 1980s, I was not working in that way. Later on, and independently of evolutionary art (which I have never personally pursued), I made a simple extension to my generative approach in order to accommodate interaction.

It did not involve a fitness function, and nor did it involve any other explicit evaluation step. What I did was to introduce the notion of "external data". These were values, stored in the computer, that were set and changed from time to time as a result of various sensor systems. For example, such an item could be the room temperature. Alternatively, it could be the degree of animation of people in front of the artwork. I made these external data available to the generative process, and wrote rules (constraints) that took account of them. I saw those rules as meta-rules, because the values detected at a given time were used to select which rules or rule-set should be used.

In my more recent work, I have added yet another mechanism. Again, in principle it is simple enough. It is, in effect, a state vector that can be varied by inputs (such as sounds picked up by a microphone, and detected behaviours by the audience), and which can be referred to just as the external data are. Thus, memory of a sort is made possible. Inputs or sensed data can cause changes at first only in the vector, but in ways that will influence the artwork's behaviour later—possibly much later (Edmonds, in press). Because of this delay, which precludes instantaneous effects on the system's behaviour, I talk about such works in terms of "influence" rather than "interaction".

IV. A TAXONOMY OF GENERATIVE ART

Our taxonomy distinguishes eleven types of art. We call them Ele-art, C-art, D-art, CA-art, G-art, CG-art, Evo-art, R-art, I-art, CI-art, and VR-art. Some of these activities, having been located within our classification, are then ignored. We pay most attention to various forms of CG-art, because these raise the most interesting philosophical issues.

This "taxonomy" is a decidedly non-Linnaean structure. Quite apart from the fact that our definitions, like most definitions, admit borderline cases and even anomalous counter-examples, there's no neat and tidy hierarchy of genus and species within which these eleven types can be located. Although there are some part–whole relations here, there are also untidy overlappings.

One type of overlapping concerns links with more traditional, or familiar, categories of art. Most cases of such art do not fall under our classification at all. But some of our concepts—namely: G-art, I-art, Evo-art, and R-art—cover artworks both inside and outside McCormack's "precious bubble". Admittedly, those which lie inside the bubble are relatively maverick examples, as we'll see. Indeed, some of them (produced by the 'conceptual' artists) were specifically intended to undermine the notion of "fine art" in terms of which the bubble is defined. For shorthand purposes, however, we locate *all* examples of non-computer art inside the bubble.

A summary list of our definitions is given at the end of this section. Meanwhile, we'll introduce them one by one, giving illustrative examples of each category.

Let us start with electronic art, or Ele-art. This wide concept covers *(df.) any artwork whose production involves electrical engineering and/or electronic technology*. So it ranges from simple analogue devices of the 1950s and 1960s such as Pask's *Musicolour* and *Colloquy* (Pask 1971; Mallen 2005) and Edward Ihnatowicz's kinetic sculpture *SAM* (Zivanovic 2005: 103)—all pioneering examples of interactive art, or I-art—to the highly sophisticated man-robot integrations recently embodied by the performance artist Stelarc (Smith 2005). And along the way, it covers the whole of computer art and media art, including those examples which exploit the advanced computational techniques of virtual reality.

Unlike mechanical art, such as Leonardo da Vinci's metal lion (who "after he had a while walked vp and downe, stoode still opening his breast, which was all full of Lillies and other flowers of diuers sortes"—Marr, forthcoming: n. 66), electronic art could not appear until the mid-twentieth century. But, as the previous paragraph implies, the technologies concerned have diversified richly since then. Accordingly, the highly inclusive label Ele-art is not very interesting for our purposes.

Surprisingly, perhaps, neither is the concept of computer art, or C-art. By C-art, we mean *(df.) art in whose productive process computers are involved*. This concept is apt for general art-historical purposes, because it covers every example that anyone might want to call computer art—including many that are commonly given other labels. It's less useful for us here, however, for two reasons.

First, it includes analogue as well as digital computers. Some of the earliest C-art work combined digital methods with specially built analogue devices. Ihnatowicz's giraffe-like kinetic sculpture *Senster* is a case in point (Zivanovic 2005). As for analogue computers as such, these were used in the early days. For example, in visual arts by Ben Laposky's work of the 1950s (Laposky 1969), and in the growth of electronic music at the same time, famously encouraged by the invention of the Moog synthesizer (Pinch and Trocco 2002).

Today, a few computer artists sometimes employ analogue *processes*, namely electrochemical reactions like those pioneered by Pask. Some of their work, including Pask-inspired 'sculptures' by Richard Brown (2001, 2006) and Andy Webster (2006–), will feature in a 2007 Edinburgh exhibition on *Gordon Pask and His Maverick Machines*. (In addition, a video on this theme called *Tuning Pask's Ear* has been shown in several European art galleries: Webster and Bird 2002.) But analogue *computers* are another matter—and are very rarely used by artists today. Because of the huge flexibility that is afforded by the general-purpose nature of digital computers, it is those machines which underlie most C-art. Indeed, to speak of computer art is typically to assume that digital computers are being used.

In other words, computer art is (usually) tacitly classed as digital art, or D-art. D-art *(df.) uses digital electronic technology of some sort*. It includes not only artworks generated by computers but also digitally manipulable (but human-produced) music and video. Common usage sometimes treats "digital art" and "computer art" as near-synonyms. In our taxonomy, they are analytically distinct—with most, but not quite all, C-art being included within D-art. (If the word "electronic" were removed from our definition, the nineteenth-century Pointillistes would count as D-artists; for their pictures were composed not of continuous brushstrokes or colour washes but of myriad individual spots of paint.)

D-art is more wide-ranging than may appear at first sight. For instance, some C-artists use visual software that is *intuitively* analogue, and so relatively 'natural' to work with. (One example is continuous vector-mapping, used instead of pixel-editing: Leggett 2000.) But they are relying on methods/hardware that are digital at base. In fact, most people who said today that they are using an analogue method (i.e.

an analogue virtual machine) would actually be working on a digital computer, used to simulate an analogue computer.

Similarly, most 'neural networks' or connectionist systems, whether used by cognitive scientists or by computer artists, are actually simulated on von Neumann machines. That's true, for instance, of Richard Brown's interactive *Mimetic Starfish*, a millennial version of the *Senster* that was described by *The Times* in 2000 as "the best bit of the entire [Millennium] dome". The starfish was built by engineering visual imagery, not metal: it is a neural-network based virtual creature (an image projected onto a marble table) that responds in extraordinarily lifelike ways to a variety of hand movements. In short, digital technology reaches further than one might think.

The second reason why the definition of C-art given above is too catholic for our purposes is that it includes cases where the computer functions merely as a tool under the close direction of the artist, rather like an extra paintbrush or a sharper chisel. Artists in the relevant community sometimes speak of this as "computer-aided" or "computer-assisted" art, contrasting it with what they call "computational" art—where the computer is more of a participant, or partner, in the art-making (e.g. Paul Brown 2003: 1). We call this CA-art, wherein *(df.) the computer is used as an aid (in principle, non-essential) in the art-making process.*

Consider video art and music videos, for instance. These popular outside-the-bubble activities qualify as CA-art in our sense. For the human-originated images and/or music are digitally stored and (usually) manipulated/transformed by the artist, using the computer as a tool. Other cases of CA-art include someone's doing a line drawing by hand on the computer screen, and then calling on a colouring program such as Photoshop to produce a Limited Edition of identical prints—or, for that matter, a unique image. This is an upmarket form of painting-by-numbers, wherein the hues for each area are chosen by the individual artist. Yet other examples include computer music that's so called because it uses electronic synthesizers and 'virtual' instruments.

In practice, the computer "aid" may be necessary for the art-making. It's impossible, for instance, to alter video images in certain ways except by using a computer. Similarly, some visual effects delivered by Photoshop could not have been produced by using oils, watercolours, or gouache. And synthesized computer music exploits sounds that had never been heard before synthesizers were developed. Nevertheless, the computer is not essential *in principle*. The relevant visual/sonic effects are specifically sought by the human artist, and might conceivably have been produced in some other way. Much as a species with iron-hard fingernails would not need chisels, so our vocal cords (or wood, metal, or cats' sinews . . .) might have been able to produce the sounds produced by synthesizers.

The subclass of C-art which interests us is the type where the computer is not used as a tool to effect some idea in the artist's mind but is in a sense (*just what* sense will be explored in Section V) partly responsible for coming up with the idea itself. In other words, the C-art that's most relevant here is a form of generative art, or G-art.

In G-art, *(df.) the artwork is generated, at least in part, by some process that is not under the artist's direct control.* This is a very broad definition. It does not specify the minimal size of the "part". It does not lay down just what sort of generative process is in question. It does not say what counts as being outside the artist's direct control. And it is silent on the extent (if any) to which the processes concerned may have been deliberately moulded by the artist before 'losing' direct control. In short, our definition of G-art is largely intuitive. In general, it picks out cases of art-making in which personal control is deliberately diminished, or even wholly relinquished, and relatively impersonal processes take over.

Those impersonal processes vary greatly. They may be physical, psychological, sociocultural, biological, or abstract (formal). And if abstract, they may or may not be implemented in a computer.

For example, in the dice music written by Haydn and Mozart the exact order of the pre-composed phrases was decided by throwing a die. Although a human threw the die voluntarily, he/she could not influence, still less determine, just how it fell. That was due to purely physical forces. Such forces also constructed the various versions of Bryan Johnson's (1969) novel *The Unfortunates*, published as twenty-seven separate sections in a box: all but the first and last were to be read in a random order, decided by shuffling or dice-throwing. One might even say, thanks to "at least in part", that Jackson Pollock's paintings examplified G-art grounded in physics. For although he certainly was not throwing (still less, choosing) paint at random, he did not have direct control over the individual splashes—as he would have done over marks made with a paintbrush.

Even more control was lost, or rather deliberately sacrificed, when Hans Haacke, in the 1960s, began to exploit—and even to high-light—the physical behaviour of water/vapour/ice, of waves, and of weather conditions. He wanted to make "something which experiences, reacts to its environment, changes, is nonstable..., always looks different, the shape of which cannot be predicted precisely..." (Lippard 1973: 38, 64 f.). He saw these works not as art *objects* but as ' "systems" of interdependent processes'—which evolve without the viewer's interaction or "empathy", so that the viewer is a mere "witness". A few years later, Jan Dibbets placed eighty sticks in the sea, a few inches below the surface, and watched them oscillate in the water from 50 feet above: "That", he said, "was the work" (Lippard 1973: 59).

The surrealists of the 1920s, by contrast, had exploited psychological processes—but of a relatively impersonal kind. Inspired by Freud, they engaged in automatic writing and painted while in trance states, in order to prioritize the unconscious mind—which André Breton declared to be "by far the most important part [of our mental world]". Indeed, surrealism was defined by Breton as: "Pure psychic automatism [*sic*] by which one proposes to express... the actual functioning of thought, in the absence of any control exerted by reason, exempt from all aesthetic or moral preoccupations" (Breton 1969). The unconscious thought was taking place in a person's mind, to be sure, but voluntary choice and personal "preoccupations" (i.e. the reality principle and ego-ideals) were not directing it.

More recently, the conceptual artist Sol LeWitt was also recommending G-art when he said that art should be designed by some formulaic rule. The crucial idea, he said, "becomes a machine that makes the art", where "all of the planning and decisions are made beforehand and the execution is a perfunctory affair" (1967: 824); once the plan has been chosen, "The artist's will is secondary to the [art-making] process he *initiates* from idea to completion" (1969: item 7; italics added). He even added that "His wilfulness may only be ego". That art-making process was nevertheless psychological, in the sense that the implications of his abstract rules were discovered not by computers but by conscious reasoning. Conscious rule-based reasoning (combined with chance) was used also in the G-art of Kenneth Martin, who—as remarked in Section II—made some artistic choices by picking numbers out of a hat.

Sociocultural processes—in the form of the United States postal system—produced Douglas Huebler's artwork called *42nd Parallel*. Here, items were posted from fourteen different towns spanning 3,040 miles on latitude 42, all sent to the Massachusetts town of Truro. The work, according to Huebler, was not the conception in his mind, nor the posted items, nor even the acts of posting. Rather, it was the widespread pattern of activity within the US postal system. But, he said, the work was "brought into its complete existence" through documents: the certified postal receipts (for sender and for receiver), and a map marked with ink to show the geographical relations between the fifteen towns. Its nature as G-art is evident in his remarks "An inevitable destiny is set in motion by the specific process selected to form such a work, freeing it from further decisions on my part", and "I like the idea that even as I eat, sleep, or play, the work is moving towards its completion" (quoted in Lippard 1973: 62).

The artist Hubert Duprat turned to biology for constructing the work of art. He put dragonfly larvae into an aquarium containing not pebbles and pondweed but tiny flakes of gold, plus a few small pearls, opals, and sapphires—and left them to "sculpt" opulent little protective cases, held together by caddis-silk (Duprat and Besson 1998). Some thirty years earlier, Haacke had experimented with the growth of grass and the hatching of chickens (as well as with water and weather), to make something "Natural", which 'lives in time and makes the "spectator" experience time' (Lippard 1973: 38).

Others have even exploited physical and biological *de-generation* to produce their G-art. The environmental sculptor Andy Goldsworthy sometimes highlights effects caused by undirected physical change: in his gradually melting ice-sculptures, for example. And in Gustav Metzger's "auto-destructive" art (notorious for the occasion on which an overnight gallery cleaner innocently threw Metzger's bag of rotting rubbish into the dustbin), the point of the exercise is to remind us of the deterioration that awaits all human constructions—and human beings, too (Metzger 1965). The artwork is originally assembled by a human artist, but it attains its final form, and its significance, through the natural processes of damage and decay.

However, such inside-the-bubble (albeit unorthodox) cases are not what the new artists normally have in mind when they refer to "generative art". Their phraseology is borrowed from mathematics and computer science, with which the maverick artists just named were not concerned. These disciplines see generative systems as sets of abstract rules that can produce indefinitely many structures/formulae of a given type, and which (given the Church-Turing thesis) can *in principle* be implemented in a computer. The GA-community outside the bubble put this principle into practice. That is, their art-making rests on processes generated by formal rules carried out by computers—as opposed to physical, biological, or psychological processes, or abstractions personally discovered by conscious thought.

In other words, the instances of G-art which most concern us here are also instances of C-art. They are computer-generated art: CG-art, for short.

A very strict definition of CG-art would insist that *(df.) the artwork results from some computer program being left to run by itself, with zero interference from the human artist.* The artist (or a more computer-literate collaborator) writes the program, but does not interact with it during its execution. In effect, he/she can go out for lunch while the program is left to do its own thing.

Such cases do exist. Cohen's AARON program (see below) is one well-known example. Nevertheless, that definition is so strict that it may be misleading. We saw in Section III that generative artists allow a "compromise" in the core concept, so as to include interactive art. This is such a prominent subclass of what's called generative art that, even though we are not aiming to capture common usage, it would be highly anomalous to exclude it.

To be sure, the definition given above does cover most interactive art, because it insists on zero interference from "the human artist", rather than from "*any* human being, whether artist or audience". However, it would be very easy for readers to elide that distinction—which, in any case, makes a questionable assumption about authorial responsibility (see Section V). Moreover, the overly strict definition of CG-art excludes those cases (also mentioned in Section III) wherein artists rely on their intuitive judgement to make selections during an artwork's evolution.

We therefore prefer to define CG-art less tidily, as art wherein *(df.) the artwork results from some computer program being left to run by itself, with minimal or zero interference from a human being.* The word "minimal", of course, is open to interpretation. It necessitates careful attention to *just what* interference goes on, and *by whom*, in any particular case. (Attention need not be paid, however, to the distinction between rule-based and step-by-step programming explained in Section II: our definition of CG-art allows for both.)

Most of what people call "computer art" is CG-art, in this sense. Indeed, the phrases "computer art" and "generative art" are often regarded as synonyms. Notice, however, that in our terminology not all C-art is CG-art. CA-art is not, because the computer is there used as a tool subject to the artist's hands-on control (and is of no more philosophical interest than a paintbrush or a chisel). That's why we called this paper "What Is Generative Art?", rather than the seemingly synonymous "What Is Computer Art?"

CG-art is intriguing on two counts. First, the generality and potential complexity of computer programs means that the possible space of CG-artworks is huge, indeed infinite. Moreover, most of the structures in that space will be images/music which the unaided human mind could not have generated, or even imagined—as the artists themselves admit.

A sceptic might object that much the same is true of a trumpet, or a cello: not even the most skilled stage-impressionists could mimic these instruments plausibly. In short, human artists often need help from machines. Trumpets, computers... what's the difference? Well, one important difference has just been mentioned, namely, the generality of digital computers. In principle, these machines can (and do) offer us an entire symphony orchestra, and an infinite set of visual images and sculptural forms—indeed, an infinite range of virtual worlds. McCormack (2003: 7) goes so far as to compare this infinite space of possibilities, way beyond our comprehension, with the Kantian sublime.

The second point is even more pertinent. Whereas there's no interesting sense in which a trumpet, or a cello, can be "left to do its own thing", a computer certainly can. And it is part of the definition of CG-art that this happens. As we'll see later, this aspect of CG-art raises some tricky problems concerning concepts such as autonomy, agency, creativity, authenticity, and authorial responsibility.

Especially well-known cases of CG-art include the successive versions of AARON. This is a drawing-and-colouring program developed over the last forty years by the one-time abstract painter Cohen (1995, 2002), and exhibited at venues all around the world—including the Tate Gallery. It has shown clear progression along various aesthetic dimensions. Indeed, Cohen (p.c.) describes the 2006 version as a "world-class" colourist, whereas he himself is merely a "first-rate" colourist: "I wouldn't have had the courage to use *those* colours", he sometimes says. (At earlier stages, colouring-AARON mixed liquid dyes and used 'painting blocks' of five different sizes to place them on paper; the current version prints out computer-generated colours instead of using liquids, but these colours too are 'mixed' at the program's behest.)

An almost equally famous example is Emmy, a computer-musician developed over much the same period by the composer David Cope (2001, 2006). This generates music in the styles of many renowned composers, and very convincingly, too—see Hofstadter (2001: 38 f.) (Nevertheless, Cope has recently abandoned it, because of the prejudiced reactions of audiences: see Section V.)

What Is Generative Art? 143

Both of those programs were based on methods drawn from what the philosopher John Haugeland dubbed GOFAI, or Good Old-Fashioned AI (although the mature Emmy also uses connectionist AI). More recent methods for constructing CG-artworks, as remarked in Section I, include cellular automata, L-systems, and evolutionary programming—all widely used in A-Life research.

Cellular automata are systems made up of many computational units, each following a small set (usually, the same set) of simple rules. In such systems, surprising patterns can emerge from the simple, anodyne, base. Further variations ensue if another 'level' of rules is added to the system. Examples in CG-art include the tessellated visual constructs within Paul Brown's *Sandlines* and *Infinite Permutations*, and other works by Paul Brown (Whitelaw 2004: 148–53; Tofts 2005: 85 f.; www.paul-brown.com).

L-systems are automatically branching structures, used by botanists to study plant form and physiology (Lindenmayer 1968; Prusinkiewicz and Lindenmayer 1990; Prusinkiewicz 2004). In the hands of CG-artists, they have led (for instance) to McCormack's *Turbulence* installation (McCormack 2004; Tofts 2005: 80 ff.). This generates images of unnatural yet lifelike vegetation growing in front of one's eyes—and in response to one's actions (thus qualifying as interactive art). Another example is the use of a "swarm grammar" based on L-systems to generate structures in (simulated) 3D space, comparable to the decentralized yet organized constructions of social insects such as termites (Jacob and von Mammen 2007).

As for evolutionary programming, this has given rise to an important subclass of CG-art: evolutionary art, or Evo-art. Examples include Karl Sims's *Genetic Images* and *Galapogos* (Sims 1991, 2007), plus many others (Whitelaw 2004: ch. 2). In Evo-art, the artwork is not produced by a computer program that has remained unchanged since being written by the artist. Rather, the artwork is *(df.) evolved by processes of random variation and selective reproduction that affect the art-generating program itself.*

Evo-art relies on programs that include self-modifying processes called genetic algorithms. To begin, a 'population' of near-identical artworks—or, to be more precise, the mini-programs that generate them—is produced by the computer. There can be any number: 9, or 16, or even more. In aesthetic terms, these first-generation artworks are boring at best and chaotic at worst. Next, each of these first-generation programs is altered ('mutated') in one or more ways, at random. Usually, the alterations are very slight. Now, some selective procedure—the 'fitness function' (decided by the artist/programmer)—is applied to choose the most promising candidate/s for breeding the next generation. And this process goes on repeatedly, perhaps for hundreds of generations. Provided that the mutations allowed are not too fundamental (see Section V), what ensues is a gradual evolutionary progress towards the type of structure favoured by the artist.

Occasionally, the fitness function is fully automatic, being applied by the computer itself. (If so, there may be scores, or even hundreds, of 'siblings' in a given generation.) This is a prime example of the computer's being "left to do its own thing". More usually (as remarked in Section III), the selection is done hands-on by the artist—or by some other human being: a gallery visitor, for instance—using intuitive, and often unverbalized, criteria. (If so, the population size rarely rises above 16, because people cannot 'take in' more than a limited number of patterns at once.) In other words, and for reasons touched on in Section V, there is usually no *programmed* fitness function. In such cases, the Evo-art also counts as I-art.

One might argue that our definition of Evo-art is faulty, on the grounds that evolutionary art need not involve a computer. It's certainly true that the very earliest G-art works of William Latham, who later became famous as a *computer* artist, were generated by repeated dice-throwing and hand-drawing. At that time, he had no idea that computers might be able to do the job for him—and do it better (Todd and Latham 1992). But that is highly unusual: virtually all art that's produced by an iterative process of random variation plus selection is computer-based. Indeed, we do not know of any non-computerized example besides early-Latham. (Someone might suggest Claude Monet's water-lily series: but although these showed gradual improvement by way of small changes, those changes were far from random.) Even Richard Dawkins's simple 'Biomorphs', which were hugely seminal for Evo-artists, were computer-generated (Dawkins 1986: 55–74). We have therefore chosen to define Evo-art as a sub class of CG-art, even though this excludes the early Latham efforts.

Another sub class of CG-art is robot art, or R-art. By R-art, we mean *(df.) the construction of robots for artistic purposes, where robots are physical machines capable of autonomous movement and/or communication.* We hope we shall be forgiven for not attempting to define "artistic purposes". As for "autonomous", the word may be understood intuitively here. At some point, however, it should be considered carefully—not least, because the concept of autonomy is closely connected also with agency and creativity (see Section V).

Clearly, not all R-art is Ele-art. Indeed, R-art covers examples built many centuries ago. A few of these ancient machines could move as a whole from one place to another—such as Leonardo's mechanical lion that "walked vp and downe" the room, or Daedalus' mercury-filled Venus which (according to Aristotle's *De Anima*) had to be tethered to prevent it from running away. Most, however, could move only their body parts—like the moving statues of nymphs and satyrs in the grotto fountains at St Germain, which enthused René Descartes as a young man.

Electronic R-art is highly varied (Whitelaw 2004: ch. 4). It includes Ihnatowicz's eerily hypnotic *Senster*, Stelarc's thought-provoking man-robot hybrids, and Ken Goldberg's *Telegarden*—wherein living plants are watered by a robot that is controlled by Everyman via the Internet (Popper 2007: 379–93).

In all those cases, only one robot is involved. Sometimes, however, groups of interacting ("distributed") robots are constructed. Usually, such groups employ the techniques of situated robotics, wherein the machines respond directly to specific environmental cues—here, including *the behaviour of other robots* (Boden 2006: 13.iii.b and iii.d). Occasionally, they exploit self-organizing techniques whereby the system gradually reaches an equilibrium state. (Futuristic though they may seem, both these methodologies were first used by mid-century cyberneticians: Grey Walter and Ross Ashby, respectively.) One example of the latter type is Jane Prophet's *Net Work* installation (Bird, d'Inverno, and Prophet 2007). One might think of this as a hi-tech version of Dibbets's oscillating sticks. But instead of eighty 'isolated' sticks, placed below the surface of the sea, *Net Work* consists of 2,500 floating, and intercommunicating, buoys—each of which is colour-emitting and wave-sensitive. (More accurately, it *will* consist in 2,500 such buoys: it has been tested in a 3 × 3 miniature on the Thames, but is planned to surround the pier at Herne Bay.)

Such mutually interacting robot-groups *do not* count as interactive art on our definition (given below), unless they are also capable of interacting with the human audience. *Net Work* does have that capability: the audience can affect it by shining torchlight on the buoys, or by remote control over the Internet. Other examples of interactive (and interacting) robot-groups include Kenneth Rinaldo's works in what he calls eco-technology. His R-art (and I-art) installation called *The Flock* comprises three wire-and-vine robotic 'arms' suspended from the ceiling, which interact with each other and with the moving/speaking human audience. Similarly, his *Autopoiesis* has fifteen robot wire-frame 'arms' distributed around the room, which sense the observer's movements and communicate with each other so as to coordinate their behaviour in various ways.

This brings us to our ninth category: interactive art. In this genre, the human audience is not a passive observer but an active participant. Audiences are never wholly passive, of course, since art appreciation involves active psychological processes. Indeed, Duchamp (1957) went so far as to say: "The creative act is not performed by the artist alone; the spectator brings the work in contact with the external world by deciphering and interpreting its inner qualification and thus adds his contribution to the creative act". Even for Duchamp, however, the spectator's contribution concerns only the work's "inner" qualification (its role, he said, is "to determine [its] weight on the aesthetic scale"). The work's perceptible nature—or, many would say, the artwork itself—does not change as a result. In interactive art, by contrast, it does.

In I-art, then, *(df.) the form/content of the artwork is significantly affected by the behaviour of the audience.* And in CI-art (i.e. the computer-based varieties), *(df.) the form/content of some CG-artwork is significantly affected by the behaviour of the audience.* Again, we are speaking intuitively here: worries about just what counts as "the artwork" are left to the next section. The word "significantly" is needed, even though it is a hostage to interpretative fortune, so as to exclude performance art—for performance is usually subtly affected by audience reception. As for the word "behaviour", this must be interpreted with generosity. In CI-art it covers voluntary actions (such as waving, walking, and touching the computer screen), largely automatic yet controllable actions (such as the direction of eye-gaze), and involuntary bodily movements (such as breathing). It even includes arcane physical factors such as the radiation of body heat.

(Occasionally, the 'interaction' involves not the audience but the physical environment: aspects of the weather, for example. Such cases fall outside our definition, unless—which is usually the case—they *also* involve interaction with the human audience.)

CI-art is generative art *by definition*. But it is not "generative" in our strictest sense (above), as AARON is. For although the artist can go to lunch and leave the program to do its own thing, the audience cannot. However, it qualifies as CG-art in our broader sense, since the artist has handed over control of the final form of the artwork to the computer, in interaction with some other human being. The degree of control attributable to the audience varies: they may not realize that they are affecting the artwork, nor (if they do) just what behaviour leads to just which changes. We'll see later that this variability is an important dimension in the aesthetics of CI-art.

I-art is not an entirely recent phenomenon: remember Haydn's dice music, for instance. But it became prominent in the mid-twentieth century. (This was often justified in political terms: I-art was seen as offering valuable *human-human* communication, in societies where the sense of community had been diluted—Bishop 2006.) It was made possible largely by cyberneticians such as Pask applying their theory of communicative feedback to art, and by the new electronic technology developed in the Second World War.

That's not to say that all these I-art efforts were examples of Ele-art. Many artists, indeed, eschewed such technology for (counter-cultural) ideological reasons: it was too strongly linked with the military-industrial complex. Even Ascott's first I-art had nary an electron in sight: it consisted of canvases with items/images on them that could be continually moved around by hand, so that the viewer of the resulting collages was their *maker* too. *SAM* and the *Senster* were early examples of I-art that did use electronics. But, as we have seen, they did not involve computers.

Today's I-art, however, is overwhelmingly computer-based. That's because the generality of digital computers enables them, in principle, to support an infinite variety of human-computer interactions.

The types of interaction explored in CI-art are already widely diverse—hence the inclusiveness of the term "behaviour" in our definition. The by-now-countless examples range from interactive CD-ROMs viewed on a desktop and altered (for instance) by touching the screen (Leggett and Michael 1996), to room-sized video or VR installations—such as Christa Sommerer and Laurent Mignonneau's *Trans Plant*. In this case, a jungle gradually appears on the walls as the audience moves around the enclosure: grass grows when the viewer walks, and trees and bushes when he/she stands still; the plants' size, colour, and shape depend on the size and bodily attitudes of the human being; and the colour density changes as the person's body moves slightly backwards or forwards. *Trans Plant* is driven by the viewer's movements, but some CI-artworks are modified also, or instead, by the sound of human voices or footsteps. This is reminiscent of the *Senster*—but these computer-generated changes are much more varied and complex than those which could be engineered in the 1960s by Ihnatowicz.

Sometimes, the relevant interactions involve online access to the Internet, automatically incorporating into the artwork items that happen to be present on the World Wide Web at that particular moment. One example is *The Living Room*, another installation built by Sommerer and Mignonneau. Unlike *Trans Plant*, this CI-artwork does not undergo changes that depend systematically on what the viewer is doing. Instead, random images and sounds, picked up from the Internet, appear in the room as a result of the viewer's movements and speech.

It's usual, as in that example, for the change in the CI-artwork (whether systematic or not) to be near-simultaneous with the observer's triggering activity. In Edmonds' most recent CI-art, however, the effects of the viewer's behaviour are delayed in time (see Section III). Partly because of the lesser likelihood that the viewer will realize—and be able to control—what is going on, Edmonds speaks of "influence" rather than "interaction" in these cases. As we'll see in Section V, whether mere "influence" can be aesthetically satisfying is controversial even *outside* the precious bubble.

Certainly, mere influence, as against instantaneous interaction, would not be enough for our final category, namely Virtual Reality or VR-art. VR-art is the most advanced version of CI-art (for examples, see Popper 2007: chs. 4–6). Already foreseen in the mid-1960s, it was not technologically possible until the late-1980s (Boden 2006: 13.vi).

In VR-art, interaction leads to illusion—of an especially compelling kind. In other words, *(df.) the observer is immersed in a computer-generated virtual world, experiencing it and responding to it as if it were real.* We do not pretend that this definition is clear: just what is it for someone to experience/respond "as if it were real"? Some relevant issues will be indicated in Section V. Meanwhile, we'll continue to rely on readers' intuitive understanding of such language.

Someone might want to argue that VR-art was initiated centuries ago. For pseudo-realistic mimetic worlds have been depicted in various forms of *trompe l'œil* (including 'realistic' panoramas) for many centuries, and even appeared in some of the wall paintings and architecture of Classical Rome. But there's a crucial difference between the relevant aesthetics in times ancient and modern. As Oliver Grau (2003: 16) has pointed out, the "moment of aesthetic pleasure" in *trompe l'œil* comes when the viewer consciously realizes that they are *not* experiencing reality.

In VR-art, by contrast, the enjoyment lies in feeling as though one is really inhabiting, and manipulating, an alternative world. The longer the awareness of its unreality can be delayed, the better. In other words, the experience of past forms of mimetic art was based only on illusion, not on immersion. Although one can say that the viewers were invited/deceived into responding to the art *as if* it were real, that "as if" was much less richly textured, much less sustained, and therefore much less persuasive, than it is now.

(Cinema is a halfway house—Grau 2003: ch. 4. It often elicits an emotional/narrative 'immersion' in the filmgoer, and sometimes—using special screens and techniques—leads to near-veridical experiences of inhabiting the cinematic world. These tend to exploit our reflex bodily responses to visual images that suggest falling, or imminent collision: so roller coasters, white-water-rafting, and tigers leaping towards us out of the screen are familiar favourites. But there's little psychological subtlety in this 'inhabitation', and no detailed interaction with the alternate world—still less, any physical manipulation of it.)

In general, VR-art aims to make the participants (often called "immersants") feel as though they are personally present in the cyberworld concerned. Normally, this world is visual or audio-visual, being presented on a VDU screen or projected onto the walls/floor of a real-world room. (McCormack's *Universal Zoologies* VR-artwork is an exception: here, the images/sounds are projected onto two large 'talking heads', in an attempt to provide a realistic illusion of human conversation—Tofts 2005: 81f.). But sometimes, VR-art leads also to convincing experiences of touch, pressure, and motion by providing the observer with special gloves and other equipment (Boden 2006: 13.vi). Sometimes, too, the observer experiences utterly *unreal* capacities, such as being able to fly or to activate highly unnatural causal chains within the virtual world.

Even when the viewer is not presented with such shockingly unfamiliar experiences as those, something about the virtual world will be perceptibly *unlike* the real world. And this is deliberate. For VR-artists are not aiming to achieve a fully detailed mimesis: what would be the point of that? Rather, they use near-mimesis to cast some aesthetically/conceptually interesting light on our usual experiences and assumptions. (Detailed mimesis may be appropriate for other purposes, of course: for instance, a VR-brain used in training neurosurgeons provides nicely realistic sensations of touch and vision when the trainee's virtualized surgical tool prods, pinches, or cuts different parts of it.)

In sum, our eleven definitions are as follows:

(1) Ele-art involves electrical engineering and/or electronic technology.
(2) C-art uses computers as part of the art-making process.
(3) D-art uses digital electronic technology of some sort.
(4) CA-art uses the computer as an aid (in principle, non-essential) in the art-making process.
(5) G-art works are generated, at least in part, by some process that is not under the artist's direct control.
(6) CG-art is produced by leaving a computer program to run by itself, with minimal or zero interference from a human being. NB: We chose to *reject* the stricter definition of CG-art (art produced by a program left to run by itself, with zero interference from the human artist).
(7) Evo-art is evolved by processes of random variation and selective reproduction that affect the art-generating program itself.
(8) R-art is the construction of robots for artistic purposes, where robots are physical machines capable of autonomous movement and/or communication.
(9) In I-art, the form/content of the artwork is significantly affected by the behaviour of the audience.
(10) In CI-art, the form/content of some CG-artwork is significantly affected by the behaviour of the audience.
(11) In VR-art, the observer is immersed in a computer-generated virtual world, experiencing it and responding to it as if it were real.

V. SOME QUESTIONS FOR AESTHETICS

Various aesthetic and/or philosophical problems arise with respect to CG-art in general, and others with respect to particular varieties of it. None of these can be explored at length here. (We have discussed them elsewhere, however. Some answers to the questions raised below are offered in Chapters 9–11 of this volume; and in Boden 1999, 2004, 2006: 13.iii.d-e and 16.viii.c, 2007, in preparation; Cornock and Edmonds 1973; Costello and Edmonds 2007; Edmonds 2006,

What Is Generative Art? 151

in press; Muller et al. 2006.) Instead, this section merely indicates the wide range of puzzles that attend the consideration of generative art.

One obvious question can be put informally thus: Is it really the case that a computer can ever "do its own thing"? Or is it always doing the programmer's (artist's) thing, however indirectly?

To answer that question seriously requires both general philosophical argument and attention to specific aspects of particular CG-art examples—in the underlying program, as well as in the observable artwork. That sort of attention is not appropriate in cases of G-art that are not computer-based. For the physical, psychological, or biological processes in which they are grounded are not specifiable in detail—not even by scientists, let alone by artists. Computer programs, in contrast, are so specifiable. That's why one can make sensible comparisons between the extent to which different CG-art programs are or are not "under the artist's direct control", and the extent to which, and the points at which, they are subject to "interference from a human being". However, one can do this only if one knows something about how the program and/or installation works. Merely observing, or even participating in, the resultant artwork is not enough.

Whether it *appears* to participants that the program/installation is independent, or autonomous, is of course another question (one which may not be easy to answer, in practice). So too is the question whether it ever makes sense to ascribe autonomy to a computer. Remember Edmonds's remarks about rule-based programming in Section III: does it really matter what the 'feel' of this activity is, if in fact it is no less directive, no less determinate, than algorithmic programming? Irrespective of the artist's phenomenology while writing the program, and/or of the participants' phenomenology when experiencing it, do some categories of CG-art have more autonomy than others? What of Evo-art, for instance: does the self-modification involved, and the automatic selection (in cases where that happens), mean that evo-programs are more autonomous than (say) AARON? With respect to AARON, can we ascribe at least a minimal level of autonomy to the computer, given that Cohen has no hands-on control over what picture will be drawn, or how?

Insofar as a program is "doing its own thing", does it take on the authorial responsibility? (Let us ignore the fact that "authorial responsibility" is often unclear here anyway, since most CG-art is produced by a team, not a lone artist.)

For instance, did AARON generate those magnificent "world-class" coloured drawings, or did Cohen do so? He admits, after all, that he himself "wouldn't have had the courage to use *those* colours". On the other hand, he says he is happy that there will be more of "his" original artworks appearing well after his death (Cohen 2002). Is he right, or is he deluded? The answer will depend not only on one's philosophy of the self but also on one's views as to whether any computer program can be seen as an author/artist. Douglas Hofstadter, for example, would be content to ascribe the posthumous works to Cohen himself (and would even deny that they are in the fullest sense *posthumous:* Hofstadter 2007); if he was emotionally moved by them, he would also resist ascribing authorship to the computer (2001).

Does Evo-art leave more room, or less, for human authorship than AARON does? That is, does the artist's choice of fitness function suffice to give him/her the authorial credit for whatever artwork emerges after many generations of random (i.e. undirected) change? Is the credit greater, or less, if instead of relying on a programmed fitness function the artist does the selecting 'by hand'?

One reason for the Evo-artist's choosing to do the selection by hand is in order to produce only works in his/her own style. This is also the reason why the mutations that are allowed are usually very slight. For an artistic style is a sustained pattern of activity, lasting over time. In Evo-art that allows radical mutations (and which does not 'ration' them to once every 2,000th generation, for instance), no pattern can be sustained for long—not even if the human artist is trying to shape the results by making the 'fitness' selection at each stage. On the contrary, huge structural changes can occur in a single generation (cf. Sims 1991). This leads to fascinated amazement on the part of the gallery audience. Nevertheless, Evo-artists do not normally allow such mutations. They prefer to explore a stylistic space which, despite many surprising variations, remains recognizable as 'theirs' to someone with an experienced eye.

There are some exceptions. The CG-artist Paul Brown (with others, including the authors of this paper) is involved in an ongoing Evo-art project whose aim is to evolve robots that will make aesthetically acceptable drawings which *do not* carry Brown's general style, or 'personal signature' (Bird, Stokes, et al. 2007; Boden, Chapter 6 of this volume; in preparation). Whether that can be done remains to be seen: Brown, after all, will be setting the fitness functions as the work proceeds.

This project raises questions also about the relation between CG-art and embodiment. Many philosophers of mind discount AI/A-Life in general (as models of mind or life) for being concerned with virtual, body-less, systems. However, these R/Evo-art creatures are robots moving in the real world, and are therefore subject to physical forces. It's known that truly fundamental changes—i.e. new types of sensory receptor—can evolve in robots as a result of unsuspected physical contingencies (Bird and Layzell 2002). (Compare the biological evolution not of a primitive eye into a better eye, but of a light-sensor where no such sensor existed before.) In principle, then, a fundamentally new style [sic] might develop in this way, whereas (arguably) that could not happen in a purely virtual, programmed, system.

Similar puzzles about authorial responsibility arise in CI-art in general, of which 'hand-selected' Evo-art is a special case. Just where, in the man-machine system concerned, is the true author? That worry affects all I-art, of course—but is there any extra difficulty where CI-art is concerned? (For present purposes, let us ignore Duchamp's suggestion that *all* art is multi-authored.) And what difference, if any, does it make if—as sometimes happens—the audience provides feedback during the construction of the CI-work, so that its final form depends not only on the decisions of the artist but also on the reactions of the audience/s who encountered it in its prototype stage? Perhaps our distinction between "decisions" and "reactions" is crucial here, debarring the audience from earning any 'extra' authorial credit in such cases?

To speak of a "worry" here, however, is perhaps to counteract what CI-artists are trying to do. Despite its sturdy roots in cybernetics and computer technology, CI-art has attracted favourable notice from post-modernists precisely because of the ambiguity of authorship involved. Ascott (2003), in particular, has always seen the value of CI-art as its democratizing ability to engage the viewer/participant *as creator*. In his words, "creativity is shared, authorship is distributed..." (1990: 238). If authorship is deliberately distributed, then to worry about its locus (about ascribing the status of *author*) is to miss the point.

(For all the heady talk of creative participation, some CI-art is fairly limiting: Kahn 1996. That's so, for instance, where the possible changes in the artwork are explicitly preset by the artist, as opposed to their emerging from the program's "doing its own thing". The limitation is especially great where they are selected by the participant's choosing from a menu.)

Another way of putting questions about authorial responsibility is to ask where the creativity lies. But what, exactly, do we mean by creativity?

It certainly involves agency—which is why considerations of autonomy and authorial responsibility are inevitable. But what is agency? The interacting 'arms' and floating buoys identified above as examples of R-art are typically described by the artists and technicians concerned as agents—a word borrowed from AI/A-Life research on distributed cognition. But does that research misuse the concept? Even if it does, does it include 'agents' of interestingly different types (Boden 2006: 13.iii.d–e), some of which are more deserving of the name than others? If so, should we at least reserve the term—and the ascription of creativity—for those cases of CG-art where the agents involved are of the more plausible variety? Again, such questions cannot be answered without careful attention to the details of the programs and communications involved.

It's commonly assumed that creativity—and art, too—involves unpredictability (Boden 2004: ch. 9). But what is its source? Is it merely lack of predictive power on the part of human minds? We have seen (in Section III) that CG-art, like complex programs in general, is indeed unpredictable for that reason. But CI-art and Evo-art are unpredictable for other reasons as well. CI-art, because the artist cannot predict the sequence of interactions that will take place, even if he/she can predict what would happen at a given moment if *that* audience movement were to occur; and Evo-art, because of the many *random* changes to the program, and because of the choices made at successive generations by the artist. Does the unpredictability of traditional art have any deeper source? And if so, is this something which cannot be ascribed to, or even simulated in, computers?

Another set of questions concerns ontology. How can we identify "the artwork" when an artist's computer program generates countless unique images, or musical compositions, none of which have been seen/heard by the artist? Is each image/music produced by AARON or Emmy an artwork—or is the artwork the program which generates them? In Evo-art, does one and the same artwork exist at differing levels of sophistication at different generations? Or does every generation produce a new artwork—or, perhaps, a new population of (sibling) artworks?

What counts as the artwork when the uniqueness is due not only to a richly generative computer program but also to the contingent (and ephemeral) behaviour of a participatory human audience? Perhaps the familiar concept of artwork is well suited only to the unchanging artefacts that form the overwhelming majority of the cases inside McCormack's bubble? A traditional artist can fully comprehend the painting or sculpture that they have executed so carefully (although whether this applies to the G-art dimension of Pollock's paintings is questionable), but CI-artists cannot fully know the CI-artwork that they constructed with equal care. This is not merely a matter of the unpredictability of detail: in sufficiently complex cases, it is not even clear that they can recognize the general potential of their own work. With regard to CI-art, then, perhaps we should speak not of the "artwork" but of the "art system"—where this comprises the artist, the program, the technological installation (and its observable results), and the behaviour of the human audience? (And perhaps, if the concept of the "artwork" falls, then that of the "artist/author" falls too?)

Or maybe we should think of each occurrence of CI-art as a performance, and the program/installation as the score? If so, the 'performance' is more like a jazz improvisation than the playing of classical music, for it can vary considerably from one occasion to another. Even if the form of each particular human-computer interaction can be completely determined by the artist (which is not so, for instance, when the computer's response can be modified by its memory of the history of previous interactions), the *sequence* of such events cannot.

Yet another problematic area concerns aesthetic evaluation. Are entirely novel aesthetic considerations relevant for CG-art in general, or for some subclass of it? And are some aesthetic criteria, normally regarded as essential, utterly out of place in CG-art: authenticity, for instance?

The devotees of CI-art, in fact, do not use the familiar (inside-the-bubble) criteria to judge different interactive installations. Or insofar as they do, these are secondary to other considerations. The criteria they see as most appropriate concern not the nature of the resulting 'artwork' (the beauty of the image projected on the wall, for example, or the harmoniousness of the accompanying sounds), but the nature of the interaction itself. There's general agreement on that point. But there's significant disagreement on just what type of interaction is the most aesthetically valuable.

Some CI-artists, especially those engaged in VR-art, stress the disturbing sense of unreality involved, and the participant's new 'take' on everyday experience that ensues. Many value the participant's conscious control of the artwork; others aim to highlight their sense of personal embodiment; while yet others stress the audience's disconcerting experience of unpredictability triggered by their own actions. All of those criteria concern the participant's *experience*—but difficulties arise if one asks how that experience can be discerned, or 'logged', by anyone other than the individual participant. (As we saw in Section III, if the observers can never come to realize that they are affecting what happens, then the "I" in "CI-art" might better be thought of as the initial letter of "influence", not of "interaction".)

There are some especially jagged philosophical rocks lying in wait for VR-artists. The concept of virtual reality has been defined in various ways (Steuer 1992). Most, like our definition of VR-art, refer to the participant's experience of being immersed in a real world, and reacting accordingly. This notion seems to be intuitively intelligible, especially if one has actually encountered a VR-installation. But just what it means, whether in psychological or philosophical terms, is very difficult to say. It is not even clear that it is coherent. Several leading philosophers of mind have addressed this hornet's nest of questions in writing about the film *The Matrix* (see especially the papers by Hubert Dreyfus and Andy Clark on the Warner Brothers website: <http://whatisthematrix.warnerbros.com>). That's not to say that *The Matrix* counts as VR-art, for it does not. Nevertheless, it raises some of the same questions that would attend highly plausible instances of VR-art. (Whether these would also be highly successful instances is another matter: we have seen that VR in art typically highlights some *unreal* dimension of the experience.)

As for authenticity, this is a tricky concept. There are several reasons, of varying plausibility, why someone might argue that it is not applicable to any instance of CG-art. And CG-artists have suffered as a result. For example, Cope (2006) has been continually disappointed by people's failure to take his music seriously—not because they dislike it on hearing it (sometimes they even *refuse* to hear it), but simply because it is computer-generated. Even when they do praise it, he has found that they typically see it less as "music" than as "computer output"—a classification which compromises its authenticity. For instance, even though each Emmy composition is in fact unique, people know that the program could spew out indefinitely many more tomorrow. (The fact that human composers die, says Cope, has consequences for aesthetic valuation: someone's oeuvre is valued in part because it is a unique set of works, now closed.) As a result of this common reaction, Cope has recently destroyed the database of dead composers' music that he had

What Is Generative Art? 157

built up over the last twenty-five years, and used as a crucial source in Emmy's functioning. (Emmy's successor will compose music only in Cope's own style; whether audiences regard this as significantly more authentic remains to be seen.)

Finally, what of the claims made by many CG-artists to be exploring the nature of life? It's clear from Rinaldo's choice of the titles *Autopoiesis* and *The Flock* (plus the rest of his oeuvre—Whitelaw 2004: 109–16), for instance, that his R-art works are not intended as mere fairground toys but as meditations on significant aspects of life. He is not alone in this: many of the CG-artists who have been influenced by A-Life see their work in that way. Concepts such as emergence and self-organization, and of course evolution, crop up repeatedly in their writings and interviews—as does the key concept of life itself. One may well agree that their work throws light on, or anyway reminds us of, important—and puzzling—properties of life. But one need not also agree with the claim sometimes made by these CG-artists, that purely *virtual* life (aka strong A-Life) is possible—and that their work, or something similar, might even create it.

VI. CONCLUSION

We have mentioned a number of philosophical questions. But we have ignored what is perhaps the most obvious one of all: "But is it art, *really?*"

Many people feel that computers are the very antithesis of art. Indeed, some philosophers argue this position explicitly (e.g. O'Hear 1995). On their view, art involves the expression and communication of human experience, so that if we did decide that it is *the computer* which is generating the 'artwork', then it cannot be an *art* work after all. A closely related worry concerns emotion in particular: if computers are not emotional creatures then—on this view—they cannot generate anything that's properly termed "art" (Hofstadter 2001). Another common way of discrediting computer art in general is to argue that art involves creativity, and that no computer—irrespective of its observable performance—can *really* be creative (for a discussion, see Boden 2004: ch. 11). And both authors of this paper have often observed someone's aesthetic approval of an artwork being instantly renounced on discovering that it is, in fact, a CG-artwork. Cope was so disturbed by this reaction, as we have seen, that he destroyed the database on which Emmy's—or should we rather say "his"?—CG-music rested.

It would not be appropriate to burden this already lengthy paper with a discussion of the slippery concept of art. But it is not necessary, either. For we have given many illustrations of the continuities between CG-art and non-computer art. Several of our analytic categories include examples drawn from both inside and outside McCormack's precious bubble—although, admittedly, most cases of traditional art elude our definitions. And those categories which apply only to CG-art cover many individual cases that are aesthetically related to traditional artworks.

Moreover, the art world itself—however suspicious it may be of computers in general, and however dismissive it may be of particular CG-art efforts—does sometimes award these new activities the coveted status of art. Sometimes, this happens in a specialized corner of the art world: for instance, London's *Kinetica* gallery (opened in 2006), which is devoted to interactive, robotic, and kinetic art. But we have also mentioned two examples (others could have been cited) where major 'traditional' galleries clearly accept that traditional and CG-art are players in the same cultural ballpark. These were the Tate's one-man show of Cohen's AARON, and the Washington exhibition featuring Edmonds's work as a development of that of the ColorField painters. The latter example is especially telling, precisely because it is not a show celebrating only CG-art. On the contrary, the Washington exhibition is putting CG-art alongside the precious bubble—or even inside it.

In response to the sceptic's challenge "But is it art, *really?*", we therefore rest our case.

REFERENCES

Ascott, R. (1966/67), 'Behaviourist Art and the Cybernetic Vision', *Cybernetica*, 9 (1966), 247–64; and 10 (1967), 25–56, reprinted as ch. 3 of Ascott (2003: 109–56).

—— (1990), 'Is There Love in the Telematic Embrace?', *Art Journal* (College Arts Association of America), 49: 241–47; repr. as ch. 15 of Ascott (2003: 232–46).

—— (1998/2003), 'Technoetic Aesthetics: 100 Terms and Definitions for the Post-Biological Era', in Ascott (2003: 375–82; 1st pub. in Japanese, trans. E. Fujihara, in R. Ascott, *Art and Telematics: Toward the Construction of a New Aesthetics* (Tokyo: NTT Publishing Co., 1998).

—— (2003), *Telematic Embrace: Visionary Theories of Art, Technology, and Consciousness* (Berkeley and Los Angeles: University of California Press).
Bird, J., d'Inverno, M., and Prophet, J. (2007), '*Net Work*: An Interactive Artwork Designed Using an Interdisciplinary Performative Approach', *Digital Creativity*, 18/1: 11–23.
Bird, J., and Layzell, P. (2002), 'The Evolved Radio and Its Implications for Modelling the Evolution of Novel Sensors', *Proceedings of Congress on Evolutionary Computation*, CEC-2002, 1836–41.
Bird, J., Stokes, D., Husbands, P., Brown, P., and Bigge, B. (2007), 'Towards Autonomous Artworks', *Leonardo Electronic Almanac* (available from jonba@sussex.ac.uk).
Bishop, C. (2006), *Participation* (Cambridge, Mass.: MIT Press).
Boden, M. A. (1999), 'Is Metabolism Necessary?', *British Journal for the Philosophy of Science*, 50: 231–48.
—— (2004), *The Creative Mind: Myths and Mechanisms* (2nd edn., expanded/revised, London: Routledge).
—— (2006), *Mind as Machine: A History of Cognitive Science* (Oxford: Clarendon/Oxford University Press).
—— (2007), 'Authenticity and Computer Art', *Digital Creativity*, 18/1: 3–10 (special issue on Creativity, Computation, and Cognition, ed. P. Brown.)
—— (in preparation), 'Can Evolutionary Art Provide Radical Novelty?', to appear is M.A. Boden and E.A. Edmonds, *From Fingers to Digits: And For a New Age*.
Breton, A. (1969), *Manifestoes of Surrealism* (Ann Arbor: University of Michigan Press), trans. R. Seaver and H. R. Lane (includes several manifestos, the first published in 1924).
Brown, Paul (2003), 'Generative Computation and the Arts', *Digital Creativity*, 14/1: 1–2 (special issue on Generative Computation and the Arts, ed. P. Brown).
Brown, Richard (2001), *Biotica: Art, Emergence, and Artificial Life* (London: RCA CRD Research).
—— (2006), 'The Electrochemical Glass', *Strange Attractor Journal Three*, available from the Strange Attractor Shoppe, <http://www.strangeattractor.co.uk>.
Burnham, J. (1968), *Beyond Modern Sculpture: The Effects of Science and Technology on the Sculpture of this Century* (London: Allen Lane).
Candy, L., and Edmonds, E. A. (eds.) (2002) *Explorations in Art and Technology* (London: Springer).
Cohen, H. (1995), 'The Further Exploits of AARON Painter', in S. Franchi and G. Guzeldere (eds.), *Constructions of the Mind: Artificial Intelligence and the Humanities* (special edn. of *Stanford Humanities Review*, 4/2: 141–60.
—— (2002), 'A Million Millennial Medicis', in Candy and Edmonds (2002: 91–104).

Cope, D. (2001), *Virtual Music: Computer Synthesis of Musical Style* (Cambridge, Mass.: MIT Press).

—— (2006), *Computer Models of Musical Creativity* (Cambridge, Mass.: MIT Press).

Cornock, S., and Edmonds, E. A. (1973), 'The Creative Process Where the Artist is Amplified or Superceded by the Computer', *Leonardo*, 6: 11–16.

Costello, B., and Edmonds, E. A. (2007), 'Playful Pleasures: A User Evaluation of Three Artworks' (University of Technology, Sydney: CCS Report 2007–1).

Dawkins, R. (1986), *The Blind Watchmaker* (Harlow: Longman).

Dorin, A., and McCormack, J. (2001), 'First Iteration/Generative Systems (Guest Editors' Introduction)', *Leonardo*, 34/3: 335.

Duchamp, M. (1957), 'The Creative Act', in M. Sanouillet and E. Peterson (eds.), *The Essential Writings of Marcel Duchamp* (London: Thames and Hudson, 1975), 138–40.

Duprat, H., and Besson, C. (1998), 'The Wonderful Caddis Worm: Sculptural Work in Collaboration with Trichoptera', *Leonardo*, 31/3: 173–82.

Edmonds, E. A. (1969), 'Independence of Rose's Axioms for m-valued Implication', *Journal of Symbolic Logic*, 34: 283–4.

—— (1988), 'Logic and Time-based Art Practice', *Leonardo*, Electronic Art supplemental issue (Oxford: Pergamon Press), 19–20.

—— (2003), 'Logics for Constructing Generative Art Systems', *Digital Creativity*, 14/1: 23–38.

—— (2006), 'New Directions in Interactive Art Collaboration', *CoDesign*, 2/4: 19–194.

—— (in press), 'Reflections on the Nature of Interaction', *CoDesign: International Journal of CoCreation in Design and the Arts*.

Eno, B. (1996), 'Generative Music: Evolving metaphors, in my opinion, is what artists do', available at <http://www.inmotionmagazine.com/eno1.html>.

Generativeart.com, <http://www.generativeart.com>.

Goodstein, R. L. (1951), *Constructive Formalism: Essays on the Foundations of Mathematics* (Leicester: University College Press).

Grau, O. (2003) *Virtual Art: From Illusion to Immersion* (Cambridge, Mass.: MIT Press).

Hiller, L., and Isaacson, L. (1958), 'Musical Composition with a High-Speed Digital Computer', *Journal of the Audio-Engineering Society*, 6/3: 154–60.

Hofstadter, D. R. (2001), 'Staring Emmy Straight in the Eye—And Doing My Best Not to Flinch', in Cope (2001: 33–82).

—— (2007), *I Am a Strange Loop* (New York: Basic Books).

Jacob, C., and von Maminer S. (2007), 'Swarm Granmars: Growing Dynamic Structures in 3D Agent Spaces', *Journal of Digital Creativity*, special issue on computational models of creativity in the arts, 18/1: 54–64.

Johnson, B. S. (1969), *The Unfortunates* (London: Panther).

Kahn, D. (1996), 'What Now the Promise?', in Leggett and Michael (1996: *Interface: Exhibition Catalogue on International Artists' CD-ROM* (Sydney: Museum of Contemporary Art), 21–30).

Kowalski, T. L., and Levy, L. S. (1996), *Rule-Based Programming* (Boston: Kluwer Academic).

Krueger, M. W. (1991), *Artificial Reality* (2nd edn., Reading, Mass.: Addison-Wesley).

Laposky, B. (1969), 'Oscillons: Electronic Abstractions', *Leonardo*, 2/4: 345–54.

Leggett, M. (2000), 'Thinking Imaging Software', *Photofile: Photomedia Journal*, 60: 28–31.

Leggett, M., and Michael, L. (eds.) (1996), *Burning the Interface: Exhibition Catalogue on International Artists' CD-ROM* (Sydney: Museum of Contemporary Art).

LeWitt, S. (1967), 'Paragraphs on Conceptual Art', *Artforum*, 5/10: 79–83; rep. in K. Stiles and P. Selz (eds.), *Theories and Documents of Contemporary Art: A Sourcebook of Artists' Writings* (Berkeley and Los Angeles University of California Press), 822–6.

—— (1969), 'Sentences on Conceptual Art', *Art-Language*, 1: 11–13; repr. in Lippard (1973: 75 f.), and in K. Stiles and P. Selz (eds.), *Theories and Documents of Contemporary Art: A Sourcebook of Artists' Writings* (Berkeley and Los Angeles: University of California Press), 826–7.

Lindenmayer, A. (1968), 'Mathematical Models for Cellular Interaction in Development, Parts I and II', *Journal of Theoretical Biology*, 18: 280–315.

Lippard, L. R. (1973), *Six Years: The Dematerialization of the Art Object from 1966 to 1972* (New York: Praeger), page references to the 1997 reprint (Berkeley and Los Angeles: University of California Press).

McCorduck, P. (1991), *AARON's Code: Meta-Art, Artificial Intelligence, and the Work of Harold Cohen* (New York: W. H. Freeman).

McCormack, J. (2003), 'Art and the Mirror of Nature', *Digital Creativity*, 14/1: 3–22 (special issue on Generative Computation and the Arts, ed. Paul Brown).

—— (2004), *Impossible Nature: The Art of John McCormack* (Melbourne: Australian Centre for the Moving Image).

McCormack, J., Dorin, A., and Innocent, T. (2004), 'Generative Design: A Paradigm for Design Research', in J. Redmond, D. Durling, and A. de Bono (eds.), *Proceedings of Futureground* (Melbourne: Design Research Society), 156–64.

Mallen, G. (2005), 'Reflections on Gordon Pask's Adaptive Teaching Concepts and their Relevance to Modern Knowledge Systems', in L. Candy (ed.), *Creativity and Cognition 2005*, proceedings of the Fifth Conference on Creativity and Cognition, 12–15 April, Goldsmiths College (New York: ACM Press), 86–91.

Marr, A. (forthcoming), ' "He Thought it the Deuil, Whereas Indeede it was a Meere Mathematicall Inuention": Understanding Automata in the Late Renaissance', in J. Riskin (ed.), *The Sistine Gap: Essays in the History and Philosophy of Artificial Life* (Chicago: Chicago University Press).

Martin, K. (1951/4), 'Abstract Art', *Broadsheet No. 1: Abstract Paintings, Sculptures, Mobiles* (London: Lund Humphries, 1951), AIA exhibition catalogue; also in L. Alloway, *Nine Abstract Artists, Their Work and Their Theory: Robert Adams, Terry Frost, Adrian Heath, Anthony Hill, Roger Hilton, Kenneth Martin, Mary Martin, Victor Pasmore, William Scott* (London: Tiranti, 1954).

Metzger, G. (1965), *Auto-Destructive Art* (London: Destruction/Creation), expanded version of a talk at the Architectural Association, updating the manifesto of 1959.

Muller, L., Edmonds, E. A., and Connell, M. (2006), 'Living Laboratories for Interactive Art', *CoDesign: International Journal for CoCreation in Design and the Arts*, 2/4: 195–207.

Nake, F.(1998), 'Art in the Time of the Artificial', *Leonardo*, 31/3: 163–4.

——(2005), 'Computer Art: A Personal Recollection', in L. Candy (ed.), *Creativity and Cognition 2005*, proceedings of the Fifth Conference on Creativity and Cognition, 12–15 April, Goldsmiths College (New York: ACM Press), 54–62.

Nees, G. (1969), *Generative Computergraphik* (Berlin: Siemens AG).

O'Hear, A. (1995), 'Art and Technology: An Old Tension', in R. Fellows (ed.), *Philosophy and Technology* (Cambridge: Cambridge University Press), 143–58.

Pask, G. (1971), 'A Comment, a Case-History, and a Plan', in J. Reichardt (ed.), *Cybernetics, Art, and Ideas* (London: Studio Vista), 76–99.

Popper, F. (2007), *From Technological to Virtual Art* (Cambridge, Mass.: MIT Press).

Pinch, T., and Trocco, F. (2002) *Analog Days: The Invention and Impact of the Moog Synthesizer* (Cambridge, Mass.: Harvard University Press).

Prusinkiewicz, P. (2004), 'Art and Science for Life: Designing and Growing Virtual Plants with L-Systems', in C. G. Davidson and T. Fernandez (eds.), *Nursery Crops: Development, Evaluation, Production and Use*, proceedings of the XXVI International Horticultural Congress, *Acta Horticulturae*, 630: 15–28.

Prusinkiewicz, P., and Lindenmayer, A. (1990), *The Algorithmic Beauty of Plants* (New York: Springer-Verlag).

Sims, K. (1991), 'Artificial Evolution for Computer Graphics', *Computer Graphics*, 25/4: 319–28.

——(2007), 'Galapogos Interactive Exhibit', <http://www.genarts.com/galapogos/index.html>.

Smith, M. (ed.) (2005), *Stelarc: The Monograph* (Cambridge, Mass.: MIT Press).
Steuer, J. (1992), 'Defining Virtual Reality: Dimensions Determining Telepresence', *Journal of Communication*, 42/4: 73–93.
Todd, S. C., and Latham, W. (1992), *Evolutionary Art and Computers* (London: Academic Press).
Tofts, D. (2003), 'Avatars of the Tortoise: Life, Longevity, and Simulation', *Digital Creativity*, 14/1: 54–63 (special issue on Generative Computation and the Arts, ed. Paul Brown.)
—— (2005), *Interzone: Media Arts in Australia* (Fisherman's Bend, Victoria: Craftsman House).
Webster, A. (2006–), *Solar Stacking* (an electrochemical sculpture), see <http://www.andywebster.info/solar/>.
Webster, A., and Bird, J. (2002), *Tuning Pask's Ear*, video (7:26) exhibited in several galleries.
Whitelaw, M. (2004), *Metacreation: Art and Artificial Life* (London: MIT Press).
Wilson, S. (2002), *Information Arts: Intersections of Art, Science, and Technology* (Cambridge, Mass.: MIT Press).
Woolf, S. (2004), 'Expanded Media: Interactive and Generative Processes in New Media Art.' unpublished DPhil thesis, Dept. Informatics, University of Sussex.
Xenakis, I. (1963), *Musiques formelles: Nouveaux principes formels de composition musicale* (Paris: Richard-Masse).
—— (1971), *Formalized Music: Thought and Mathematics in Composition* (Bloomington, Indiana University Press).
Zivanovic, A. (2005), 'The Development of a Cybernetic Sculptor: Edward Ihnatowicz and the Senster', in L. Candy (ed.), *Creativity and Cognition 2005*, proceedings of the Fifth Conference on Creativity and Cognition, 12–15 April, Goldsmiths College (New York: ACM Press): 102–8.

8

Agents and Creativity

When Alice had finished reciting "*You are old, Father William*", at the Caterpillar's request, the following exchange ensued:

"That is not said right," said the Caterpillar.

"Not *quite* right, I'm afraid," said Alice, timidly: "Some of the words have got altered."

"It is wrong from beginning to end," said the Caterpillar decidedly.

After that, Lewis Carroll tells us, there was silence for some minutes.

The silence was hardly surprising. How can you compare two things—still less, judge the closeness of their relationship—if they are different (or "wrong") in *every* respect? Without a series of intermediate structures, the one cannot be understood in terms of the other. Even if they do share some similarities, these have to be noticed—and they have to be recognized as significant. Had Alice pointed out that her poem, presumably like the one the Caterpillar had in mind, contained several instances of the word "the", the creature would not have been persuaded. Where poems are concerned, metres, rhyming patterns, and many individual words are significant, but "the"-counts are not. To argue with the Caterpillar, Alice would have had to identify the important features of her poem, and of his, before being able to compare them.

What has this got to do with creativity, and with agents? Well, creativity involves coming up with something novel, something different. And this new idea, in order to be interesting, must be intelligible. No matter how different it is, we must be able to understand it in terms of what we knew before. As for agents, their potential uses include helping us by suggesting, identifying, and even evaluating differences between familiar ideas and novel ones. (You'll be relieved, perhaps, if I don't attempt to define just what an agent is—and isn't.* Instead, I'll rely on

---

* This is discussed in M. A. Boden, *Mind as Machine: A History of Cognitive Science*, 2 vols. (Oxford: Oxford University Press), 15, iii. d–e.

the intuitive notion that an agent is a part of a program which can act, and/or be asked to act, in relative independence of others.)

No one would choose the Caterpillar as an assistant: he was both grumpy and unhelpful. What Alice wanted to know was just where she had "gone wrong", just where her recital differed from what she had learnt before. But the Caterpillar was in no mood to tell her. A computerized agent cannot be grumpy. Whether it can be specifically helpful, to someone trying to come up with (or to assess) creative ideas, is what we must consider.

How is creativity possible? How can a person, or a computer for that matter, generate novel ideas? Many scientifically minded individuals would argue that there is nothing especially problematic about creativity. A creative idea, they would say, is merely a novel (and valuable) combination of familiar ideas. Accordingly, creativity could be explained by a scientific theory showing how such novel combinations can come about.

Up to a point, they're right. Samuel Taylor Coleridge's questions about "the hooks and eyes of memory", for instance, could be answered by psychological theories describing the associative processes in the poet's mind (or brain). Indeed, current computer models of neural nets provide some preliminary ideas about just how such associations could happen. Using those ideas, we can lay computational foundations for *The Road to Xanadu* described in a fascinating literary study of the sources of Coleridge's poetic imagery (Boden 1991: ch. 6; Livingston Lowes 1951).

Moreover, we can see, in outline, how such theories might lead to helpful agents of diverse kinds. For example, the units (on various levels) within a computer model of a rich semantic network could communicate not only with each other but also with a human user. A writer might use the set of intercommunicating agents as an intelligent thesaurus, or even a computerized literary critic. For agents of this type might aid someone stuck for a new image, or someone attempting to assess (or interpret) one suggested by another writer. And they might help to show whether (and how) a series of images fits together, or to diagnose the mixture in a mixed metaphor. An agent within a semantic network could not only effect an association but also trace the associative pathways involved, which in itself might prompt the user to new insights. If such agents were unable always to tell the difference between an interesting image and an inappropriate one, they would be little the worse for that. Human brainstorming sessions, too, produce a lot of rubbish. Nuggets can be found within the rubbish, even though they may require further polishing.

Analogy, too, is the novel combination of familiar ideas. In analogy, the structural similarity between the two ideas is especially important. Moreover, the analogy (unlike many associations of ideas) may be systematically developed, for purposes of rhetoric or problem solving.

Several current computer models suggest how two ideas can be seen as analogous, being matched in various ways according to the context of thought (Boden 1991: pref. and ch. 7). Some are relatively rigid, in the sense that analogies are sought between things having pre-given descriptions, which descriptions are not altered if a new analogy is found (Falkenhainer et al., 1990; Holyoak and Thagard 1989). We can think of these programs in agentive terms if we focus separately on the various criteria they use in seeking analogies (semantic, structural, or pragmatic). Interactive versions might be helpful to human writers or problem solvers wanting to find, assess, or compare analogies. (As in the discussion of associative agents, above, this presupposes the availability of a rich database of potentially relevant concepts.)

One analogy model, in particular, is readily seen as a community of agents. The *Copycat* system (Hofstadter et al., in press; Mitchell 1993) uses many independent descriptors in trying to interpret a given analogy and to find a new (but similar) one. These descriptors, or "codelets", are applied in parallel, competing with one another to find the strongest analogy. The domain this program works in is very simple: alphabetic letter-strings. But there are hidden complexities even in this simple domain. For instance, one and the same structure can be described differently on different occasions, according not only to probabilistic variations but to the specific context surrounding it. Thus the ministring *mm* will be described as a letter repetition if it occurs within the larger string *aaffmmppzz*, but as two separate letters (identified respectively as the last and the first member of successor triplets) if it occurs in the string *abcfghklmmno*. A description can be used for a while and then discarded, as *Copycat* finds a more integrated, high-level, analogy involving other descriptions.

This program has come up with many unexpected alphabetic analogies, some of which are highly persuasive. For example, it was told that *abc* is analogous to (can be changed into) *abd*, and was asked to find a matching analogy for *xyz*. Among the many answers it offered were not only *xyd*, *xyzz*, and *xyy*, but also the surprising and elegant *wyz*. This involves, among other things, mapping *a* onto *z* and *left* onto *right*, and also swapping *successor* and *predecessor*. In embryo, then, we have a set of agents which can say not only "Think of it this way" and "Think of it that way," but also "Better still, think of it like this". If these techniques were made available in an interactive system, they might help human users to see analogies in some unexpected places.

Combinational creativity, then, can be thought of in agentive terms—and might be aided by computer systems made up of many largely independent agents. But is that enough? Can we explain *all* creativity by reference to novel combinations? If not, could we explain other cases in other terms—and would these also be suitable for computer implementation?

Creative ideas include scientific theories; musical compositions; literary genres; instances of choreography, painting, and architecture; theorems of mathematics; and the inventions of engineers. Some of these can be understood as mere novel combinations of familiar ideas. But many cannot—especially those which not only solve the creator's initial problem but also engender a whole new set of problems, to be solved perhaps by the creator's successors over many years. Exploring the implications of a radical new scientific theory, or of a new visual or musical genre, is not a matter of mere combination-juggling. On the contrary, it is a structured, disciplined, sometimes even systematic search for the meanings promised by the new idea.

But how can this be? How can a new idea be pregnant with such promise? Imagine someone trekking through a desert and up a barren mountainside—only to see, from the crest of the hill, a verdant valley stretched out before him. The promise, the possibilities, are enormous. But to find them, he will have to explore the valley—sketchily at first, perhaps, but later seeking treasures in many a nook and cranny. Creative thinkers (which means all of us, on a good day) explore the possibilities inherent in their own minds, wherein the spaces are not geographical but conceptual.

A conceptual space is a style of thinking, a mental skill that may be expressed in marble, music, or movement, in poetry, prose, or proof (Boden 1991: esp. ch. 4). It is defined by a set of constraints (the dimensions of the space) guiding the generation of ideas in the relevant domain. Some of these constraints are accepted, by the thinker and by the relevant social group (the Caterpillar?), as being more inescapable than others. And some are more fundamental than others. Together, they form a mental landscape with a characteristic structure and potential.

Conceptual spaces are analogous to geographical ones in several ways: they can be mapped, explored, and superficially altered, with many valuable results. In one way, however, they are very different. Unlike physical terrain, a conceptual space can be fundamentally transformed. The result of such a transformation is the appearance of a new space of possibilities, a mental terrain which simply did not exist before. It does not follow that creativity involves only transformations, although many of the most exciting examples do. Many creative achievements result from exploring conceptual spaces in systematic and imaginative ways.

For exploring and transforming our thinking styles—and for understanding and appreciating the results—we need good "maps" of the relevant space. Intuitive maps exist within our heads, mostly inaccessible to consciousness. In more explicit form, they can be found (though usually only in outline) in the humanities: in literary criticism and musicology, in the philosophy of science and aesthetics, and in the history of art, science, and mathematics.

Think of the disciplined beauty of a Palladian villa, for instance, with its symmetrical plan and elegant facade. Or consider the clean lines and interconnecting volumes of a Frank Lloyd Wright open-plan Prairie House. Think of the conventions of New Orleans jazz, and how they differ from Dizzy Gillespie. And remember how organic chemistry was changed by Kekule's discovery of the benzene ring, which engendered not just one molecular structure but a vast space of structural potential (aromatic chemistry), whose contents, pathways, and boundaries have now been largely mapped.

Even the Caterpillar might be able to sense the similarity between one Palladian villa and another, or between the various Prairie Houses. And a twentieth-century Caterpillar might be able to recognize New Orleans jazz, and distinguish it from later varieties. But Alice's invertebrate friend would not be able to specify the relevant similarities. A well-educated Caterpillar could enumerate the dimensions of the space of benzene derivatives, for these have been made explicit by theoretical chemists. With respect to architecture and jazz, however, things are much less clear—to humans, as to caterpillars.

Generations of architectural historians have disagreed on just what principles of design underlie Palladian design. And an expert on Lloyd Wright's work pronounced the (intuitively evident) architectural balance of his Prairie Houses to be "occult" (cited in Koning and Eizenberg 1981: 322). However, the crucial stylistic similarities concerned have been explicitly identified within a computer program (Hersey and Freedman

1992) and a computationally inspired "space-grammar" (Koning and Eizenberg 1981), respectively. Each of these formal systems describes the relevant conceptual space, making it possible to say just why two structures share (or do not share) the same style, and just how (and how fundamentally) they differ.

In addition, each of these systems can generate an indefinite number of structures lying within the relevant conceptual space. Some of these match buildings already designed by Palladio or Lloyd Wright. Others are new, depicting houses of the same general type.

For instance, the plan of a Palladian villa is designed by starting with a rectangle (certain proportions being preferred), and generating internal rectangles—the rooms—by making vertical and horizontal "splits" of various kinds. (Palladio himself described this method.) Not any splits will do, if the resulting design is to be one which Palladio would have approved. Splits are unacceptable if they produce internal corridors; long, thin rooms; too many rooms; rooms of greatly disparate size; many internal (windowless) rooms; and the largest rooms lying off the central axis. Early versions of the Palladian program made all of these mistakes, but the relevant design constraints have now been incorporated. Further non-Palladianisms, produced in the past by human imitators (such as Lord Burlington), include rectangular bays jutting out from the rectangular perimeter.

Other "mistakes" would be more debatable. For instance, Palladio almost never built cylindrical rooms. Should we say that an architect (or a program) who includes circles within the plan is faithful to Palladio's inspiration, or not? And if not, should we credit him (or it) with transforming Palladio's style into another, fundamentally similar, one? Whatever our answer, the grounds of judgement have been made explicit. So there is more chance of fruitful debate, and even of agreement.

As well as designing plans, this program designs Palladian facades appropriate to a given plan. It knows (among other things) the difference between Doric, Ionic, and Corinthian columns, and the constraints governing the placement of windows and pediment. On several occasions, it has produced a plan-and-facade design virtually identical to one drawn by Palladio himself. In short, the Palladian program, and the Lloyd Wright shape-grammar too, has generated new architectural designs (though not new architectural styles).

Our question here, however, is not whether an entire program can do something "creative", or even useful, but whether an agent can help a person to do so. The computational work on architectural styles suggests some ways in which computer agents might help a human architect.

For example, someone designing a Palladian villa, or even combining aspects of Palladianism with some other style, might find it helpful if an informed agent were to suggest—or to forbid—a split at a certain place in the plan. This would be especially useful to architects, or architectural students, with little experience of working in this genre. Left to themselves, such a person might design asymmetrical splits, overly narrow rooms, or bays spoiling the clean perimeter-line. Similarly, once the house plan had been approved, various agents might offer advice on the facade. Some could suggest the number, and the type, of columns. Others might argue for and against an attic storey, or for and against a particular type of pediment or architrave.

The agent-initiators and critics could communicate among themselves as necessary (to check for bilateral symmetry, for instance, or for numbers of rooms). But they need not insist on universal agreement. If they are being used as assistants to human beings, then responsibility for the overall integration of the design could be left to the person. In some circumstances, however, the human could not be relied on to achieve a satisfactory design, because of either inexperience or complexity. In producing a set of computerized agents (a program) for practical use, careful judgements would have to be made about just which decisions and evaluations could be left entirely to the user, and which should be monitored, or even made, by the agents. (This is a special case of the familiar problem about the use of "expert systems" in general.)

Agents could be used to help people to map, explore, tweak, and (ultimately) transform conceptual spaces of many different kinds. It is not necessary to restrict ourselves to examples like Palladian architecture, which has long been described in formalist, mathematical, terms. Once a conceptual space has been mapped, agents could help us to move around it in some surprising ways.

Take jazz, for instance. Suppose that the Caterpillar in *Alice's Adventures in Wonderland* had been holding not a hookah, but a saxophone. And suppose that Alice, an uncommonly precocious child, had taken some jazz cassettes with her to Wonderland, and played them to the Caterpillar. Could the Caterpillar have been helped to learn to play music in that style by a set of computer agents (also presciently provided by Alice)? Surely, this idea is too nonsensical even for Lewis Carroll? The spontaneous creativity of jazz improvisation, you may feel, is simply not the sort of thing where computers could help.

Well, that feeling might not survive experience of a program that can help people to improvise jazz (Hodgson 1990, in preparation; Waugh 1992). This program knows about various dimensions of the musical space of jazz, and various ways of travelling through it. For instance, it can produce fragments of ascending or descending scales, ensuring that the scale chosen is the one relevant to the harmony at that particular point. It can provide "call" and "reply" over two or more bars. It can replace the current melody note by another note drawn from the same scale, or provide a chromatic run between this melody note and the next. It can "cut and paste" a library of melodic and rhythmic patterns, or play fractionally ahead of or behind the beat. And it, and the human user, can vary the frequency with which it does any of these things.

If left to wander through the space by itself, this program will improvise—on a given melody, harmony, and rhythm—by making (random) choices on many dimensions simultaneously. Working in this fashion, it often creates novel musical ideas which professional jazz musicians find interesting, and may wish to develop in their own playing. Alternatively, the human—or Caterpillar—user can make the program concentrate on one (or more) dimension at a time, and explore it (or them) in a very simple way. This is why it can help jazz novices, who can focus on the aspect of jazz which is currently causing them difficulty.

The separability of the various musical dimensions suggests the activity of a number of independent musical agents. An improved version of this system might include evaluative modules (agents) which could discriminate between equally legal phrases, or identify weaknesses in an improvisation (its own or the user's) and show how they can be avoided. A really knowledgeable system might even be able to teach the user how to recover from, or even make the best of, a mistake that had not been avoided. (Oliver Sacks has described a patient with Tourette's syndrome who is a jazz drummer, able to turn his unpredictable muscular tics into the seeds of exciting jazz improvisations.) In general, mistakes can be thought of as a sort of serendipity. If knowledgeable agents were developed to help us make the best of our mistakes (not just avoid them), they could lead to some real surprises.

Mention of mistakes raises the question, inevitable in discussions of creativity, "When is a mistake not a mistake?" The answer, sometimes, is "When it is a transformation". Going beyond the familiar conceptual space—generalizing a constraint, specializing it, dropping it, negating it, adding another . . . —could always be described as a mistake, relative to the original style of thinking. Indeed, it often is so described: one of Kekule's contemporaries dismissed his account of the benzene ring as "a tissue of chemical fancies", and new art forms are commonly rejected when they first appear.

A transformation may be more or less fundamental: changing a string molecule to a ring molecule, by closing the formerly open curve, is more fundamental than switching between methyl and ethyl alcohol by making different attachments to the hydroxyl group. And several transformations may be combined: one could include both bays and cylindrical rooms in a basically Palladian design. But not everything can be transformed at once. The new conceptual space is generated from its predecessor, and must be intelligible in terms of it if it is to be accepted. If Alice's recital was literally "wrong from beginning to end", the Caterpillar wouldn't know what poem she was reciting.

Heuristics for transforming conceptual spaces, including the space of heuristics, have been applied in a number of programs (Lenat 1983). One of these, whose task is to generate new mathematical concepts from very simple bases, also has criteria for evaluating the mathematical "interest" of the results. Some of the evaluations are mutually exclusive (if the union of two sets either *has* or *does not have* some property possessed by both the original sets, that is counted, rightly, as interesting). Likewise, some heuristics are opposites: to specialize a concept, and to generalize it, for instance. There is nothing wrong with that, for a concept does not need to satisfy every possible criterion to be interesting, nor does every heuristic need to be applied simultaneously.

These generative heuristics and evaluative rules can all be thought of as agents. Despite being called the "Automatic Mathematician", this program was often used interactively. A human mathematician would guide it into certain pathways, for example by giving some concept a name—which the program would interpret as a hint to give that concept priority for a while. Versions of this program might be developed for other domains, in which the knowledge and judgement of human users could aid, and be aided by, the application of the transformational and evaluative heuristics. Indeed, its heuristic-altering successor has been applied to several different problem-areas, and has generated at least one patentable idea (in US law, an idea "not obvious to one skilled in the art").

The most surprising—though not necessarily the best—transformations would be able to change the conceptual space in unpredictable ways and at unpredictable levels. The clearest example at present is given by genetic algorithms. A crossover operator, for instance, might be thought of as an independent agent which transforms, at random, certain types of constraint represented in the target code.

The targeted constraints may be more or less restrictive. In one graphics program, for example, the crossovers and mutations can get right into the heart of the image-generating code (Sims 1991). The results are always "viable", in the sense that the newly transformed code will generate some visible image or other. But the process is utterly undisciplined. Although it could be used to help graphic designers come up with images they would never have thought of themselves, it cannot be used to explore or refine an image space in a systematic way. That is possible, however, if the mutating agents are allowed to alter only the superficial parameters of the code. Significantly, these less powerful agents are preferred by a professional artist working on "computer sculpture", who uses them to explore specific classes of 3D forms (Todd and Latham 1992).

In both these cases, the evaluation is done by the human user. At each generation, he chooses the image or image pair to be used in "breeding" the next generation. In principle, evaluation could be made automatic (in whole or in part). And it might be useful for the artist to be able to avoid having to consider certain sorts of image, or to be presented up front with the most "promising" ones. But if one's interest here is in the development of agent systems for interactive use, evaluation should not be entirely handed over to the computer.

I've concentrated on the practical question of whether agent systems might help to further human creativity. But my discussion can be seen also as an outline of how creativity might be scientifically understood. Many different psychological processes are involved, ranging across combinational and exploratory-transformational thinking. And many questions remain unanswered, or unasked. Despite all the unclarities, however, we are beginning to understand the computational resources that underlie creativity in its various forms.

Creativity at Lewis Carroll's level seems magical, but there is no reason to think that it is magic. Wonderland (and the world behind the Looking-Glass, too) owes many of its surprising features to tweakings and transformations of conceptual spaces familiar even to a child. Other Wonderland surprises are grounded in serendipitous associations within the author's mind. We shall never know what all of these were (still less could they have been predicted beforehand). Who can say where the hookah came from? But the Caterpillar and his mushroom may have owed their existence to a real caterpillar and a real mushroom, falling under Carroll's eye on that golden summer afternoon.

REFERENCES

Boden, M. A. (1991), *The Creative Mind: Myths and Mechanisms* (expanded edn., New York: Basic Books; London: Abacus).

Falkenhainer, B., Forbus, K. D., and Gentner, D. (1990), "The Structure-Mapping Engine: Algorithm and Examples", *Artificial Intelligence*, 41: 1–63.

Hersey, G., and Freedman, R. (1992), *Possible Palladian Villas (Plus a Few Instructively Impossible Ones)* (Cambridge, Mass.: MIT Press).

Hodgson, P. (1990), 'Understanding Computing, Cognition, and Creativity', MSc thesis, University of the West of England.

—— (in preparation), 'Modelling Cognition in Creative Musical Improvisation', (provisional title), DPhil thesis, University of Sussex.

Hofstadter, D. R., Mitchell, M., French, R., Chalmers, D., Moser, D. (in press), *Fluid Concepts and Creative Analogies* (Hemel Hempstead: Harvester Wheatsheaf).

Holyoak, K. J., and Thagard, P. (1989), "Analogical Mapping by Constraint Satisfaction", *Cognitive Science*, 13, 295–356.

Koning, H., and Eizenberg, J. (1981), "The Language of the Prairie: Frank Lloyd Wright's Prairie Houses", *Environment and Planning B*, 8: 295–323.

Lenat, D. B. (1983), "The Role of Heuristics in Learning by Discovery: Three Case Studies", in R. S. Michalski, J. G. Carbonell, & T. M. Mitchell (eds.), *Machine Learning: An Artificial Intelligence Approach* (Palo Alto, Calif.: Tioga).

Livingston Lowes, J. (1951), *The Road to Xanadu: A Study in the Ways of the Imagination* (2nd edn., London: Constable).

Mitchell, M. (1993), *Analogy-Making as Perception* (Cambridge, Mass.: MIT Press).

Sims, K. (1991), "Artificial Evolution for Computer Graphics", *Computer Graphics*, 25/4 (July), 319–28.

Todd, S., and Latham, W. (1992), *Evolutionary Art & Computers* (London: Academic Press).

Waugh, I. (1992), "Improviser" *Music Technology* (Sept.), 70–3.

9
Autonomy, Integrity, and Computer Art

I. INTRODUCTION

Autonomy is a key notion in certain forms of computer art—where the autonomy in question is ascribed to the computer system itself. This applies, for instance, to many examples of interactive art, and to evolutionary art in general. But the senses in which these artworks are autonomous differ.

In non-technological contexts, there are two very different forms of autonomy: physical and mental/intentional. These are typified, respectively, by biological homeostasis and human freedom. Accordingly, there are two very different classes of 'artificial' autonomy. One is quasi-physical, and closely related to homeostasis (and other forms of biological self-organization); the other is quasi-mental, and related to freedom. Artists strongly influenced by the scientific field of artificial life (A-Life) pay more attention to the first, whereas some interactive computer artists prioritize the second. The kind of autonomy that's achieved in the computerized work of art differs accordingly.

Or perhaps one should speak of 'quasi-autonomy' here? For the claim made above may seem counter-intuitive, even absurd: how can *any* notion of autonomy properly be applied to *any* computer system? As for freedom of choice, this seems even more distanced from these impersonal machines.

Likewise, perhaps one should speak only of 'quasi-art' in this context? Insofar as the appreciation of art in general depends on the (tacit) attribution of autonomy or freedom to the artist, it would seem that computer art lies beyond the pale—so much so, that it isn't really 'art' at all? At best, someone might say, it retains its status as art only because autonomy/freedom can be ascribed to the human computer artist who created it.

However, that last response is rather too quick. For the sense in which the human can be said to have created the artwork is importantly different in traditional and computer art—and in any art that's produced by largely impersonal processes. The proper 'location' of the autonomy is problematic accordingly.

In short, autonomy is a concept that has a place in the understanding of computer art: not only in one's understanding of the computer artist but also in one's appreciation of the artworks concerned. We shall see, however, that it can't be applied (or withheld) merely by observing the finished product. In particular, when this concept is being attached (or not) to the computer artwork itself, the critic must have some knowledge of how it works, and/or how it was generated. The epistemology of art criticism, one might say, is more taxing for computer art than it is for more traditional art forms.

II. HOMEOSTASIS AS AUTONOMY

Homeostasis isn't stasis. On the contrary, it's an active process. Nonetheless, it constitutes a form of stillness, or constancy. For homeostasis is the ability of living organisms to keep certain aspects of their physical state constant, irrespective (up to a point) of what's going on in the environment.

One familiar example is the maintenance of blood temperature in mammals and birds. It's not that the temperature of the blood never changes: it does. But incipient changes—due, perhaps, to increased or decreased heat in the outside world—are soon compensated by other bodily changes (the diameter of blood vessels, for instance, or the secretion of chemicals by the pituitary gland . . .). The end result is the maintenance of the blood temperature.

Because homeostasis conveys independence of the environment, it counts as a form of autonomy, or self-direction. Indeed, all forms of biological self-organization do so (various examples are mentioned below). The biological system does its own thing, and achieves constancy despite varying environmental factors. It works by means of perturbations producing constancy: PPC, for short. The organism itself controls the various bodily perturbations that occur, directing them towards the final state that it wanted all along—98.4° Fahrenheit, perhaps.

That's a misleading way of putting it, of course. For non-human mammals and birds don't actually *want* a normal blood temperature.

Even human beings very rarely *want* that. Occasionally, however, they do—and then they may take active, deliberate, steps to achieve it. As we'll see, this reiterates the point remarked above, namely that there are two very different kinds of autonomy.

III. AUTONOMY AND PARADOX

The term PPC, if considered in the abstract, may seem incoherent: how can perturbations possibly *produce* constancy? Surely, those two notions are contradictory? It's only because we're so familiar, nowadays, with examples of physiological homeostasis that talk of 'PPC' doesn't faze us. Talk of 'autonomy', however, still may. That's why autonomy is an intriguing, and enticing, concept for many artists. For it can seem to be close to magic—or, in the context of computers, to paradox.

References to autonomy and self-determination trip fairly easily off the tongue. But just what do these terms mean? Even more puzzling, how did the self-determining 'self' (the system) get there in the first place? If the answer we're offered is that it spontaneously generated and/or organized *itself*, this risks being seen as empty mystification. The fact that this answer has been given by some very distinguished people—from Kant (in 1790) and the *Naturphilosophien*, through the philosophers Henri Bergson and Hans Jonas, to the autopoietic biologist Humberto Maturana and his psychologist colleague Francisco Varela—doesn't prevent its being embarrassingly vague. Indeed, the A-Life pioneer (and cybernetician) William Ross Ashby complained that the term *self-organization* was 'fundamentally confused and inconsistent' and 'probably better allowed to die out' (Ashby 1962: 269). He saw it as potentially mystifying because it implies that there's an organizer when in fact there isn't.

For all that, Ashby's own mid-century work on the Homeostat machine showed, in general terms, how it is possible for self-organization to happen (Ashby 1947, 1948; cf. Boden 2006: 4.viii.c–d, 15.i.b). The Homeostat looked pretty boring: nothing to excite artists there, it seemed. (And no professional artists were excited by it, at that time.) But it threw a powerful theoretical searchlight on the autonomy of living organisms, including human behaviour and experience.

Ashby's contraption consisted of four square boxes, each with an induction coil and a pivoting magnetic needle on the top; each needle carried a wire dipping into a trough of water, with electrodes at each end. To cut a long story short, the interconnections between the boxes were such that the machine could maintain the set of needles in a constant state. It could return to that state if a needle was temporarily moved, and it could even reach that equilibrium from a random starting point. (The PPCs, here, consisted in electrical feedback affecting the movements of the needles: changes in the current flowing through a coil would make its needle move, which would move the wire, which would cause changes in the electric potential of the water.)

The Homeostat was named in honour of homeostasis, of course. But it was inspired also by two other—then highly mysterious—examples of PPCs: George Stratton's experiences (in the 1890s) of visual reorganization when wearing inverting spectacles for a week or so, and Roger Sperry's 1940s discovery that animals can recover from the surgical 'cross-wiring' of antagonistic muscles. Ashby was as fascinated as anyone else by Stratton's intriguing introspective reports. But he was less surprised, because he regarded the brain as yet another feedback-controlled homeostatic system, alongside blood temperature and blood sugar. In general, he said, homeostasis (alias self-equilibration) is an adaptive activity that maintains/recovers the critical values of the variables that are necessary for life. In short, the Homeostat, in theoretical terms, was much more ambitious than it looked.

More recent research on self-organization, based on various types of computer modelling, has disarmed the PPC paradox still further. A very simple example was A-Life's three-rule explanation of the self-organizing phenomenon of flocking (Reynolds 1987), soon picked up by Hollywood for the computer animation of flocks of bats and dinosaurs.

More complex—and sometimes almost as entertaining—instances are based on computerized neural networks. These are driven by so-called 'weak' constraints, and turn perturbations into constancy (equilibrium) by a method called parallel distributed processing (PDP). The body of data/evidence that is input to the system may be incoherent, some items contradicting others. But, provided that the degree of conflict is not too great, the system as a whole can reach an appropriate decision (by processes of internal self-equilibration). This is known in the trade as multiple constraint satisfaction, whereby the system satisfies *the greatest possible number* of the many constraints concerned, and ignores the remainder.

Some computer artworks depend on being able to tolerate such ambiguities. Consider Richard Brown's *Mimetic Starfish*, for instance.

This intriguing installation appears to the gallery visitors to be a knobbly, multicoloured starfish trapped—and periodically struggling—inside a marble table. In fact, the 'starfish' is a coloured image projected from the ceiling down onto the surface of the table. Its varying (but always lifelike) changes, which are experienced by observers as movements of a starfish, are generated by a neural network that responds to the bodily movements of the human beings near the table. However, the significance (to the system) of these body movements may conflict. If two people are standing by the table and both of them happen to lift their fingers at the same time, the tip of the third 'arm' of the starfish may be disposed to turn *both* to the left *and* to the right—which is impossible even in an image, never mind a real live starfish. Multiple constraint satisfaction takes care of this problem, hiding the conflicting interactive signals within plausible images as of a living starfish.

Further examples of PPC in action have included scientific work on the autopoiesis of cell membranes (Zeleny 1977; Zeleny et al. 1989), and on computer models of self-organization within neural networks (e.g. von der Malsburg 1973; Linsker 1988, 1990). The latter case showed that ordered sets of orientation detectors, comparable to those found in mammalian visual cortex, can arise spontaneously from a randomly connected base. (So the fact that newborn kittens already possess orientation detectors *does not* prove that these are 'innate' in the sense of being specifically predetermined by the genes.) There is even a computerized version of Stratton: a two-eyed robot, modelled closely on the Homeostat, which can gradually recover from having the input to its two eyes reversed (di Paolo 2000).

Since none of that empirical research relied on magic, it has helped us to understand self-organization much more clearly. In both natural and artificial examples, self-organization is *the spontaneous emergence (and maintenance) of order, out of an origin that's ordered to a lesser degree.* It concerns not mere superficial change but fundamental structural development. And it's spontaneous, or autonomous [*sic*], in the sense that it results from the intrinsic character of the system rather than being imposed by some external force (or program).

It follows that we can now say with a clear intellectual conscience what's been confidently, though vaguely, asserted for over two hundred years: namely, that self-organization is the central feature of living things. And we can now see that various other concepts often used in defining 'life', *and in describing certain areas of computer art*, are special cases of it: emergence, autonomy, unity/wholeness, autopoiesis, homeostasis, evolution, adaptation, and responsiveness. Self-organization, in fact, is a term for a form of autonomy where the system's independence is especially strong: it is not merely self-controlled, but also self-generated. In short, talk of autonomy and self-organization isn't empty after all.

That's partly why many computer artists are excited by A-Life (Whitelaw 2004), a field of computational research that has given us a wide range of examples of autonomy and/or self-organization. Some artists are using evolutionary programming to generate novel (and largely unpredictable) artwork, while others employ systems called cellular [sic] automata to make unexpectedly complex patterns emerge from a simple base. A few are even utilizing millennial versions of Ashby's deceptively 'boring' machine: Jane Prophet's *Net Work* installation (planned to surround the pier at Herne Bay) consists of 2,500 intercommunicating floating buoys, each of which is colour-emitting and wave-sensitive (Bird, d'Inverno, and Prophet 2007). Other computer artists rely on the A-Life techniques of 'situated' robotics, in which robots respond in ways that aren't arbitrarily programmed into them but result from their own physical structure (Boden 2006: 13.iii.b). Two examples are Kenneth Rinaldo's installations *The Flock* and *Autopoiesis* [sic], in which wireframe robotic 'arms' hanging from the ceiling interact autonomously with each other and with the moving/speaking human audience.

In brief, computational work on autonomy has thrown explanatory light in places previously so intellectually dark as to be nigh-invisible. Moreover, this work has already inspired some professional artists in their day-to-day practice. The autonomy and self-organization of their computer artworks are *real*, despite having been engineered by human beings.

Nevertheless, sometimes 'self' really does mean (personal) *self*, not just (impersonal) *system*. And that, again, should alert us to the second class of autonomous systems—which are typically ignored in A-Life.

IV. TWO KINDS OF AUTONOMY

The air of paradox isn't the only unclarity concerning the concept of autonomy (Boden 1996). There's complication, too. And if the paradox has been resolved by work in A-Life (see above), the complication hasn't.

The difficulty, here, is that there are three aspects of an organism's—or, more generally, a system's—behavioural control which are crucial to its independence. Moreover, these don't necessarily run alongside each other, nor keep pace with each other even when they do.

The first is the extent to which response to the environment is direct (determined only by the present state of the external world) or indirect (mediated by inner mechanisms that depend in part on the system's previous history). The second is the extent to which the controlling mechanisms were self-generated rather than externally imposed. And the third is the extent to which any inner directing mechanisms can be reflected upon, and/or selectively modified in the light of general interests and/or the particular problem and current context.

In general, an individual's autonomy is the greater, the more its behaviour is directed by self-generated (and idiosyncratic) inner mechanisms, nicely responsive to the specific problem-situation yet reflexively modifiable by wider concerns. Clearly, then, autonomy isn't an all-or-nothing property. There are various types, and varying degrees, of autonomy. And—even more confusing—the senses in which autopoietic systems or self-organizing networks are autonomous differ from each other, and from the sense in which situated robots (often used in computer art) are autonomous.

For our purposes here, however, the most important difference is that between autonomy *as ascribed to non-human systems* and autonomy *as ascribed to adult human beings* (though not to babies or infants). The latter form has a special name of its own: freedom.

Human freedom is a special case of self-organization that's commonly regarded as the epitome of autonomy. A-Lifers, who generally concern themselves with organisms well below *Homo sapiens* in the phylogenetic scale, rarely mention it explicitly. Occasionally, they admit that their work doesn't cover it (e.g. Bird, Stokes et al. 2007: 2.1). But sometimes, their words seem to imply that they confuse it with autonomy as such. That's a mistake. The examples of autonomy considered in A-Life show varying degrees of independence from direct outside control. But none has the cognitive/motivational complexity that's required for freedom (remember the third aspect of autonomy listed above).

That's why traditional, or 'top-down', methods of artificial intelligence—often disparagingly referred to as GOFAI: 'Good Old-Fashioned AI'—have got closer to an understanding of freedom than A-Life has done. For freedom is best understood in terms of a particular form of complex computational architecture (Dennett 1984; Boden 2006: 7.i.g–i, 12.ix.b).

It requires a range of psychological resources, which combine to generate decisions/actions selected from a rich space of possibilities. These resources include reasoning, means-end planning, motivation, various sorts of prioritizing (including individual preferences and moral principles), analogy recognition, the anticipation of unwanted side effects, and deliberate self-monitoring. The decisions—choices—concerned involve concepts of intention, desire, and belief, and the attribution of such concepts both to the self and to others. In other words, they require cognitive resources commonly referred to as Theory of Mind. (It's because these psychological resources aren't yet fully developed in infants, who haven't even acquired the concepts needed for a Theory of Mind, that they can't properly be said to be free.)

In the paradigm case, the choice is largely conscious. But an action may be termed "free" because, given the computational resources possessed by the person in question, it *could* have been consciously considered by them, and the decision could have differed accordingly.

Freedom is often compromised as a result of physical force, threats, bribery, or just plain ignorance. But it can also be compromised in more exotic circumstances. Under hypnosis, for instance. Or when someone obeys hallucinated instructions, perhaps believed to come from 'saints' or 'aliens'. Or when brain damage affects the planning of everyday actions, so that the person repeatedly forgets what goal/sub-goal they were following, or performs plan steps in the wrong order (e.g. licking the letter instead of the stamp).

All those 'exotic' phenomena, wherein a person's autonomy is significantly lessened, are intuitively mysterious. Yet psychologists have helpfully theorized and/or modelled all of them in partly GOFAI terms (Boden 2006: 7.i.h–i; 12.ix.b). In short, the third aspect of behavioural control isn't modelled in A-Life but does feature in (some) GOFAI. And for that aspect of control, 'self' really does mean self. There's not only reflection on one's own thinking, but structured patterns—a self-image, as well as a self-ideal—that affects the choices made.

(These features of adult minds underlie a special case of autonomy that's often used as a criterion in art criticism: namely, moral and/or stylistic integrity. This will be briefly discussed in Section VI.)

Another way of putting all this is to say that the autonomy of non-human organisms is purely physical, whereas the autonomy of adult human beings is both physical (blood temperature, again) and mental (or, philosophers would say, intentional). These provide physical constancy and mental constancy—where, in each case, the 'constancy', or stillness, isn't stasis but may involve continual effort and change. The goal-forgetting example, above, is an especially clear case of the *lack* of (teleological) constancy in the afflicted person's behaviour and thinking.

(The previous paragraph was written in a philosophical shorthand, because to write it out in longhand would be a lengthy—and here unnecessary—enterprise. The autonomy of many other 'higher' animals is arguably partly mental, too. Chimpanzees, for example, appear to have a minimal Theory of Mind, and vervet monkeys engage in communicative behaviour which—unlike blood temperature—can't be described or explained in purely physical terms: Heyes 1998; Cheney and Seyfarth 1990. Whether their behaviour is intentional in the sense in which that of language-using humans is, however, is quite another matter. See Boden 2006: 7.vi.b-c.)

In the context of computer art, this analysis raises the question of which type/types of autonomy are being attempted—or perhaps even achieved?—by the artists in question.

V. AUTONOMY AND COMPUTER ART

It follows from the discussion above that the autonomy one can ascribe to the computer artist and to the computer artwork are fundamentally different. Both involve various types of independence, and both can result in some form of constancy. But there are important distinctions to be drawn.

Consider interactive art, for instance. In general, the computer systems involved here are reactive, or responsive. They do what they do, and change from moment to moment, as a result of environmental input.

Most of them are 'autonomous' in the same sense that situated robots are autonomous. Indeed, some interactive artworks are comprised of one or more such robots, interacting with the audience and/or with each other. One example, mentioned above, is Rinaldo's *Autopoiesis*. Occasionally, however, the changes within an interactive artwork are carried out by self-equilibrating processes that are deliberately modelled on homeostasis—or, more accurately, on Ashby's Homeostat: the *Net Work* installation, also mentioned above, illustrates this point. Similarly, the interactive *Mimetic Starfish* relies on PPCs (perturbations producing constancy) that are mutually equilibrated by the structure of the neural network concerned. In such cases, the system's autonomy is not merely a matter of internal (as opposed to external) control, but also a matter of the self-organization of the system as a whole.

In practice, what happens in an interactive artwork is usually a function—commonly, a direct function—of the human observer's behaviour. The 'observer' may be a viewer, or a listener, or a viewer-and-listener, or even a sniffer or a feeler . . . . Indeed, all of these terms are perhaps better replaced by 'participant', for it is part of the aesthetic point of interactive art that the human audience—again, a potentially misleading term (since 'audience' may be taken to imply passivity)—plays a crucial part in the creation of the artwork in its final form.

The relevant input may be the movements of the observer's body, even including the movements of their eyes, or perhaps the sounds emitted/caused by them. Or it may be something more abstract, such as the density of viewers located in a particular area of the gallery floor. It may even depend to some degree on past events: if the artwork has a memory of past interactions, the cue-response rules may vary accordingly.

Sometimes, non-human input is relevant too: changes in air temperature, for example, or the density of autumn leaves falling in the wind. However, allowing such non-human factors to have an influence threatens to lessen the viewer's sense of engagement with the artwork concerned. And that sense of engagement is aesthetically crucial. The characteristic feature of interactive art—as opposed to traditional paintings, sculptures, or music—is that the audience doesn't merely engage with it intellectually, or even emotionally: they *change* it, too. (This is why, as remarked above, the location of the creativity involved is problematic: some computer artists insist that the audience helps to 'create' the work—e.g. Ascott 1990.)

Whether they can decide *just how* to change it is another matter. If the observer/participant is able to follow an agenda, producing a desired end-result in the artwork in question, their sense of engagement (control) will be much greater than if they can cause only unpredictable, apparently random, changes in the piece. Many interactive artists, then, value their installations more highly if the causal influences are relatively clear, or at least if they can become relatively clear after the participant has interacted with them for a while. Some observers, however, may prefer to luxuriate in the experience of caused-but-uncontrolled unpredictability.

It's the computer artist who decides just how unpredictable the artwork's responses will be. They also decide just what the environmental cue/cues will be, and just how the system will respond to them. Whether the observer is able, with experience, to discover what the particular artwork's cue-response rules are depends on whether the computer artist wanted that to be so.

One can give an aesthetic rationale for wanting the audience to have this capacity, which could give them some voluntary ('free') control over what happens to the artwork; and one can equally give a rationale for not doing this, so that the changing artwork remains unpredictable (see Chapter 11). In the first case, the autonomy (independence) of the artwork is lessened, and the autonomy (freedom) of the viewer is increased. In the latter case, the artwork is less manageable, so appears more autonomous.

What about the autonomy of the computer artist? They exercise their freedom in deciding what sort of artwork to produce, and why. Even a relatively 'formless', or unpredictable, artwork is a result of the artist's free choice. That isn't to say that they will have foreseen all that the artwork will do: in general, they cannot. But they may want to engender certain fairly specific types of experience in the observer. In other words, the artist may be aiming for a particular aesthetic effect to arise constantly [*sic*] as a result of the interaction.

Since the viewer's behaviour too is autonomous (in the strong sense), that constancy can't be guaranteed—unless the system is very highly constrained, not to say boring. But, with skill and understanding (of the human audience as well as the computer artwork itself) on the artist's part, it can be approximated. In such cases, the artist's autonomy is overriding the autonomy both of the artwork and of the viewer.

An increasingly popular genre is evolutionary art, which is inspired by A-Life and the near-miraculous self-organizing powers of biological evolution (Whitelaw 2004). This employs genetic algorithms (GAs) to make random alterations in the images/sounds produced. Evolutionary artists regard their artworks as having a stronger claim to autonomy than the more traditional computer artworks do, because the system's detailed performance (its evolutionary history) is less dependent on human choice.

There are different kinds of evolutionary art, however, wherein the influence of the observer varies. As a result, the degree of autonomy that can be ascribed to the program varies too.

On the one hand, an evolutionary artwork may run in complete independence [*sic*] of the audience. In such cases, *both* the nature of the images/sounds produced *and* the selection at each generation are wholly automatic. As in the non-evolutionary cases, the autonomy of the human programmer is crucial—even though the results are less predictable (because random mutations are involved). But the autonomy of the viewer is irrelevant, since it can't affect what the program does.

On the other hand, the evolutionary artwork may be interactive—in one or both of two senses. First, in a work of art (e.g. a video installation) that responds to the movements of the viewer, the cue-response rules themselves may evolve as the engagement proceeds. So one and the same movement can have different effects in different generations. Second, the selection of images/sounds at each generation may be done by the viewer. This gives the viewer a better chance of moulding the artwork to his/her own preferences.

In principle, there could also be a third type of interaction, wherein the viewer can choose the type/s of mutation to be used. For instance, suppose that the artwork allows not only for superficial parameter changes (altering numerals in an image-generating procedure, for example), but also for the hierarchical nesting of an entire image-generating procedure into another and/or for the concatenation of such procedures (cf. Sims 1991). The viewer might be able to 'switch off' the nesting and/or the concatenation at will [sic]—in which case, the newly evolved images will be much less varied, much less surprising.

The reason for limiting the degrees of freedom possessed by the artwork in this way might be that the viewer finds the images of generation x aesthetically interesting, and wants the program to explore only images of that general type rather than jumping into a very different (e.g. hierarchically more complex) space of possibilities. That, in effect, is the choice that's been made by the sculptor William Latham, in order to produce images within a clearly recognizable aesthetic style (Todd and Latham 1992). Exploratory creativity, here, is preferred over transformation.

Even if the selection at each generation is done automatically (not interactively), the artist's freedom constrains the autonomy of the artwork itself. For it's the artist who chooses the fitness function, or functions. These are the ways in which the evolutionary program measures the success of the phenotype in the Darwinian sense. (This choice is usually made 'once and for all', but it could vary during the development of the program.)

This tension between the autonomy (independence) of the program and the autonomy (freedom) of the artist is one of the issues being explored in a current art project based in evolutionary robotics (Bird,

Stokes, et al. 2007; Chapter 6 in this volume). Here, a group guided by the computer artist Paul Brown is trying to evolve line-drawing robots whose drawings *do not* display his 'personal signature'. (This telltale signature wasn't deliberately intended, or freely chosen, by him; to the contrary, he has been trying for many years to expunge it—for broadly modernist reasons.) One way of putting this is to say that the team is trying to maximize the autonomy of the program, at the expense of the autonomy of Brown himself. To be sure, Brown is the prime mover here—and the prime chooser of the fitness function. But he is hoping to *lose* the 'constancy' that characterizes all his previous work, including his computer art.

VI. AUTONOMY AS INTEGRITY

As remarked in Section IV, integrity in adult human minds is a special case of autonomy—one that's enabled by the processes and structures of human freedom. Integrity involves not only having a constant and coherent set of self-organizing principles, but also holding to them in the face of various sorts of temptation from outside. 'Temptation' (not just pressure), because whereas physiological homeostasis can't be abandoned without dying, it's always possible—and usually somehow easier and/or more convenient—to abandon one's integrity. Moreover, in ascribing integrity to someone we usually imply that the principles by which they are maintaining their independence (their autonomy) are ones which we can respect, even if we do not share them.

Those principles may be moral/political or aesthetic. So, for example, a self-proclaimed champion of peace would be false to his/her moral principles if they were to write a poem or paint a canvas glorifying torture or war. And stylistic melanges and switches are almost as unwelcome as moral equivocations. We don't ascribe artistic integrity to someone who produces art in indefinitely many styles on request (as some commercial graphic designers can do), and who doesn't keep to a single style even if there are no 'requests' from third parties. We say, rather, that they haven't found their own voice, or that their work has no unity.

Computer art, too, can show—or lack—both kinds of integrity. Some individuals will be prepared to compromise their moral principles—for commercial gain, perhaps, or for fame. It may be difficult to decide, in a particular case, whether the person is indeed doing that. A virtual-reality installation shot through with sadism, for instance, might be a deliberately shocking expression of the artist's contempt for such behaviour in real life. (More likely, it's a computer game aimed at young males and written primarily for money.) But the same is true of more familiar forms of art. The line between pornography and erotic art, for example, or between erotic art and the innocent depiction of nudes, is hard to define.

Some individuals, too, will be happy to produce computerized works 'to order' in many different styles, and perhaps (IT-skills permitting) even using various methodologies. If presented as 'art', however, a series of computer-generated images that didn't fall into any recognizable style would be down-valued for lacking artistic integrity. Indeed, some evolutionary artists deliberately avoid the more fundamental kinds of mutation (such as nesting and concatenation), which can lead to radical stylistic changes, for that very reason. They aim not for sudden transformations (as in Sims 1991), but for the gradual exploration of a consistent style (as in Todd and Latham 1992).

As well as the integrity of the visible style, one can consider the integrity of the underlying method. Mixed-media art in general challenges conventional values of aesthetic unity. Computer art could be considered in that light too—not just in respect of the materials/means used in the resulting artwork, but also with regard to the technical methods employed to generate it. However, to consider the latter question the critic would need to know just which computational methods were being used, and (if more than one) just how they were related. If they were merely juxtaposed, thrown into a methodological melting pot without any coherent rationale, the work as a whole would lack (technical) unity—or, in other words, integrity.

We've already seen (in Sections III and IV) that there are various technical methods available to the computer artist. And it's a sociological fact, within AI/A-Life no less than in computer art, that the proponents of one of these methods tend to decry the others. This isn't simply a matter of methodological preference, but (often) of withering—and unmerited—scorn for the other 'camp' (Boden 2006: 4.ix). Partly as a result of this, and partly also because of the technical difficulty involved in building mixed (hybrid) systems, today's computer artists don't favour hybrid artworks. But what if they did? To combat the criticism that hybrid systems lack integrity, one would need to show that some valuable feature had been achieved by the mix of methods which could not have been achieved without it.

To take an example from psychology, consider a hybrid system that models human action—and pathological cases of action error (Norman and Shallice 1986). This system combines perception (and perceptual reminding) with planning, both of which are crucial for intentional actions. It uses PDP networks to model the perception, and GOFAI programs to model the planning—with sensible ways of switching appropriately between the two. However, those switches can be rendered less 'sensible' in order to model common types of action error, which all of us experience occasionally and which in some brain-damaged people (after a stroke, perhaps) can be so frequent as to be debilitating. For instance, think of the times that you have gone upstairs to your bedroom to look for something that you need in order to complete a task that you're doing downstairs, only to forget all about it on entering the bedroom and to come down with something else instead. Your plan told you to fetch one thing, but your perception (and associated habits) captured your attention and led you to pick up another.

In that hybrid system, there's a clear psychological rationale for using a mix of computational methods. (There's a neurological rationale too, for there's evidence that different parts of the brain are active at the contrasting action-points: Cooper et al. 1995.) A computer artist using a hybrid system would need to provide a comparable rationale in aesthetic terms. Otherwise, they might be accused of a lack of (methodological) integrity. But if they are to be charged with this 'sin' by an art critic, the critic must be able to understand that distinct methodologies are in play, and to evaluate the strengths of the system in which they are combined. Merely observing the final results, without any knowledge of their computational basis, would not be enough.

Integrity implies coherence, for if the artist's principles conflict then to keep faith with one will be to betray another. Someone might say that we should not speak of *principles* here at all, but rather of warring—and maybe fleeting—preferences. In general, however, that would be too severe. Even theologians and moral philosophers struggle to achieve (never mind follow) a fully coherent set of moral principles. And in artistic contexts, internal tensions can be exciting, even illuminating. Hence Walt Whitman was content to say: 'Do I contradict myself? Very well then I contradict myself. (I am large. I contain multitudes.)' But the contradictions must be carefully controlled, and either hidden or appropriately (intelligibly) highlighted, if the art is to escape the charge of incoherence. As the *Mimetic Starfish* shows, a computerized artwork may be able to maintain its unity even in the face of contradictions. Too many, however, and the art—and the integrity—will be overwhelmed.

VII. CONCLUSION

Prima facie, it may seem absurd to speak of autonomy in the context of computers, and to speak of integrity (a special case) in the context of computer art. Nevertheless, many computer artists value their work in part because, on their view, it exploits autonomous processes in the computer.

They see their projects, accordingly, as more aesthetically interesting than computer artworks that result from conceptualizing the computer as a mere slave. To be sure, even in cases like that (e.g. the AARON program: Cohen 2002), the human artist/programmer can't knowingly predetermine the machine's every step; often, they can't even predict more than the broad outlines of the artwork that results. Moreover, the works generated by 'slave' programs can be very attractive indeed. But computer artists who stress the autonomy of their art-making machine value that autonomy not only for the results it produces but for its own sake.

Or, more accurately, they value it as an analogy of the processes of self-organization and/or self-direction in living things. They are less influenced by traditional (symbolic) AI, or even by connectionist AI, than by A-Life. However, they often fail to see—as A-Life scientists typically do too—that there are different kinds of autonomy. Human freedom, for instance, is very different from homeostasis. It's also very different from the relatively rigid behaviour of insects (Boden 2006: 15.vii), and even from the 'self-direction' of a dog or a chimpanzee. All these forms of autonomy should be recognized, if computer artists wish to celebrate life's diversity.

REFERENCES

Ascott, R. (1990), 'Is There Love in the Telematic Embrace?', *Art Journal* (College Arts Association of America), 49: 241–7; repr. as ch. 15 of Ascott (2003: 232–46).

—— (2003), *Telematic Embrace: Visionary Theories of Art, Technology, and Consciousness* (Berkeley and Los Angeles: University of California Press).

Ashby, W. R. (1947), 'The Nervous System as a Physical Machine: with Special Reference to the Origin of Adaptive Behaviour', *Mind*, 56: 44–59.
—— (1948), 'Design for a Brain', *Electronic Engineering*, 20: 379–83.
Bird, J., d'Inverno, M., and Prophet, J. (2007), '*Net Work*: An Interactive Artwork Designed Using an Interdisciplinary Performative Approach', *Digital Creativity*, 18/1: 11–23.
Bird, J., Stokes, D., Husbands, P., Brown, P., and Bigge, B. (2007), 'Towards Autonomous Artworks', *Leonardo Electronic Almanac* (available from jonba@sussex.ac.uk).
Boden, M. A. (1996), 'Autonomy and Artificiality', in M. A. Boden (ed.), *The Philosophy of Artificial Life* (Oxford: Oxford University Press), 95–108.
—— (2006), *Mind as Machine: A History of Cognitive Science*, 2 vols. (Oxford: Oxford University Press).
—— (in press), 'The Aesthetics of Interactive Art', in C. Makris, R. L. Chrisley, R. W. Clowes, and M. A. Boden (eds.), *Art, Body, Embodiment* (Newcastle: Cambridge Scholars Publication).
Boden, M. A., and Edmonds, E. A. (forthcoming), 'What Is Generative Art?' Reprinted as Chapter 11 in this Volume.
Cheney, D. L., and Seyfarth, R. L. (1990), *How Monkeys See the World: Inside the Mind of Another Species* (Chicago: University of Chicago Press).
Cohen, H. (2002), 'A Million Millennial Medicis', in L. Candy and E. Edmonds (eds), *Explorations in Art and Technology* (London: Springer), 91–104.
Cooper, R., Shallice, T., and Farringdon, J. (1995), 'Symbolic and Continuous Processes in the Automatic Selection of Actions', in J. Hallam (ed.), *Hybrid Problems, Hybrid Solutions* (Oxford: IOS Press), 27–37.
Dennett, D. C. (1984), *Elbow Room: The Varieties of Free Will Worth Wanting* (Cambridge, Mass.: MIT Press).
di Paolo, E. A. (2000), 'Homeostatic Adaptation to Inversion of the Visual Field and Other Sensorimotor Disruptions', in J.-A. Meyer, A. Berthoz, D. Floreano, H. Roitblat, and S. W. Wilson (eds.), *From Animals to Animats 6: Proceedings of the Sixth International Conference on Simulation of Adaptive Behavior* (Cambridge, Mass.: MIT Press), 440–9.
Heyes, C. M. (1998), 'Theory of Mind in Nonhuman Primates' (with peer commentary), *Behavioral and Brain Sciences*, 21: 101–48.
Kember, S. (2003), *Cyberfeminism and Artificial Life* (London: Routledge).
Linsker, R. (1988), 'Self-Organization in a Perceptual Network', *Computer*, 21: 105–17.
—— (1990), 'Perceptual Neural Organization: Some Approaches Based on Network Models and Information Theory', *Annual Review of Neuroscience*, 13: 257–81.
Norman, D. A., and Shallice, T. (1986), 'Attention to Action: Willed and Automatic Control of Behavior', in R. Davidson, G. Schwartz and D. Shapiro (eds.), *Consciousness and Self Regulation: Advances in Research and Theory*, vol. 4 (New York: Plenum), 1–18.

Reynolds, C. W. (1987), 'Flocks, Herds, and Schools: A Distributed Behavioral Model', *Computer Graphics*, 21: 25–34.

Sims, K. (1991), 'Artificial Evolution for Computer Graphics', *Computer Graphics*, 25/4: 319–28.

Todd, S. C., and Latham, W. (1992), *Evolutionary Art and Computers* (London: Academic Press).

von der Malsburg, C. (1973), 'Self-Organization of Orientation Sensitive Cells in the Striate Cortex', *Kybernetik*, 14: 85–100.

Whitelaw, M. (2004), *Metacreation: Art and Artificial Life* (London: MIT Press).

Zeleny, M. (1977), 'Self-Organization of Living Systems: A Formal Model of Autopoiesis', *International Journal of General Systems*, 4: 13–28.

Zeleny, M., Klir, G. J., and Hufford, K. D. (1989), 'Precipitation Membranes, Osmotic Growths, and Synthetic Biology', in C. G. Langton (ed.), *Artificial Life: The Proceedings of an Interdisciplinary Workshop on the Synthesis and Simulation of Living Systems* (held Sept. 1987) (Redwood City, Calif.: Addison-Wesley), 125–39.

10
Authenticity and Computer Art

I. INTRODUCTION

One of the meanings of "authentic" listed in my dictionary is "entitled to acceptance". This sits alongside other meanings such as "genuine", "trustworthy", "authoritative", and "of established credibility". That's hardly surprising: if something is indeed genuine, trustworthy, authoritative, and of established credibility then, for sure, it's entitled to acceptance.

But if not, not—and there's the rub. A very common reaction to computer art is to withhold acceptance in principle, to refuse to regard it as authoritative under any circumstances because, inevitably, it lacks authenticity. This paper considers some of the reasons given for that attitude—which so annoyed one computer artist, as we'll see, that he has recently taken extreme action in an attempt to counter it.

As is usual for dictionary definitions, the terms listed together are closely linked. The concept of authenticity implies some originating agent, whose honesty (compare "genuineness"), and perhaps whose competence (compare "authoritative"), can be "trusted"—and to trust someone is to "accept" what they say or do. Nevertheless, the listed terms aren't exact synonyms. In particular, "entitled to acceptance" doesn't mean the same—no more, and no less—as "authentic". Lack of authenticity is only one possible ground for non-acceptability (see Section II). However, it's the one that's in focus here.

At this point, three terminological warnings are in order. First, I sometimes use the expression "computer artist" to denote the computer itself, and sometimes to denote the human being who programmed it. The context should make clear which meaning is intended in each case. As we'll see, both senses are philosophically problematic.

Second, my phrase (above) "the human being who programmed it" should more strictly have been "the human being who programmed it or inspired it". For the person who actually did the programming is not always the person whose artistic vision is embodied in the system. One well-known example of this is the evolutionary artwork of Stephen Todd and William Latham (1992), where the IBM computer scientist Todd wrote the code (and doubtless offered some aesthetic insights along the way) but Latham, an RCA-trained sculptor, provided the artistic inspiration and guidance. Except for a brief reminder in Section V, I'll ignore such complications. I'll write as though the inspirer/artist is always the same person as the programmer. (With the spread of IT among young people, this is increasingly true.)

Third, and most important, I'll mention "computer art" and "artworks" throughout the text. This is a shorthand way of denoting specific visual, auditory, or literary compositions in whose origin a computer had a hand. Like the word "hand" in that sentence, my terms "art" and "artwork" don't carry a heavy load of philosophical baggage. I'm not prejudging the question of whether it's possible for a computer to generate anything that's properly called a work of art. The answer to that question, as we'll see, depends partly on what role authenticity plays in aesthetics.

II. IRRELEVANT UNACCEPTABILITY

Sometimes, people who refuse to accept computer art do so—or anyway, claim that they are doing so—purely on the grounds of its intrinsic qualities. They look at a particular computer-generated image, listen to some computer-generated music, or read a computer-generated story or poem, and announce that it's uninteresting and/or faulty in various ways.

An unusual example of this type of reaction was directed at the products of the "Emmy" program discussed below (Sections III and IV). Emmy writes music in familiar styles, to be played by human musicians on the usual range of instruments. Some of these performances were recorded, and Emmy's programmer offered the tape-recording to a commercial CD company specializing in computer music. To his amazement, they refused to take it on because, in their view, it wasn't authentic: as they put it, "it didn't sound like computer music" (Cope 2006: 352). For them, "computer music" didn't mean 'music composed (and possibly also performed) by a computer', but 'music (whether composed by human or computer) that uses computer-synthesized sounds instead of, or as well as, traditional musical instruments'. (Happily, after many more rejections, another CD company was eventually found which was willing to publish Emmy's music. Unhappily, as we'll see, the music then met a number of very different criticisms.)

If a critic of computer art really is responding only to the intrinsic properties of a particular artwork (as this CD company was doing), their arguments aren't relevant here. After all, fully-human works presented as art are often criticized too. Not everything produced by a self-styled artist, or even by a publicly recognized 'name', is entitled to acceptance. Indeed, even human beings can be accused in various ways of a lack of authenticity (hypocrisy, for instance) that undermines their work's acceptability.

To be sure, the "entitlement to acceptance" is a matter of aesthetic judgement, not a matter of fact. In that sense, it's as problematic as any other such judgement. But these are judgements that we're accustomed to making, and which can even achieve a high degree of consensus.

A judgement of this type, when directed to a computer artwork, may be generalizable up to a point. Suppose that the observed aesthetic flaw is a lack of balance in a computer's drawing, or a lack of expression in its musical performance. It may be that the particular technology and/or programming style that was used is inherently incapable of providing the balance or expressiveness required. If so, that technology or style is as aesthetically constraining for the computer artist (in either sense) as a drunken haze, a muscular cramp, or a bad habit acquired during training, would be for a traditional painter or pianist. In such cases, the critic can justifiably argue that no computer art generated in that particular way will be entitled to acceptance. But "that particular way" must, of course, be specified.

It must be specified because it's always possible that some other approach might avoid the aesthetic flaw in question. For example, the music program discussed in Sections III and IV had no way of representing musical expression: it laid down what notes to play, not how to play them. You may feel that that's no surprise: surely, you may be muttering, no computer could model musical expressiveness. You'd be wrong. That seemingly unanswerable challenge has been met with remarkable success, dealing with familiar compositions by Romantic composers such as Chopin (Longuet-Higgins 1994).

These generalized criticisms, too, are irrelevant for our purposes—unless they can be generalized still further. The critic would need to show (at least) that any computer art that's feasible in the foreseeable future would have the same shortcoming, or (more strongly) that any conceivable computer art would necessarily have it too. In other words, they'd need to show that computer art isn't just unsatisfactory here and there but, as the Caterpillar said of Alice's recital of '*You Are Old, Father William*', 'wrong from beginning to end'.

III. EMOTIONAL AUTHENTICITY

The arguments most germane to our discussion, then, are those which suggest a principled reason why no computer could possibly produce an authentic work of art. I'll mention two examples in this section, taken from two very different writers. But they're highly similar in spirit, as we'll see.

The first example comes from Douglas Hofstadter. He's a cognitive scientist, who for many years has been developing computer models of creativity—specifically, creative analogies of various kinds, including typographical fonts (Hofstadter and FARG 1995; Hofstadter 2002). In addition, he has commented at length on other such work, in literary, visual, and musical domains. But he hasn't attempted to model the art that's closest to his heart: music. And that's no accident. For his view is that music involves emotions (in both creator and listener), which computers cannot have.

Presumably, he'd allow that a programmer might deliberately set out to model emotions, and then use this model in enabling a computer to compose music. And he'd certainly admit that a programmer might set out merely to generate compositions having one of several distinct emotional tones. Indeed, that has been done by several people, including another Douglas—Douglas Riecken (1989, 1994, 2002). But for Hofstadter, no matter how successful the result (in inducing sadness, or joy, or. . . in the listener), there would be no genuine emotion in the music. For the composing computer isn't an emotional agent. In other words, the program's compositions wouldn't be authentic—just a clever fraud.

How extraordinary it would be, then, if a programmer who wasn't even trying to make his composing machine express, or suggest, emotion managed to do so regardless. And how embarrassing (for Hofstadter), if the computer music concerned were to engage the emotions of musically sensitive listeners—even a highly sceptical listener, such as himself—in the same sort of way that human-originated music does.

Well, such a program already exists: the Emmy system, whose music was spurned by the specialist CD company mentioned in Section II. It was written by David Cope, a professor of music at the University of California (Santa Cruz) and a recognized composer in his own right. The program has been developed and improved over the last twenty-five years (Cope 1991, 2000, 2001, 2006). Its first name was EMI (the acronym for Experiments in Musical Intelligence), but it soon became known as Emmy. This system is briefly described in Section V. Here, let's just note that it composes music in the style of X (where X may be anyone from Monteverdi to Joplin, and including non-European music too)—and that it does so with remarkable success.

Hofstadter has the honesty to admit this. As a fine amateur musician, he found even the early version of Emmy impressive despite—or rather, because of—his initial confidence that "little of interest could come of [its classical AI] architecture". Indeed, Emmy was so impressive that the experience shocked him to the core:

> I noticed in [the pages of Cope's 1991 book] an Emmy mazurka supposedly in the Chopin style, and this really drew my attention because, having revered Chopin my whole life long, I felt certain that no one could pull the wool over my eyes in this department. Moreover, I knew all fifty or sixty of the Chopin mazurkas very well, having played them dozens of times on the piano and heard them even more often on recordings. So I went straight to my own piano and sight-read through the Emmy mazurka—once, twice, three times, and more—each time with mounting confusion and surprise. Though I felt there were a few little glitches here and there, I was impressed, for the piece seemed to *express* something... [It] did not seem in any way plagiarized. It was *new*, it was unmistakably *Chopin-like* in spirit, and it was *not emotionally empty*. I was truly shaken. How could emotional music be coming out of a program that had never heard a note, never lived a moment of life, never had any emotions whatsoever?
>
> [... Emmy was threatening] my oldest and most deeply cherished beliefs about ... music being the ultimate inner sanctum of the human spirit, the last thing that would tumble in AI's headlong rush toward thought, insight, and creativity. (Hofstadter 2001a: 38 f.; italics in original)

One could argue that Hofstadter was allowing himself to be over-impressed, here. For what psychologists call the "effort after meaning" (Bartlett 1932) imbues our perception of music as well as of visual patterns and words. The human performer naturally projects emotion into the score-defined notes, much as human readers naturally project meaning into computer-generated haikus (Boden 2004: 170 ff.). So, given that Chopin-like scores had been produced, it wasn't surprising that Hofstadter interpreted them expressively. What was surprising was the fact that Chopin's composing style had been captured so well in the first place.

However, the important point here is that Hofstadter—like many others—regards the very essence of music as the expression and communication of human emotions. A similar position has been taken about art in general by the philosopher Anthony O'Hear (1995).

O'Hear sees art, by definition, as involving communication between one human being and another. This often goes beyond the communication of relatively unfocused emotions, as happens in music, for it may express positive or negative concerns about specific aspects of the world. Think of the many Annunications and Madonnas, for example, or of Pablo Picasso's *Guernica*. But for any communication whatever to be possible, O'Hear insists, both artist and audience must share human experience.

Computers are therefore excluded. O'Hear refuses to refer to computer-generated products as "art", no matter how superficially beautiful or seemingly interesting they may be. He grants that music, pictures, and poems produced in this way may sometimes (as in Hofstadter's recollection) appear to satisfy some of our psychological and/or aesthetic needs. But were we to discover that they'd come from computers, he says, the satisfaction would evaporate. For we'd have been deceived: tricked (thanks to the ubiquitous effort after meaning) into responding to an item as though it were an artwork, whether good or mediocre, when really it was nothing of the kind.

Insofar as this is an empirical claim about people's psychological responses, there's some evidence for it. I myself have seen this sudden switch of attitude on several ocasions, the people concerned being adamant that their initial, spontaneous, reactions had been inappropriate. On the other hand, Hofstadter wrestled gamely to make his satisfaction evaporate—but couldn't do so.

However, O'Hear is offering us prescription rather than description. He's talking about an item's entitlement to appreciation as an art object. And since he grounds the status of "art object" in human authenticity (of artist and observer), he sees talk of art-making by computers as philosophically confused, not to say absurd.

O'Hear doesn't bother to argue for his claim that computers can't have experiences—whether of emotions, or colours, or anything else. Like Hofstadter, he regards this as obvious. If asked about the few programs that specifically model emotions, he'd insist that they can't actually experience them. And he'd have many allies besides Hofstadter. For this opinion, or intuition, is shared by the vast majority of people—including visitors to art galleries.

Some tough-minded computationalists insist that they're mistaken (Dennett 1991; Sloman 2000). In a nutshell, these philosophers see conscious experience (alias qualia) as a matter of subtle discriminatory and action-oriented functions, occurring in a hugely complex, and self-reflexive, mental architecture. Emotions, on this view, are much more than feelings. At heart, they are essential scheduling mechanisms in a multi-motive intelligence. Conscious emotional feelings are only the tip of the functional iceberg (and, as such, they themselves are functional too).

If these computationalists are right, then Hofstadter's attack on the authenticity of any conceivable computer art must fail (although today's computer art certainly isn't produced by programs having the requisite complexity). O'Hear's challenge must fail too, unless one puts more weight on the word "human" than on the word "experience" (which would also rule out chimpanzee art or Martian art, even though chimps do, and intelligent Martians would, have emotions of some kind).

Carefully considered, the functionalist analysis of qualia isn't as crazy as it seems at first sight (Boden 2006: 14.xi.b–d). But whether it's correct or not, this position is a minority taste even among philosophers of cognitive science. For sure, it's not widespread in the general public, still less in the art world. Computer artists, then, can expect to encounter the 'orthodox' opinion, which is that computers don't, and can't, have emotions in any sense.

Critics of computer art who agree with Hofstadter and O'Hear are demanding authenticity in two senses. On the one hand, they're saying that an artwork must involve some genuinely human communication, springing from genuinely human experience. On the other hand, the communication must be honest—which is why, as suggested above, the charge of hypocrisy undermines an artist's entitlement to acceptance. However, it's not clear that human-ness and honesty are enough. For "acceptance" is ambiguous as between aesthetic and moral acceptance, and the relation between these is notoriously problematic. Perhaps artistic authenticity also involves a moral dimension?

Suppose that the experiences being communicated by a human being are hatred, cruelty, and rage, directed onto an intentional object with respect to which such emotions are morally repulsive. Think of a Nazi film or newspaper cartoon depicting Jews, for example, or the cruelty-soaked writings of the Marquis de Sade. One may have to allow that these items are skilful, even hugely powerful in their emotional effect. But whether one should ascribe aesthetic value to them is a highly controversial matter.

In relation to our present discussion, the stories written by a 'sadistic' computer might arouse strong feelings in its readers, much as Emmy's music did in Hofstadter. But O'Hear, and perhaps Hofstadter too, would say that we should not be repelled by it, because there's no real (authentic) cruelty there.

IV. WHY DO COMPUTER ART?

If computer art is apparently so problematic, why do people do it in the first place? There are three main reasons.

The first is to overcome the technical challenges involved in programming a plausible computer composer, painter, or poet. This sometimes includes exploring the potential of some relatively new technology: evolutionary programming, for example. In that case, the programmers concerned may think of themselves primarily as artists (see Whitelaw 2004), or they may not (e.g. Sims 1991). The second reason for doing computer art is to explore the psychological processes involved when human artists go into action. And the third is simply to produce works of art.

These are very different motivations. It's possible for one and the same person to be driven by all three. Often, however, one of them is paramount. When the prime reason is the third, namely to produce works of art, there's usually a further aim: to exhibit those artworks to the public, thereby gaining—or consolidating—one's reputation as an artist.

In such cases, how the public in fact responds will be important to the aspiring artist. If, like Hofstadter and O'Hear, most people—and influential art critics—see computers (for whatever reason) as essentially incapable of producing art, then the third aim will be frustrated. At best, the originator will be recognized as someone who could have produced good art, if only they'd left their computer in its box. (Hence my warning, in Section I, that both senses of "computer artist" are problematic.) In short: no computer art, no computer artists.

That unappreciative public reaction has often been directed at Cope, the originator of the Emmy program. In one case, there wasn't even any pretence on the part of the critic that he had identified specific aesthetic flaws in the computer-composed music. For his review was published fully two weeks before the performance that he was 'reviewing': Emmy's first public concert, given in 1989 (Cope 2006: 345). Moreover, when phoned by Cope to invite him to attend the occasion, he refused.

His main objection to the music wasn't that it didn't spring from emotion. Nor did he complain that the concert pieces were musically crude, perhaps even faulty—how could he, if he hadn't heard them? Rather, he poured scorn on the very idea of a concert devoted to what he termed "computer forgeries".

In the art world, a forgery is the epitome of inauthenticity or bad faith. (And of bad luck too, if you pay a fortune to buy it.) To present the public with a work notionally by a long-dead artist when in fact it was made only yesterday is a betrayal of trust. Whether, and how, the devaluation of forgeries can be justified on strictly aesthetic grounds is controversial (see e.g. Stalnaker 2005; Davies 2004: 13 ff., 200–5). But if—like O'Hear, for instance—one sees art as a form of human communication then forgery must be condemned, because it's deceitful. This suggests that the reviewer's deliberately insulting reference to "computer forgeries" shouldn't be taken literally. For Cope hadn't attempted to deceive anyone. To the contrary, the interest of Emmy's music lay largely in the fact that it clearly hadn't been composed by any famous names of the past.

The charge of forgery was compounded, in this reviewer's eyes, by the risk of contaminating the listener's musical knowledge, or expectations. Given that too few people, he said, know the music of C. P. E. Bach (one of the composers mentioned in the advance programme), it was "unforgivable to dilute the repertoire" with Emmy's versions of it. He was complaining not only of the lack of authenticity in any music composed by computers, but also of the inauthenticity involved in aping (riding on the back of?) specific—and sometimes sadly under-appreciated—human musicians.

Cope was especially chagrined by this criticism because he'd had no intention of "diluting" the repertoire. To the contrary, he'd already decided that he'd never release more examples of a given genre than the original human composer had done. So, for instance, he has officially published only 371 Bach-style chorales (although he confesses that

5,000 were put on his website for downloading in 2005, alongside 1,000 Chopin nocturnes). The reason was precisely to avoid risking the originals' being "lost amid greater numbers of new compositions in the same style and form" (2006: 364).

Indeed, he'd started out with no intention to imitate other composers, still less dishonestly to produce "forgeries". His original aim had been to write a program to produce music in his own style. However, he soon realized that he was "too close to [his] own music to define its style in meaningful ways", so he switched to the well-studied classical composers instead (2001: 93). By "well-studied", he meant not merely familiar, but musicologically documented. Dozens of musicians and scholars had already started to identify the stylistic patterns found in classical music. Those patterns could be applied not only in assembling Emmy's database, but also in designing the procedures used to generate new compositions.

He was annoyed, too, at the reviewer's tacit downplaying of his own musical skills, and his near-invisibility qua artist. For he, not the computer, was the true composer of Emmy's music. Indeed, he still feels it necessary to insist that Emmy's music is, in truth, "my own" (2006: 346). (Notice that if we take this seriously, then O'Hear's and Hofstadter's criticisms fail. For the music must now be regarded as an artwork of human origin, communicating human experience—including emotion—to other human beings.)

The fact that he wrote the program code isn't the main point here: as remarked in Section I, someone else might have done that. (As it happens, Cope was technically highly adept; for instance, he invented a way of describing music formally, before the MIDI format was available.) The point lies, rather, in his musical skills—which were crucial in two main ways.

On the one hand, he identified the items to be used in the database for each human composer being studied, and chose the musicological principles guiding the program's composition. On the other hand, and less obviously, he decided just which instances of Emmy's output would be put before the public—in concerts, for example. He was determined to release only the best. These would be "the tip of the iceberg", with respect to the entire mass of Emmy's production. (The now-complete list of "the best" comprises about 1,000 items, recalling thirty-five composers—2006: 385–9.) Deciding which items were the best required subtle musical judgements. For instance, Cope usually rejected Emmy-compositions that he judged to be "vague paraphrases" of entries in the database. Occasionally, however, he accepted them because the composer in question, e.g. Mahler, "seemed so fond of self-referencing" (2006: 346).

However, such self-defence fell on deaf ears. If the reluctant concert-goer's vitriolic review was the first public attack that Cope had to endure, there were plenty more where that came from. And they hurt. They didn't injure only his personal pride, but also his perceived status as an artist.

Eventually, they elicited an unexpected response. He has recently destroyed much of a quarter-century's work—not in a fit of petulance or pique, but specifically in order to highlight the artistic authenticity of his oeuvre. This dramatic incident, as we'll now see, sharpens the question of why an artist would even want to do computer art.

V. A CASE HISTORY

To understand this story, one needs to know a little about how Cope coaxed his computer to compose music "in the style of X".

Emmy's basic method has been described by Cope as "recombinatory", and was summarized by Hofstadter (2001a: 44) as "(1) chop up; (2) reassemble". Both these descriptions underplay what the program was doing, for—taken at face value—they suggest that Emmy works by random generation. In fact, the program's "recombinations" were highly constrained, in musically acceptable ways. For Emmy explored generative structures, as well as recombining motifs. It showed both combinational and exploratory creativity—but not, as Hofstadter (2001b) was quick to point out, transformational creativity (Boden 2004). A 'new' style could appear only as a result of mixing two or more existing styles, such as Bach/Joplin or Thai/jazz.

The program's database was a set of 'signatures' (note patterns of up to ten melodic notes) exemplifying melody, harmony, metre, and ornament. These had all been selected by Cope himself, as being characteristic of the composer concerned. Emmy would start applying statistical techniques to identify the core features of these snippets. Then, guided by general musicological principles, she/it would use them to generate new structures.

(Some results worked less well than others. Cope has described some of these unsatisfactory results, saying just what he thinks is wrong with them—e.g. 2001: 182 f., 385–90. In other words, he himself criticizes

Emmy's compositions in specific ways, as considered in Section II. When choosing "the best" pieces for public exhibition, however, he tries to avoid faulty examples.)

The early versions of Emmy were exercises in traditional, symbolic, AI. That's largely why Hofstadter, already a long-time critic of GOFAI, was so amazed at their emotional power. From 1990 on, a connectionist network was added, giving Emmy increased flexibility (Cope says it had become "truly creative"). Today, its successor program uses a fully integrated associative network; even so, it still employs the core principles that inspired Emmy.

Emmy soon became famous, even to people who had no interest in computers. Part of its notoriety was spread by scandalized gossip: "There doesn't seem to be a single group of people that the program doesn't annoy in some way" (Cope 2001: 92). But as well as relying on newspaper features and word of mouth, people could read about it, and examine some Emmy scores, in Cope's books. Enthusiasts could even try it out for themselves, following his technical advice, by using one of the cut-down versions ("ALICE" and "SARA") provided on CDs packaged inside his books.

They could listen to Emmy's compositions, too. Some stand-alone CDs were released in the late 1990s, and several live concerts of Emmy's music were staged to public audiences. (These featured human instrumentalists playing Emmy's scores, because the program didn't represent expressive performance. As remarked in Section II, it laid down what notes to play, not how to play them.)

However, the concerts were mostly arranged by Cope's friends. The musical establishment was as loath to support them as was the anticipatory reviewer mentioned in Section IV. Cope now recalls: "Since 1980, I have made extraordinary attempts to have [Emmy's] works performed. Unfortunately, my successes have been few. Performers rarely consider these works seriously" (2006: 362). For someone aspiring to be accepted as an artist, that dismissive attitude was very hard to take. (I say "aspiring", even though he was already accepted as an artist in respect of his 'normal' music, because he wanted his computer music to be regarded as art too.)

The problem, as he sees it, was that the dismissive performers (like most people) regarded Emmy's music as computer "output", whereas he had always thought of it rather as music. Naturally, he wanted listeners to approach it as music. But many were unable, or anyway unwilling, to do that. The fact that it was computer-generated swamped the fact that its human originator was looking for an innocent aesthetic response on their part. As suggested in Section II, their putatively aesthetic criticism was largely "rhetoric [that is] simply a subterfuge engineered to avoid confronting the music directly" (2006: 351).

A large part of the difficulty was that the term "output", besides suggesting inhuman tin cans, implies infinite extensibility. This, Cope found, makes people devalue music considered as output. The fact that human artists die, he remarked, is part of what makes us value their work. Rarity is important for our unsullied aesthetic response, not only in the grubby context of the auction room: "Part of what's involved in experiencing any work of art is knowing that while it may be imitated, it is unique" (2006: 363). Put another way, an artwork's authenticity is grounded in its being a specific communication that a specific individual has chosen to make—where the number of such choices is always finite.

This is why, just over a year ago, Cope took the drastic decision to destroy Emmy's historical database (2006: 364). There will be no more new Bach-style fugues from the program. The old ones still exist, however, both on CDs and in printed scores (and on Cope's website). As Cope puts it, they constitute a "completed oeuvre", which can be studied by musicians just as any other composer's work can be. He even feels that the uniqueness of this collection will render the individual pieces "musically more valuable than they seemed when each new day brought the possibility of many new creations" (2006: 363). As a result, he hopes, they will be performed by others besides his close friends and colleagues.

(It must be said that Cope's sensitivities about uniqueness aren't shared by all computer artists. Harold Cohen, for instance, welcomes the prospect of indefinitely many novel examples of his [sic] art continuing to appear after his death: Cohen 2002. This difference in attitude may reflect the fact that Cohen, unlike Cope, has never aimed to make his program produce art in someone else's style.)

Emmy has gone out with a bang, not a whimper. The program's "farewell gift" to the historical-music world was a fifty-two-page score for a new symphonic movement in the style of Beethoven. This required "several months of data gathering and development as well as several generations of corrections and flawed output" (Cope 2006: 366, 399–451). From now on, Emmy—or rather, Emmy's much-improved successor—will be composing in Cope's own personal style, as "Emily Howell" (2006: 372 ff. and pt. III *passim*). (Emily's database will be drawn largely from Emmy's music, so this new, unique, creative entity—Cope's words—will be reminiscent of its mothballed predecessor.)

This tale can be read as a dire warning to people motivated by the third aim listed at the outset of Section IV. It wouldn't be surprising if some still-struggling computer composers were so discouraged by Emmy's poor reception—from professional instrumentalists and other musicians, as well as the general public—that they renounced computer art entirely. An artist who has already invested years of effort in computer art will be less ready to abandon it. Cope himself, for instance, hasn't done this: Emily Howell is proof of that. But ambitious youngsters, hearing about Cope's difficulties in getting his works "considered seriously", might decide not to enter the field in the first place.

If you're persuaded that virtually no one is going to credit you with producing authentic works of art, why bother? At best, your work will be confined to a niche market.

VI. CONCLUSION

Whether Cope's future listeners will, as he hopes, be willing to regard Emily's output as authentic music remains to be seen. They may or may not like it, but that's not the issue. (Someone who doesn't appreciate atonal music may accept Schoenberg as a real artist, and his oeuvre as an authentic body of art.) As we've seen, most members of the art audience approach putative artworks with certain philosophical assumptions in mind, which prevent them from taking computer art seriously.

These assumptions have nothing to do with the intrinsic qualities of specific examples of computer art. Rather, they concern the authenticity—or, as most people would have it, the inauthenticity—of computer art in general. They include the following: (1) art must spring from human agency; (2) art must be grounded in emotion; (3) art must involve the communication of human experience; (4) art must be honest, and/or produced in good faith; (5) art must be unique/rare; and (6) art must be transformational.

The first four assumptions could be satisfied if one were prepared to ascribe the human concepts concerned to computers too. As we saw in Section III, a few philosophers are in principle willing to do that. But even they have to admit that current and foreseeable computers don't/won't have the necessary complexity, so this isn't promising as a way of saving the authenticity of computer art. Alternatively, one might seek to neutralize the first four assumptions by identifying the human computer artist as the true originator of the artwork (compare Cope: Emmy's music is "my own"). However, problems then arise due to the indirectness of the (often) highly complex computational processes that actually generate the works.

(One might even quibble about the word "human" in assumptions (1) and (3), not only to allow computer art but also to admit chimpanzee art and Martian art. With respect to the latter two genres, constraint no. (2) would be satisfied, since—as noted in Section III—both chimps and suitably intelligent Martians have, or would have, emotions. However, assumption (4) would exclude the chimps, if not the Martians. Having a relatively primitive Theory of Mind, chimps can't lie—so they can't be honest, either: cf. Tomasello et al. 2003.)

The fifth assumption can be countered by deliberately limiting the productive capacity of a given program, as Cope did with respect to Emmy. But 'killing' a program for this reason is arbitrary, even inauthentic—unlike the all-too-authentic phenomenon of a human artist's death.

The sixth assumption could be countered in two ways. First, one could point out that not all of the art that's heard in concert halls, read in books, or seen on gallery walls, is transformational. Much of it springs from combinational or exploratory creativity, which are available to computers in principle—and, up to a point, in practice (Boden 2004). Cope's work is an excellent example, wherein exploratory and combinational creativity are combined. However, it's true that much of the art that we value most highly is transformational, so to that extent the assumption must be granted.

Second, one could argue that evolutionary programming enables computers to engage in transformational creativity too. Indeed, this technique can sometimes generate results that are not only unpredictable but bear no recognizable relation to their 'ancestors' (Sims 1991; Boden 2004: 318–20). However, whether purely programmed (as opposed to embodied and/or world-linked) systems can generate transformations that are truly fundamental, such that the system surpasses the limits initially inherent in it, is a difficult and controversial question (Boden 2006: 15.vi.d).

In sum, none of these six assumptions about the nature of art can be confidently rejected (although the last must be qualified), and none can be unequivocally satisfied by computers. If they remain in play in people's minds, the status of computer artists as recognized artists will remain problematic.

REFERENCES

Bartlett, F. C. (1932), *Remembering: A Study in Experimental and Social Psychology* (Cambridge: Cambridge University Press).
Boden, M. A. (2004), *The Creative Mind: Myths and Mechanisms* (2nd edn., expanded/revised, London: Routledge).
—— (2006), *Mind as Machine: A History of Cognitive Science* (Oxford: OUP/Clarendon Press).
Cohen, H. (2002), 'A Million Millennial Medicis', in L. Candy and E. Edmonds (eds.), *Explorations in Art and Technology* (London: Springer), 91–104.
Cope, D. (1991), *Computers and Musical Style* (Oxford: Oxford University Press).
—— (2000), *The Algorithmic Composer* (Madison: A-R Editions).
—— (2001), *Virtual Music: Computer Synthesis of Musical Style* (Cambridge, Mass.: MIT Press).
—— (2006), *Computer Models of Musical Creativity* (Cambridge, Mass.: MIT Press).
Davies, D. (2004), *Art as Performance* (Oxford: Blackwell).
Dennett, D. C. (1991), *Consciousness Explained* (London: Allen Lane).
Hofstadter, D. R. (2001a), 'Staring Emmy Straight in the Eye—And Doing My Best Not to Flinch', in Cope (2001: 33–82).
—— (2001b), 'A Few Standard Questions and Answers', in Cope (2001: 293–305).
—— (2002), 'How Could a COPYCAT Ever be Creative?', in T. Dartnall (ed.), *Creativity, Cognition, and Knowledge: An Interaction* (London: Praeger), 405–24.
Hofstadter, D. R., and FARG (The Fluid Analogy Research Group) (1995), *Fluid Concepts and Creative Analogies: Computer Models of the Fundamental Mechanisms of Thought* (New York: Basic Books).
Longuet-Higgins, H. C. (1994), 'Artificial Intelligence and Musical Cognition', in M. A. Boden, A. Bundy, and R. M. Needham (eds.), *Artificial Intelligence and the Mind: New Breakthroughs or Dead Ends?* (Special Issue of the *Philosophical Transactions of the Royal Society*: Series A, 349, no. 1689), pp. 103–13.
O'Hear, A. (1995), 'Art and Technology: An Old Tension', in R. Fellows (ed.), *Philosophy and Technology* (Cambridge: Cambridge University Press), 143–58.

Riecken, R. D. (1989), 'Wolfgang: Musical Composition by Emotional Computation', in H. Schorr and A. Rappaport (eds.), *Innovative Applications of Artificial Intelligence* (Menlo Park, Calif.: AAAI Press), 251–69.

—— (1994), 'A Conversation with Marvin Minsky about Agents', *Communications of the Association for Computing Machinery*, 37/7: 23–29.

—— (2002), 'The Wolfgang System: A Role of "Emotions" to Bias Learning and Problem-Solving when Learning to Compose Music', in R. Trappl, P. Petta, and S. Payr (eds.), *Emotions in Humans and Artifacts* (Cambridge, Mass.: MIT Press), ch. 10.

Sims, K. (1991), 'Artificial Evolution for Computer Graphics', *Computer Graphics*, 25/4: 319–28.

Sloman, A. (2000), 'Architectural Requirements for Human-like Agents Both Natural and Artificial (What Sorts of Machines Can Love?)', in K. Dautenhahn (ed.), *Human Cognition and Social Agent Technology: Advances in Consciousness Research* (Amsterdam: John Benjamins), 163–95.

Stalnaker, N. (2005), 'Fakes and Forgeries', in B. Gaut and D. M. Lopes (eds.), *The Routledge Companion to Aesthetics* (2nd edn., expanded/revised, London: Routledge), 513–26.

Todd, S. C., and Latham, W. (1992), *Evolutionary Art and Computers* (London: Academic Press).

Tomasello, M., Call, J., and Hare, B. (2003), 'Chimpanzees Understand Psychological States: The Question is Which Ones and to What Extent', *Trends in Cognitive Science*, 7: 153–6.

Whitelaw, M. (2004), *Metacreation: Art and Artificial Life* (London: MIT Press).

11
Aesthetics and Interactive Art

I. INTRODUCTION

As a practice, interactive art—wherein the form of the art object is partly determined by the actions of the audience (or, occasionally, by non-human forces)—is by now well established. It's not mainstream, to be sure. But it's an identifiable genre (Krueger 1991; Candy and Edmonds 2002; Ascott 2003; Whitelaw 2004).

However, there's no established aesthetics associated with it. Forty years ago, the prize set aside for a pioneering exhibition of computer art wasn't awarded, because the committee—which included Umberto Eco—felt that it was too experimental for them to be able to make a reasonable decision (Reichardt 2008: 80). Instead, they listed the works they found most "interesting". Computer art is still experimental today, and there's still confusion about which aesthetic criteria are relevant. That's especially true in respect of *interactive* art. For here, the nature of the interaction is considered to be at least as important as that of the art object itself. But interaction doesn't figure as a consideration in traditional aesthetics. Moreover, the artists concerned disagree among themselves about what type of interaction is most interesting and/or most humanly significant.

A related unclarity concerns the attribution of creativity, or artistic responsibility, for the artwork. Such responsibility is sometimes distributed over several people in traditional art, too. (Think of the teamwork in a Renaissance master's studio, for instance.) But there, the gallery audience isn't part of the "team". Many interactive artists not only insist that the audience are participants in the art-making, but claim that this distributed responsibility has value in itself, so is a factor in their aesthetic evaluation. The aim of enabling the human audience to be creative in its own right is not achieved, of course, where the relevant interactions depend on purely physical forces. So interactive artworks that depend on such forces, no matter how interesting and/or beautiful they may be, won't satisfy these people.

Those are the main issues explored in this chapter. Section II outlines the theoretical ideas that encouraged the development of interactive art. Just what's *new* about it is clarified in Section III, which also explains why it is that there's so much room for dissension about the aesthetics of the field. Section IV explores the fact that the *nature of the interaction* is held to be aesthetically relevant. Finally, Sections V and VI consider how the dependence on interaction suggests a new understanding of the identity of the maker, or artist—in other words, of the source of creativity.

A caveat, before we begin: I referred above to the "art object", by which I meant *the images/sounds that result from the interaction*. Many, perhaps most, interactive artists understand the term in that way too. But one might argue that the "art object", here, should rather be regarded as the program. In that case, the issues about artist's identity that are explored in Section V would be less problematic—for there's normally no ambiguity about who designed, and usually also wrote, the program. ("Normally", because evolutionary art is arguably an exception: see Section VI.)

Alternatively, one might follow those practitioners—such as Ernest Edmonds, for example (Cornock and Edmonds 1973)—who deliberately avoid talk of art objects, preferring the term "art system"—comprising the program, technical equipment, relevant aspects of the environment, and the human participant. Many art systems involve interdisciplinary teams, consisting of artist, programmer, engineers, lighting technologists and so on. The "creativity", these writers say, is distributed over all the team members, albeit mostly inspired by the so-called artist. Even under their usage, however, the questions about artist's identity that are discussed in Section V still arise.

II. THE REBIRTH OF INTERACTIVE ART

Strictly speaking, interactive art has existed for centuries. Its seeds included the dice music of Haydn and Mozart, and—earlier still—the moving statues of nymphs and satyrs seen by the young Descartes in the gardens of the royal palace at Saint-Germain. The interactions in those cases involved manual dice-throwing, and stepping—intentionally or otherwise—on mechanical triggers placed on the ground.

Today's interactive art may involve those actions too. So where Descartes's Paris had individual plates or levers hidden in the grass, the Pompidou Centre showing Karl Sims's work in 1993 offered an array of sixteen footplates (each attached to a TV screen showing a different image) whereby visitors could affect the evolution of the art object (Sims 1991; Whitelaw 2004: 26 f.). But it can also involve any other action—including involuntary ones, such as breathing. It can even depend on causal interactions where no human being is present (weather conditions or wave movements, for example). In short, most recent examples of interactive art are very different from those which delighted Descartes. Indeed, the term is now normally understood to mean *art that involves interactions mediated by computers*. (Interactive theatre, wherein human actors respond to a human audience, is an exception—although even here, the audience may communicate its views by using computers.)

Having germinated centuries ago, interactive art flowered in the 1950s and 1960s, thanks to cybernetics (Brown et al. 2008, chs. 2–5; Boden 2006: 4.iii.e and 13.vi.c). Cybernetics provided two theoretical motivations for this type of art. On the one hand, it encouraged artists to focus on, and to engineer [*sic*], relations of *feedback* between audience and art object. On the other hand, it weakened the previously stark distinction between living organisms and machines—so that a machine could sensibly be seen as an artwork, and the idea of an artist's *engineering* anything at all no longer seemed absurd. (It hadn't seemed absurd to Leonardo da Vinci, of course—but the "two cultures" had long since shoehorned people into mutually mistrustful camps: Snow 1959.)

So by the late 1950s, the young British painter Roy Ascott—who soon became one of the most influential voices in the field—was exhibiting "change-pictures". These consisted of several partially overlapping transparent panels, which the viewer could (manually) rearrange in various ways. Ascott made a point of interpreting them in explicitly cybernetic terms. At around that time, too, the Russian mathematician Aleksei Lapunov, who founded the journal *Problems of Cybernetics* in 1958, urged the construction of wall-mounted displays that required the viewer to slide, fold, open, or close the moving parts. Like Ascott's change-pictures, each one resulted in a varied, and varying, range of artworks. Or, perhaps, a single artwork with various instantiations.

The self-styled "cybernetic sculptor" Edward Ihnatowicz created a sensation in the late 1960s with his *SAM* construction (Sound Activated Mobile)—and even more so with his *Senster* of the early

1970s (Zivanovic 2005, 2008). *SAM* was a metallic "flower", equipped with electronic sensors, that moved towards the source of sound. The *Senster* was a large Meccano-ish (steel-strut) creature, strongly suggestive of a giraffe, that would move its neck and lower its head towards someone whom it heard walking or speaking in its vicinity. A loud shout, however, would make it retreat—and stay timidly dormant for a while. The emotional effects of these lifelike interactions on the human audience/participants were startling, and as the *Senster*'s fame spread it spawned a constant pilgrimage to Phillips, Eindhoven, where the sculpture was installed for several years.

The highly creative cybernetician Gordon Pask, from 1950 on, was especially prescient. Indeed, his early work is still bearing fruit, inspiring current artists—and researchers in artificial life, too (Boden 2006: p. xii, 4.v.e, 15.vi.d). He applied his ideas not only to machines but also to human groups, and to social-psychological studies as well as to art. (His simulations of the interactions between the police and the criminal underworld drew visits from the writers of TV's *Z Cars*, and was so convincing that it was used for training at the Bramshill Police College—George Mallen, p.c.).

His suggestions for a future interactive art included a cybernetic theatre, in which audience reaction would influence the unfolding of the plot on stage—an idea that's now being claimed as "new" by enthusiasts for interactive media and virtual reality. He led the team of scientists and artists planning Joan Littlewood's 'Fun Palace Project', which would provide a host of challenging diversions not found in ordinary theatres (Ascott 1966/7: 119). He outlined how an architectural space (room, building, public arena...) might, in effect, *learn* and *adapt* to some of its users' goals, and their physiological and psychological reactions (Pask 1969). Some of this learning and adaptation could be automatic (using sensor technology, variable lighting, and moveable walls/screens), some would require feedback-driven modifications by human architects. This work anticipated today's ideas on "intelligent buildings", and is regarded by some as one of the "critical writings for the digital era" (Dong 2003; Spiller 2002: 76 f.).

As well as making visionary plans for the future, Pask built some functioning (and sometimes malfunctioning) interactive technology. One example was his *Musicolour* system for dance halls, an array of coloured lights that adapted to the musicians' performance. This was installed in a couple of Mecca dance halls in the early 1950s, but didn't catch on because it often broke down. Another was his *Colloquy* of mutually adaptive mobiles. Descendants of *Musicolour*, these mobiles communicated by both sight (colour and pattern) and sound (pitch, rhythm, and simple phrases). They also provided what Pask (1971) called an "aesthetically potent" environment for interactivity, enabling humans to include meaningful interpretation in the loop.

The *Colloquy* was one of the works exhibited in 1968 at the ICA's *Cybernetic Serendipity* event, a pioneering international exhibition of computer art (Reichardt 1968, 2008; MacGregor 2008). This show was highly influential; besides inspiring many budding artists, it was favourably reviewed in publications as diverse as *Nature*, *Practical Electronics*, and *Vogue*. The *SAM* mobile was featured there also. Both these pieces attracted significant interest.

Pask and Ihnatowicz were almost alone in providing *interactive* examples for the ICA's exhibition. Gustav Metzger's proposal for *Five Screens with Computer*—a huge auto-destructive artwork wherein the changing seasons, the quality of light and shade, and the actions of spectators using photo-electric switches would trigger the ejection of the work's components—was described at the show (Reichardt 1968: 31). But, being way ahead of the current technology, it hadn't actually been built. (And despite further planning over the next few years, it never was—Ford 2008: 165–8.) The 1968 exhibition could be mounted nonetheless, because not all computer art is interactive (see Chapter 7).

Complex interactions require powerful digital computers. (There were only two digital computers in the ICA show, and these were inevitably primitive.) Moreover, the computers must be accessible: before the advent of personal computers in the 1980s, even non-interactive computer art could be done only on laboratory-based (or, occasionally, home-tinkered) machines. So this genre developed relatively slowly. However, huge advances in computer power and man-machine interfaces have enabled interactive art to blossom luxuriantly over the past quarter-century.

One well-known artist whose work illustrates the changing potential provided by these technological advances is Stelarc, who has been exploring the notion of self-as-cyborg for over twenty years (Stelarc 1986, 1994, 2002a and b; Smith 2005). He began, in the late 1960s, with purely mechanical man-machine linkages: not an electron in sight. Specifically, he relied on meat hooks inserted into his skin, and attached to pulleys (Stelarc 1984). More recently, he has focused on increasingly diverse human-computer interfaces. For instance, he links/integrates his own muscles with robots, or with random or human-originated messages from the Internet—so that his body becomes a prosthesis for other people. Stelarc is normally labelled a performance artist, but he could also be seen as the pioneer of an especially intimate—and philosophically challenging—form of interactive art. Indeed, we'll see in Section V that interactive art in general can be regarded as a variety of performance art, for the prime interest is less in the sensory qualities of the product than in the mental and/or bodily processes that produced it.

Each interactive artist, of course, is part-driven by aesthetic considerations. However, as remarked in Section I, there's no generally agreed aesthetic in this area. As Linda Candy has put it: "[A] satisfactory critical framework of new forms in art technology has yet to be developed" (2002: 266). This isn't merely a question of different artists having different signatures (see Chapter 6), or even different styles. The point, rather, is that many—perhaps most—questions about the aesthetics of interactive art are still open.

For instance, many interactive artists aim to end up with final products that are pleasing and/or interesting—even though they may differ (as other artists do) about just what counts as aesthetically valuable. In that sense, they're doing old-fashioned art in a novel (computer-based) way. By contrast, a number of their colleagues—including Ascott, Edmonds, and Myron Krueger (1977)—have explicitly claimed that the properties of the visual or auditory product are aesthetically secondary, even irrelevant. What matters is the nature of the interaction itself.

Is that a reasonable position? And if so, just what aspects of the interaction should be assigned aesthetic value? Why should one type of interaction be valued above another? To answer those questions, we must first ask what is so *new* about interactive art, which leaves its aesthetics still so controversial?

III. WHAT'S NEW?

If one merely looks at (and/or listens to) the final products of interactive art, it's not immediately obvious that there's any special aesthetic problem. One may warm to them or not, as one may or may not warm to the work of a newly discovered painter hung on a gallery wall. But there's no huge surprise, no instant recognition of a brand new genre—especially if one is already familiar with video art. There's no disorientating shock comparable, for instance, to that experienced on first encountering conceptual art.

As explained in Chapter 5, conceptual artists, like some (but not all) interactive artists, explicitly deny the importance of the sensory qualities of the art object. That's partly why the movement has been described as seeking "the dematerialization of the art object" (Lippard 1973). Accordingly, they deliberately downplay the artist's making-skills. Only two things are held to be important. One of these is the interest of the particular idea, or concept, involved. Indeed, the art object itself (if one can speak of it in that way) may be made accessible *only* as an idea.

For example, consider Walter de Maria's *Vertical Earth Kilometer*. This is a perfect cylinder, made of highly polished solid brass, exactly 5 centimetres in diameter and 1,000 metres long (and weighing nearly 19 tons). But instead of displaying its finely crafted material splendour to admiring eyes, de Maria buried it in the earth so that it's invisible. The only indication of its existence is its 5-centimetre-wide circular top, level with the ground and kept free of grass by its "keepers". In short, the aesthetic interest is held to lie in the *concept* of the buried object, not in any visual/tactile experience of it.

The second challenging aspect of conceptual art is its lack of concern with the artist's making-skills. In orthodox art, these are admired insofar as they can generate aesthetically valued (sensory and symbolic) properties in the object. In conceptual art, they're typically held to be irrelevant (although the appeal of the *Vertical Earth Kilometer* surely lies partly in the fact that its manufacture is known to be so materially perfect). On the one hand, this allows for the exhibition/celebration of readymades, as opposed to handcrafted unique objects—for example, Marcel Duchamp's urinal *Fountain*, or de Maria's manufactured brass cylinders. On the other hand, anything that is in fact handmade doesn't have to be made "skilfully". Tracey Emin's embroidered tent, for instance, which carries the names of all her past lovers, isn't supposed to be judged by the skilfulness of her embroidery.

Interactive art is different. It doesn't denigrate making-skills—although, as we'll see in Section V, it does sometimes interpret and value the "making" in a new way. Nor does it (usually) ignore the sensory/symbolic properties of the product—although, again, it often sees them as much less important than they are normally taken to be.

The making-skills of orthodox art are material skills. An obvious example is the adept use of paint, whether in meticulously detailed sixteenth-century images of formal ruffs and Dutch interiors, or in the rougher paint-marks of the post-Impressionists, or Jackson Pollock's carefully controlled (yes!) action paintings. The making-skills of interactive art, one might say, aren't material skills at all, but technological/computational abilities—in a word, programming.

To be sure, they result in a visible and/or audible (occasionally, seemingly tactile) end product, which has many sensory properties comparable to those of orthodox art. But that end product is a form of virtual reality, not something one can pick up or use as a doorstop. It's a computer-generated image, or series of images, displayed on a VDU screen (occasionally, framed like a painting and hung on a wall) or projected onto the gallery walls. Or it's a set of sounds with no visible instrument being visibly played. In the extreme, it's an episode in a multisensory immersive virtual reality, in which the audience (wearing special gear) can *feel* the result much as one can feel a real sculpture, and even—so it seems—pick it up and heft its weight.

If the introduction of new making-skills were all, however, our topic would be less interesting than it actually is. It would be like the introduction of a new material, or of a new medium for pursuing already accepted artistic aims: oil paint, for instance, or photography, or step-by-step animation using drawings or plasticine. Each of these developments required artists to learn new skills, and each—especially photography—raised new questions in philosophical aesthetics too. But interactive art goes beyond those examples, in two ways.

First, while introducing the skill of designing (programming) novel possibilities for human-computer interaction, it also suggests that much or all of the aesthetic interest lies in *the nature of that interaction itself*. The focus, in other words, is not (or not primarily) on the intrinsic properties of the final product, but on the interactive processes that led up to it. Second, it suggests that the "human" in this human-computer interaction needn't be thought of only as *the person who has laboriously acquired the new skills* (i.e. the "artist"), but also as *the participatory audience*, whose voluntary and/or involuntary actions help determine the perceptible form of the virtual art object.

Both these points arise out of the key novelty of the genre, which distinguishes it from all others: the (computer-mediated) constructive interaction between audience and art object. The viewer isn't just a viewer, but a playful participant—even a co-creator. As one practitioner has put it, interactive art is therefore "*a whole new field of creative endeavor* that is as radically unlike each of [the] established genres as they are unlike each other" (Ascott 1990: 245; italics added). It's even a radical departure from most computer art, which uses computers merely as "rather complicated tools, extending the range of painting and sculpture, performed music, or published literature" (ibid.).

IV. WHAT SORTS OF INTERACTION SHOULD BE VALUED?

The nature of the audience/art interaction is typically held to be more important than the (conventional) aesthetics of the product because, as we've just seen, the fact of there being any interaction at all is what's unusual (if not wholly "new": see the opening of Section II). But it doesn't follow that the conventional aesthetics are wholly irrelevant. Even if (and it's an arguable "if") it's not strictly necessary for the product to have any intrinsic value, one might still reasonably regard an interactive artwork that produces conventionally pleasing and/or interesting products to be aesthetically superior to one which does not.

But perhaps some particular conventional values are to be favoured over others, in this new artistic context? Should the presence of interaction, and/or of some specific type of interaction, lead us to expect that such-and-such a property (of the product) is even more—or even less—important than we've conventionally taken it to be?

For instance, suppose that there are certain aspects of music which are especially hard to achieve in interactive art (as opposed to fully automatic musical composition: e.g. Cope 2001, 2005). One example might be the type of polyphony where several melodies, either different or the-same-with-time-delay, are generated alongside each other. Should we regard this achievement as relevant to aesthetics, or only to technology and/or the IQ of the artist-programmer? In other words, is *difficulty* aesthetically relevant?

Turning now to the interaction itself, there's no "conventional" aesthetics to be considered. That's primarily because the occurrence of any sustained interaction at all is still relatively novel. It's not surprising, then, that questions about what effects the interactive artist should aim for still remain unsettled.

There's a second reason why such questions are unsettled—indeed, why one might say that *they needn't even arise*. Namely, by the turn of the millennium conventional aesthetics—in many people's minds—had died the death with respect to art in general: postmodernist pluralism reigned. Accordingly, any notion of laying down an aesthetic convention for others to follow (as opposed to following it oneself) was anathema. It wasn't acceptable to say that the artist "should" aim for such-and-such effects. (Even so, various characteristics became favoured, if not quite de rigueur, their presence/absence being specifically praised/lamented by art critics. One was the deliberate juxtaposition of images and symbols from far-distant cultures around the world, an expression of or comment on late twentieth-century globalization—Stallabrass 2004: ch. 2.)

However, even if a question needn't arise, it doesn't follow that it won't arise. The question "What should the interactive artist aim for?", or at least "What makes for a successful/satisfying interactive project?", was often raised by the pioneering interactive artists (before the rise of pluralism in art), and it's sometimes still raised now. So, despite the general art-world's flight from prescriptive aesthetics, it's not unreasonable to take it as our "text for today".

Asking what aspects of the interaction are especially valuable isn't a question that's easily answered. For there are many possibilities—and many actualities too, in the sense that not all interactive artists would give the same reply.

Consider attributability and predictability, for example. Some interactive artists say that the changes in the computerized product/environment should be clearly attributable by the human person (i.e. the audience) to his/her own actions. The artists may or may not deem it acceptable for this attributability to dawn slowly on the person concerned, as opposed to being near-instantly recognizable. But for other artists in this genre, it is enough that the visible/audible changes be actually caused by the audience, irrespective of whether the audience realizes that fact.

The changes may be, and perhaps—to establish the artist's *creativity*? (see Chapter 2)—they aesthetically should be, surprising. For instance, they may be types of change that are normally beyond our control. In some virtual worlds, for example, the movements of the audience can counter the usual effects of gravity, or cause an object to move from one spot to another without traversing the intervening space. Is that merely entertaining gimmickry, or does it have intrinsic artistic value?

Irrespective of the nature of the changes, one common position holds that it should be clear to the human being, at least after playing around with the artwork for a while (how long is too long?), that it's *their* actions which are causing the changes to happen. I say "actions", but initially they will be involuntary movements, or actions that are *not* directed at causing the changes in question. Only after the attributability link has been established can the viewer intentionally *act* so as to cause specific types of change. According to this view, a recognizable direct dependence, even (perhaps?) the growth of predictability—and therefore of creative control—as the audience becomes more adept, is the name of the game.

Others disagree. Some interactive artworks are deliberately designed to make such predictability impossible. But here too, there's room for aesthetic maneouvre.

The artist may aim for near-complete unpredictability. Indeed, randomness, and the computer's role in approximating it, was often praised in the early days of interactive art, and was explicitly mentioned in the official description of *Cybernetic Serendipity*. The exhibition was said to show, among other things, "the links between the random systems enployed by artists, composers and poets, and those involved in the use of cybernetic devices" (Reichardt 1968: 5). The cognitive psychologist Bela Julesz's random-dot figures attracted artistic interest—and imitators—accordingly (Reichardt 2008: 72; Julesz 1971). But not all these artists welcomed it. Edmonds, for example, says: "In my mind, randomness... is inherently uninteresting. My goal was to make work that is complex enough to be engaging, but not so complex as to seem random" (2008: 351). And he adds that "complexity can occur in many ways, and may not occur on the surface at all". In short, there are many specific ways in which these general points could be implemented. How are we to compare those, in assessing their aesthetic merits?

What counts as "engaging", of course, is open to question. Some artworks entice the human participant to build up expectations over time, only to negate them (repeatedly?) once they've developed. For instance, one artist programmed a VDU maze, to be explored with a cursor. The viewer has some fun in trying to approach the centre... but then, all of a sudden, the maze reconfigures itself. The cursor remains at the same spot as before, but it's no longer just one or two turnings away from the goal. In effect, the viewer must start all over again. That type of teasing unpredictability will probably win one's approbation, and one's engagement—but only for a while. When the maze reconfigures itself a second time, approbation and amusement are likely to give way to frustration and boredom. Is it reasonable to regard an art object that can be enjoyed *only once* as something of high aesthetic value?

As another example of unpredictability, consider the installation *The Living Room*, built in 2001 by Christa Sommerer and Laurent Mignonneau. Here, the movements and speech of the viewer cause images drawn from the Internet to be projected onto the walls, and

Internet sounds to be broadcast too. But there's no rhyme or reason: the constantly changing images/sounds are picked more or less at random from those current on the Internet at each particular moment. There's therefore no way in which the viewer can control the specific contents of the result (see Section V).

The unpredictability is much less in *Plant Growing*, the first (in 1992) of several "biological" installations designed by Sommerer and Mignonneau (Whitelaw 2004: 64–71). Five potted plants (ferns and a small cactus) are placed on pedestals, in front of a large video-projection screen. Initially, the screen is blank. But as the audience brush against the plants, or actively touch them, images of imaginary plants appear—and move and grow, sprouting new leaves and branches as the humans engage with the real plants. (Unknown to the audience, the potted plants are fitted with small electrodes connecting them to the unseen computer.) The graphic "species" depending on any given pot plant is fixed, but the particular touches of the human viewer determine just what *this* species member will look like. The determination isn't random, but systematic—so to some extent predictable. Each person can act individually, or a group of people can coordinate their touches to achieve relatively coordinated effects on the screen.

Sommerer and Mignonneau's later work includes a variation of *Plant Growing* called *Trans Plant*, developed in 1995/6. Here, a jungle forms on the semicircular walls surrounding the viewer as he/she moves around the room. The relations are systematic and predictable: grass grows where the viewer walks, and trees and bushes grow when and where he/she stays still. In addition, the size, colour, and shape of the virtual plants depends on the size and bodily attitudes of the human being. Children will co-create plants different from those brought into being by their parents, although the system can be "cheated" if the child stretches out his/her arms. The colour density will change if the person moves their body slightly backwards or forwards.

Another interactive installation, also inspired by the biological world, is a room with a number of fine strings hanging from the ceiling. The walls bear projected images of trees of various species. When the viewer's body brushes against a string, another tree (or trees) appears, its location and species depending on the particular string and/or movement. It's possible for the viewer not even to notice the newly appearing trees for a while. When they do, they don't necessarily realize that it's their own movements which are causing the virtual forest to grow. And it may take a long time (if ever) before they realize the systematic relation between their movements and the locations/species of the new trees.

Does the fact that this interactive systematicity is (a) present, and (b) ultimately recognizable, make this installation aesthetically superior to one in which the newly appearing locations/species would be random? If so, why?

One answer to that question might be justified in terms of the issues discussed in Section V. Namely, the more voluntary control the viewer has over the movement-induced changes, the more he/she can be regarded—and can regard him/herself—as not merely an active participant but also a creative/guiding one. If (as some claim) the aesthetic of interactive art in general is one which stresses the creative role of the audience, then systematic "tree planting" is preferable to random placements. (Even so, questions remain about *which sorts* of systematicity are preferable.)

Alternatively, one might say that clumps of same-species trees are aesthetically preferable to having individual trees dotted around at random—either because this arrangement is more botanically plausible and/or because it gives added visual structure, and therefore interest, to the image. One way of achieving that would be to have certain strings assigned to certain potential clumps, such that the viewer—once they'd realized the "projection rules" involved—could design a multi-species forest more or less at will.

A clue would (or rather, could) be provided if the viewer happened to touch the same string several times, perhaps because they were standing right next to it while still looking at the original image on the walls. For then a new—or newly enlarged—clump would "happen" to appear, and catch the viewer's eye. This clue would increase the degree of control and predictability, from the point of view of the audience. If those two dimensions are taken to be aesthetically valuable, then a clue-providing interactive installation, whether this one or any other, is to that extent a "good" one.

Another way of approaching such questions would be to focus on predictability/control not in the abstract, but rooted in human embodiment. Presumably, this would make it easier for the viewer to learn the causal relationships, and also easier to manipulate them once they'd been learnt.

For example, there might be a direct and "sensible" mapping between the human and the computerized end product. So any movements made by the viewer's left arm or leg, or the left-hand side of the body in general, would cause changes only on the left-hand side of the room; similarly, forward movement of the viewer's body or body parts could cause visible changes seeming to bring the current focus of interest nearer. Or, instead, there could be a direct but "nonsensical" mapping. For instance, left and right, forward and back, could be systematically reversed: a Looking-Glass world in one's actual experience, unlike the purely imaginary descriptions bequeathed to us by Lewis Carroll. In principle, John Tenniel's illustrations could be borrowed to provide clues as to what was going on.

My guess is that Tenniel's Red Queen wouldn't be needed, because the embodied participant would become aware of the reversal easily enough. Projection rules even more bizarre than straightforward 180° reversal are of course possible. Whether they would be realized by the participants is an open, and interesting, question. (Such exploitations of embodiment would probably work best in room-sized installations rather than VDU-screened videos, but similar principles could be applied in the small-scale versions too.)

Temporal relations could be varied, too. The "sensible" scenarios would have fast and slow body movements being reflected by fast and slow changes in the display. "Nonsense" would, up to a point, map fast onto slow and vice versa. In a fully immersive virtual world, the absence of time-faithful mapping would be especially disconcerting.

But what's wrong with disconcerting one's audience? It's a common artistic strategy, at least in modernist and—especially—postmodernist art. If (and as we've seen, this is a genuine "if") what one seeks to achieve is predictability, then my guess would be that the more the viewer's embodiment is systematically emphasized in the ways sketched above, the sooner the predictability will be recognized. To that extent, reflections of embodiment would be aesthetically valuable. (One might still argue, however, that the recognition shouldn't be too prompt, that the participant should do some "work" to gain the insight.)

The artist might have additional reasons for respecting, and drawing the audience's attention to, human embodiment. For the topic, or theme, of the artwork might be embodiment *as such*. If so, the semantic content of the images (and the accompanying verbal text, if any) could somehow draw attention to bodies and/or to the general human experience, or predicament, of being embodied. The rules of image change in such cases would be body-grounded (though not necessarily "realistic"), as discussed above. But now, they wouldn't stand alone.

Rather, they would reinforce the body-centred semantics, or theme, of the installation.

Body-grounded rules of projection need not be fixed: they could change occasionally. For instance, one might start out realistically, on this side of the Looking-Glass, but go through to the other side after ten minutes or so. Is that inherently interesting, and aesthetically desirable? Or is it confusing, a sort of artistic sadism inflicted on the audience?

However, if the artist is seeking to convey some specific concept or message, as opposed to presenting a contentless but entertaining series of images, then any changes in the projection rules should be semantically coherent with meaningful changes happening in the images being shown. (This leaves open the question of how far "coherence" should be regarded as an aesthetic value in its own right; Marc Chagall's dreamscapes, for instance, are incoherent by everyday standards.) Even if the artist isn't aiming at sending a specific message, he/she may wish to encourage meaning-centred responses from the human participants. For instance, we saw in Section II that Pask valued his *Colloquy of Mobiles* partly because it led to meaningful interpretations by the audience.

Do apparently boring things such as the speed of computation matter? Certainly, the experience one has in interacting with a virtual environment or a robot will be very different depending on whether its responses are speedy or sluggish. Too slow, and the audience's causal responsibility may not even be recognized. Too fast, and it may not be analysable—so cutting down on the delicacy of control. Just right (perhaps), and the viewer will sense an unfolding rather than an immediate response—which may or may not be regarded as a valuable aspect of the art object.

What about multimedia? Is an effective audio-visual example inherently "better" than a purely visual or purely auditory one? If so, why? To be sure, it may display the ingenuity and skills of the artist to greater effect, so that the artist is better satisfied with it as an emblem of ego. But from the point of view of the audience, why (if at all) is a multi-sensory experience aesthetically preferable to a single-sensory one? If the VR example is aiming at verisimilitude, then multi-sensory results (provided that they are plausible) are certainly preferable. And in a training simulator for an airline pilot, or for a fighting soldier (e.g. the US Army's JFETS, or Joint Fires & Effects Trainer System: see www.ict.usc.edu), verisimilitude is pragmatically desirable. But what's to say that VR designed for artistic purposes has to aim for verisimilitude?

Again, how can one weigh these two types of "unrealistic" installation against each other: (1) a VR environment that is unrealistic in deep ways (such as the absence of gravity, mentioned above) but otherwise very like normality, and (2) a wholly fantastic virtual environment? Is bemusement (as opposed to surprise) on the part of the viewer to be regarded as an aesthetically relevant dimension? If so, is it important that the bemusement can eventually fade, allowing systematic negotiation/creation of even the fantastic world? Or is an endlessly bemusing fantasy, perhaps even having the appearance of chaos, just as acceptable in artistic terms?

You may not even want to try to answer these questions. You may say, instead: "Let a hundred flowers blossom!" And in effect, that's what interactive artists themselves say. For as remarked above, there's no agreed aesthetic in this area. The artists aim for different effects. Some don't make their aesthetics explicit. Others do, but differ in the justifications they give. The discussion here isn't aimed at laying down the law about such matters. Rather, its intention is to indicate some of the dimensions that might be thought relevant.

In particular, it's aimed at uncovering dimensions of experience which—unlike the "beauty" of the resulting images, for example—can arise *only* in relation to this new (interactive and computer-based) artistic genre. It's because these possibilities for interaction are so unprecedented (thanks to the limitless potential of the general-purpose computer) that it's plausible to argue that a fundamentally new technology demands a radically new aesthetic.

Whether that aesthetic should reflect *specific properties of the underlying technology as such is* another question. We'll see in Section VI, for example, that some interactive art is based on evolutionary algorithms. Many of the artists concerned regard it as crucially important that the audience be aware of this fact. One must ask why they feel that this awareness has aesthetic relevance.

V. AUDIENCE AS ARTIST

Interactive art, as remarked in Section II, can be thought of as a form of performance art, wherein the prime interest is in the mental and/or bodily processes that produced it. Arguably, *all* art, even including the *Mona Lisa*, is performance art in that sense (Davies 2004: esp. chaps. 7–10). If so, then interactive art isn't quite as marginal as a more conventional aesthetics would imply. And certainly, all art audiences are participatory, in the sense that they actively construct their experience and interpretation of what they see or hear. That's largely what distinguishes the spontaneous enjoyment of craftwork from the culture-based appreciation of fine art (see Chapter 4). Conceptual art puts a special burden on the active engagement of the audience: specifically, on their power of mental association (see Chapter 5). But interactive art is participatory in an even stronger sense.

In other genres, the art object is made—or, as in some cases of conceptual art, described—by the artist, where the artist's identity is clear. (Or relatively clear: Jeff Koons, for example, is notorious for having "his" canvasses painted on his behalf by his assistants.) In interactive art, by contrast, the audience is the maker. Not the only maker, to be sure, for it was the named "artist" (with the cooperation of the engineers and/or programmers) who made the interaction possible in the first place. Nevertheless, the final form of the art object is generated by the actions of the audience.

These actions are highly various, as we've seen. They may be simple button presses; or noise making (from footsteps, through breathing or humming, to speech); or voluntary/involuntary contact with surfaces or hanging strings; or changes of body position with respect to the floor; or specific movements of legs and/or arms. Or even, in Stelarc's case, mental volitions—which result in movements of robotic arms attached to and/or directly connected with Stelarc's human body. It is the artist (I'm using this word as a term of convenience here) who determines which actions will be effective, and what their effects will be. But only the audience decides, or unknowingly determines, just which actions—and therefore just which effects—will take place on a particular occasion.

This fact has three interesting implications. One is that the audience's sense of active engagement, or participation, is much stronger than usual. Another is that the engagement with the art object becomes "fun", wherein the audience explores and experiments in an open and playful manner. And the third is that the audience can take some responsibility for the creation of the art object—perhaps accompanied by a sense of pride, or perhaps by disappointement and frustration.

Many interactive artists regard this last implication as especially important. Far from jealously guarding their own creative ownership of the art, they welcome the so-called audience as a partner in the creative act. Ascott, one of the pioneers of the genre, has always been explicit about this.

Ascott's first forays into interactive art didn't involve computers, but canvasses with physical items/images on them that could be continually moved around by the viewer. So the "viewer" of the resulting collages was their physical *maker* too. This aspect was retained, and strengthened, in the computerized art that followed. The value of computer-based interactive art, for Ascott, is its ability to engage the viewer/participant *as creator*, in ways much more wide-ranging than rearranging material things on a canvas (Ascott 1964, 1966/1967; cf. 2003). By the same token, he holds that its aesthetic crux is the nature of the interaction itself, not the (visual and/or musical) end result.

Inevitably, the authority of the single artistic signature is undermined. For crucial creative choices are now being made by the viewer. Indeed, the "viewer" may in fact be many viewers. Given the advent of the Internet and the Web, authorship of the "telematic" artwork may be very widely dispersed:

[The] status of the art object changes. The culturally dominant objet d'art as the sole focus (the uncommon carrier of uncommon content) is replaced by the interface. Instead of the artwork as a window into a composed, resolved, and ordered reality, we have at the interface a doorway to undecidability, a dataspace of semantic and material potentiality   (Ascott 1990: 237).

Telematic culture means, in short, that we do not think, see, or feel in isolation. Creativity is shared, authorship is distributed, but not in a way that denies the individual her authenticity or power of self-creation, as rather crude models of collectivity might have done in the past. On the contrary, telematic culture amplifies the individual's capacity for creative thought and action . . . *Networking supports endless redescription and recontextualization such that no language or visual code is final and no reality is ultimate* (Ascott 1990: 238; italics added).

In short, interactive art as conceptualized by Ascott is a buttress of postmodernism. Instead of "the death of the author" (Barthes 1977), we have the death of the artist—or, perhaps better, the continuous augmentation of the "artist" so as to include one or more (maybe many more) "viewers". Ascott's longtime colleague Edmonds is less explicitly postmodernist in approach. But he, too, welcomes what he calls "re-designating the role of the artist". As he puts it: "The artist could potentially enable or frame creative behaviour [on the part of the audience] rather than only produce objects to be consumed" (2008: 350).

The term "audience" is ambiguous, covering as it does both a single viewer and a group—even one (as in Network art) made up of people widely dispersed over time and space. For a viewer who wishes to bask in the flattering aura of creative artistry, of course, the satisfaction will be reduced in cases where there are *many* people determining the final result. Perhaps a committed postmodernist such as Ascott wouldn't want to pander to such individualistic impulses. Others, however, might regard the degree of the individual viewer's control as a positive criterion for an interactive aesthetics. In that case, multiple viewer-creators might be specifically avoided, or allowed only if deliberate cooperation on their part were possible.

Certainly, the intentions of the originating artist, even supposing that they can be ascertained, may not be crucial to the audience's response to the artwork. Any intentions the interactive artist may have had about the final forms that will result may be frustrated to a greater or lesser degree by the actions/choices of the participatory public. The more diverse the system's potential, the greater freedom the audience has. This provides an extra dimension for the new aesthetics involved. In Section IV, we considered predictability/unpredictability *from the point of view of the participant audience*. Here, we're concerned with predictability/unpredictability *from the point of view of the interactive artist*.

It's up to the artist to decide whether they want to constrain the possible results within a particular range, or style, or whether they want them to be more open-ended. In other words, there's a choice as to how far the specific intentions of the artist should be evident in the final products. Unlimited open-endedness would swamp them entirely, risking either mere uninteresting chaos or *complete* creative control on the part of the audience. In practice, of course, the range of possibilities is always limited. But there can be genuine aesthetic disagreement about the extent to which the artist's intentions *should* survive the vicissitudes of the interaction.

(To the extent that they don't, does the artist become downgraded to a mere technologist? Compare: the programmers of a PC's operating system, or of software such as Photoshop, make the user's creative work *possible*—but they're not credited with the results.)

VI. INTERACTION AND EVOLUTIONARY ART

The vicissitudes of the interactions are especially great in evolutionary art, a genre that has been growing steadily since the early 1990s

(Whitelaw 2004). The first examples were done by hand (e.g. Todd and Latham 1992: 2–6), but the term is normally used to apply to a particular type of computer art.

Here, random mutations change the original structure (e.g. image) in various ways, and the artist—or, sometimes, the gallery audience—continually chooses which "descendants" should be selected for further "breeding". As in non-evolutionary interactive art, the programmer can decide whether or not to constrain the results to fit his/her own aesthetic intentions closely.

Sometimes, the allowable mutations can be deep. They may include, for example, nesting an entire mini-program inside another one (Sims 1991). In such cases, the results are hugely unconstrained and unpredictable. In particular, fundamental changes in the nature of the image can and do happen. There's no recognizable family-resemblance between widely separated generations, or even (sometimes) between one generation and the next.

Fundamental transformations in general constitute what I call "the third road to surprise". This type of creativity is highly valued, whether in art or science, because the results are not merely surprising but seemingly *impossible* (Boden 2004: 5 f., chs. 3–4). Since (by definition) some accepted stylistic rules will have been broken in effecting the transformations, there will be disagreement about the value of the novel results. Transformational results are very rarely accepted as valuable by everyone, immediately. Nevertheless, transformational creativity is usually regarded as the most interesting, and mysterious, type (as compared with "combinational" and "exploratory" creativity—Boden 2004: 3–6, chs. 4–6). To that extent, then, this interactive program might appear to be aesthetically significant. And some pleasing images, almost *irrespective* of one's aesthetic preferences, will usually result.

For all that, the artistic interest of such "wild-mutation" programs is small. One *can't* say that an interactive system of this (transformational) type is in general aesthetically preferable to other, less adventurous, ones. For there's no disciplined attempt to achieve a particular (aesthetically valued) aim, or to explore an aesthetically interesting space of possibilities. To do that, the types of mutation that are allowed must be less luxuriant.

That's why William Latham, trained as a sculptor and working as a professional artist, ensured that the evolutionary programs he designed (with Stephen Todd) could make only relatively superficial changes to the existing image (Todd and Latham 1992). Admittedly, even superficial changes, if continued over hundreds of generations, can produce surprises: images which the artist admits he couldn't (not just didn't) imagine for himself. But there are no fundamental transformative changes. All the images are clearly members of the same species, or style. (They are close to exploratory creativity, especially if one allows that exploratory creativity may involve superficial variations, or "tweaking", of the stylistic rules). It follows that if one finds the general style aesthetically pleasing/interesting, one will find all/most of the evolved images valuable too.

Most of the evolutionary artists interviewed by Mitchell Whitelaw (2004) take the biological inspiration of this technology seriously. That is, they see themselves as producing artworks—sometimes, audience-interactive artworks—which celebrate and explore the phenomenon of life. Some even aim to create life itself, albeit within a computer (an aim that is fundamentally misconceived: see Chapters 1 and 12). In general, and especially when their works enable audience participation, they deem it important that people realize the evolutionary nature of the technology, and its biological provenance—namely, life. With respect to the underlying technical details, of course, the audience is faced with a black box. But their knowledge *that the box contains an evolutionary, life-imitating, process* is—according to this aesthetic—crucial. That is, the life-related aspects of the artwork provide it with much of its *value*.

In principle, the selection at each generation could be done automatically. But even so, the fitness function—the measure of adaptive/aesthetic value—would normally be decided by the human artist. Normally, but not necessarily: the computer might be able to learn, for instance, which colour combinations the artist—or anyone else—prefers, and add that dimension to the fitness function. And/or it might be able to evolve higher-order fitness functions for itself, even though the basic selection criteria had been fixed by the programmer. That might be possible, for example, if there were unanticipated interactions between the environment and the program—or physical robot.

In some cases of automatic evolution, unexpected results of amazing subtlety can arise. For instance, the neural-network "brain" of a simple evolutionary robot can come to include a mini-circuit comparable to the orientation detectors found in mammalian cortex (Cliff et al. Husbands 1993). One wouldn't normally attribute this result to the ingenuity, still less the foresight/intention, of the roboticists. Analogously, a surprising but aesthetically valuable result of an "artistic" evolutionary program wouldn't naturally be attributed to the programmer-artist.

The preceding two paragraphs may have been strictly irrelevant to our topic. It's not clear that a fully automatic evolutionary system should be classed as interactive art, since the "interactions" involved all take place within the computer. There's no human choice guiding the evolution of the novel forms. The only "human-computer interaction" is in the original programming. That's not what is usually meant by the term, which is why most computer-based art isn't counted as interactive art—even though it was produced by human movements (finger taps on keyboards) influencing computers. The interactions concerned must come *after* the programming. In a fully automatic evolutionary system they do, but they aren't *human-computer* interactions.

If a fully automatic evolutionary system doesn't count as interactive art, should it be classed as "art" at all? If it is, then who is the artist? The programmer is the only (human) candidate. (Whether a computer, in principle, could ever generate a work of art is controversial; for those who define "art" as involving human communication, it could not: O'Hear 1995.) But the programmers of the robot mentioned above had absolutely no idea that an orientation detector might emerge. It would seem perverse to attribute a similarly unexpected result in an apparently artistic medium to the unknowing programmers. Facilitators, they may be. But artists, surely not? Paradoxically, we would have what appear to be artworks, without any artist.

VII. CONCLUSION

This paper has raised many more questions than it has answered. For taking the aesthetics of interactive art seriously isn't a simple matter. It involves a host of considerations about conventional aesthetics, about technology, about the psychology of perception and creativity, and about the identity/role of the "artist". No doubt, the ingenuity of interactive artists will raise even more questions in the future.

REFERENCES

Ascott, R. (1964), 'The Construction of Change', *Cambridge Opinion*, 1: 37–42, special issue on 'Modern Art in Britain', repr. as ch. 1 of Ascott (2003: 97–107).

Ascott, R. (1966/7), 'Behaviourist Art and the Cybernetic Vision', *Cybernetica*, 9 (1966), 247–64; and 10 (1967), 25–56; repr. as chap. 3 of Ascott (2003: 109–56).

—— (1990), 'Is There Love in the Telematic Embrace?', *Art Journal*, 49/3: 241–7; repr. as chap. 16 of Ascott (2003) (page references are to the reprinted version).

—— (2003), *Telematic Embrace: Visionary Theories of Art, Technology, and Consciousness* (Berkeley and Los Angeles: University of California Press).

Barthes, R. (1977), 'The Death of the Author', in S. Heath (ed., trans.), *Image, Music, Text* (New York: Hill), 142–8.

Boden, M. A. (2004), *The Creative Mind: Myths and Mechanisms* (2nd enlarged edn., London: Routledge).

—— (2006), *Mind as Machine: A History of Cognitive Science* (Oxford: Clarendon Press).

Brown, P., Gere, C., Lambert, N., and Mason, C. (eds.) (2008), *White Heat Cold Logic: British Computer Art 1960–1980* (Cambridge, Mass.: MIT Press).

Candy, L. (2002), 'Defining Interaction', in Candy and Edmonds (2002: 261–6).

Candy, L., and Edmonds, E. A. (eds.) (2002), *Explorations in Art and Technology* (London: Springer).

Cliff, D., Harvey, I. and Husbands, P. (1993), 'Explorations in Evolutionary Robotics', *Adaptive Behavior*, 2: 71–108.

Cope, D. (2001), *Virtual Music: Computer Synthesis of Musical Style* (Cambridge, Mass.: MIT Press).

—— (2005), *Computer Models of Musical Creativity* (Cambridge, Mass.: MIT Press).

Cornock, S., and Edmonds, E. A. (1973), 'The Creative Process where the Artist is Amplified or Superseded by the Computer', *Leonardo*, 16: 11–16.

Davies, D. (2004), *Art as Performance* (Oxford: Blackwell).

Dong, A. (2003), 'A Cybernetics-Based Design Process for Intelligent Rooms', *Proceedings of the 37th Conference of the Australia and New Zealand Architectural Science Association, Sydney*, 1: 267–74.

Edmonds, E. A. (2008), 'Constructive Computation', in Brown et al. (2008: 345–60).

Ford, S. (2008), 'Technological Kindergarten: Gustav Metzger and Early Computer Art', in Brown et al. (2008: 163–74).

Julesz, B. (1971), *Foundations of Cyclopean Perception* (Chicago: Chicago University Press).

Krueger, M. W. (1977), 'Responsive Environments', *American Federation of Information Processing Systems*, 46 (13–16 June), 423–33; repr. in K. Stiles and P. Selz (eds.), *Theories and Documents of Contemporary Art: A Sourcebook*

of Artists' Writings (Berkeley and Los Angeles: University of California Press, 1996), 473–86.
—— (1991), Artificial Reality (2nd edn., Reading, Mass.: Addison-Wesley).
Lippard, L. (1973), Six Years: The Dematerialization of the Art Object 1966–1972 (New York: Praeger).
MacGregor, B. (2008), 'Cybernetic Serendipity Revisited', in Brown et al. (2008: 83–93).
O'Hear, A. (1995), 'Art and Technology: An Old Tension', in R. Fellows (ed.), Philosophy and Technology (Cambridge: Cambridge University Press), 143–58.
Pask, G. (1969), 'The Architectural Relevance of Cybernetics', Architectural Design, 7 (Sept.), 494–96.
—— (1971), 'A Comment, a Case-History, and a Plan', in J. Reichardt (ed.), Cybernetics, Art, and Ideas (London: Studio Vista), 76–99.
Reichardt, J. (ed.) (1968), Cybernetic Serendipity: The Computer and the Arts, special issue of Studio International, published to coincide with an exhibition held at the Institute of Contemporary Arts, 2 Aug.–20 Oct., 1968 (London: Studio International).
Reichardt, J. (2008), 'In the Beginning...', in Brown et al. (2008: 71–82).
Sims, K. (1991), 'Artificial Evolution for Computer Graphics', Computer Graphics, 25/4: 319–28.
Smith, M. (ed.) (2005), Stelarc: The Monograph (Cambridge, Mass.: MIT Press).
Snow, C. P. (1959), The Two Cultures: The Rede Lecture (Cambridge: Cambridge University Press).
Spiller, N. (ed.) (2002), Cyber-Reader: Critical Writings for the Digital Era (London: Phaidon).
Stallabrass, J. (2004), Art Incorporated: The Story of Contemporary Art (Oxford: Oxford University Press).
Stelarc (1984), Obsolete Body: Suspensions, compiled/ed. with James D. Paffrath (Davis, Calif.: J. P. Publications).
—— (1986), 'Beyond the Body: Amplified Body, Laser Eyes, and Third Hand', NMA (New Music Articles), 6 (1986–7), 27–30; repr. in K. Stiles and P. Selz (eds.), Theories and Documents of Contemporary Art: A Sourcebook of Artists' Writings (Berkeley and Los Angeles: University of California Press, 1996), 427–30.
—— (1994), 'Prosthetics, Robotics and Remote Existence: Postevolutionary Strategies', Leonardo, 24: 591–5.
—— (2002a), Alternate Interfaces, with M. Grzinic, B. Massumi, and T. Murray (Melbourne: Faculty of Art and Design, Monash University).
—— (2002b), 'From Zombies to Cyborg Bodies: Extra Ear, Exoskeleton and Avatars', in Candy and Edmonds (2002: 115–24).

Todd, S., and Latham, W. (1992), *Evolutionary Art and Computers* (London: Academic Press).

Whitelaw, M. (2004), *Metacreation: Art and Artificial Life* (London: MIT Press).

Zivanovic, A. (2005), 'The Development of a Cybernetic Sculptor: Edward Ihnatowicz and the Senster', in L. Candy (ed.), *Creativity and Cognition 2005: Proceedings of the Fifth Conference on Creativity and Cognition, 12–15 April, Goldsmiths College* (New York: ACM Press), 102–8.

—— (2008), 'The Technologies of Edward Ihnatowicz', in Brown et al. (2008: 95–110).

12
Is Metabolism Necessary?

I. INTRODUCTION

The motivating question of this paper is whether strong A-Life is possible. In other words, could a virtual creature—existing only in computer memory, and manifested on the VDU screen—properly be regarded as alive? (Strong A-Life is so called by analogy with strong AI (Searle 1980).) In addressing this question, one must first consider the concept of metabolism. Metabolism is typically included within the definition of life, and is especially problematic for proponents of strong A-Life.

Metabolism concerns the role of matter/energy in organisms considered as physically existing things. It is not an abstract functionalist concept, divorced from the specific material realities. By contrast, the other features typically mentioned in definitions of life—self-organization, emergence, autonomy, growth, development, reproduction, adaptation, responsiveness, and (sometimes) evolution—can arguably be glossed in functionalist, informational, terms.

The core concept of self-organization, for example, involves the emergence (and maintenance) of order, out of an origin that is ordered to a lesser degree. It concerns not mere superficial change, but fundamental structural development. The development is spontaneous, or autonomous, in that it results from the intrinsic character of the system (often in interaction with the environment), rather than being imposed on it by some external force or designer. Similarly abstract definitions can be given of the other items on the list. Thus emergence is the appearance of novel properties that seem (at least at first sight) to be inexplicable in terms of earlier stages or lower-level components. Growth is increase in quantity; development is autonomous structural change leading to a higher degree of order; adaptation is improved response

I am grateful to Michael Wheeler and an anonymous reviewer for helpful comments.

to the environment by means of structural and/or behavioural change (which may be heritable); reproduction is self-copying; and evolution is adaptive change by means of reproduction, heredity, variation, and selection.

It is because no comparable definition can be given for metabolism that it is problematic for strong A-Life. A-Life in general is a functionalist enterprise. That is, A-Life researchers typically think of vital phenomena in terms of information and computation, not matter or energy. For example, John von Neumann defined the general requirements of reproduction in logical-computational terms, and pointed out that copying-errors (an informational notion) could result in adaptive evolution (Burks 1966, 1970). Similarly, in the 'Call for Papers' for the first conference identifying 'Artificial Life' as a unitary project, Christopher Langton said: 'The ultimate goal of A-Life is to extract the logical form of living systems' (Levy 1992: 113).

Of course, none of these A-Life researchers doubts that living things are material entities of some sort. In other words, life is not pure information. Langton makes this explicit in his statement that life is 'a property of the organization of matter, rather than a property of the matter which is so organized' (Langton 1989: 2). So far, then, the question 'Are matter and energy essential to life?' seems to be answered with a guarded 'Yes'. Some matter is organized, somehow. But the nature of the material stuff is philosophically irrelevant to the status of the physical system as a living thing. It could, for example, be silicon. And nothing can (or need) be said about the general type of physico-chemical processes that must be going on, except that they are organized in the relevant ways.

In this, A-Life scientists resemble functionalist philosophers of mind. Putnam's original definition of functionalism could in principle be satisfied by squads of angels jumping on and off immaterial pinheads (Putnam 1967/1975). But functionalists normally do assume a material base, whether wetware or hardware, on which mental properties somehow supervene. Indeed, this is why functionalism was welcomed by scientifically inclined philosophers of mind as an advance on, as opposed to a wholesale rejection of, the identity theory and central state materialism.

However, Langton (1986) also says: 'The ultimate goal of the study of artificial life would be to create "life" in some other medium, ideally [*sic*] a virtual medium where the essence of life has been abstracted from the details of its implementation in any particular model.' Such 'life' would inhabit cyberspace, a virtual world of informational processes grounded in computers. The virtual creatures would be defined in purely informational terms, as strings of bits or computer instructions. But their activity (the execution of the instructions)—without which, they could not be regarded even as candidates for life—would require the computer. So, like biological creatures, they would have some physical existence: namely, the material ground, in computer memory, of the relevant information processing. The 'matter which is organized' would be the stuff of which the relevant computers are constructed—which might be almost anything (according to John Searle (1980), even including old beer cans). As Langton's word 'ideally' makes clear, the molecules and physico-chemical processes involved would be of no concern to the A-Life functionalist. The virtual creatures' only interesting properties, qua living things, would be abstract, informational ones.

This claim of Langton's is disputed even by many A-Life researchers, so his 'ultimate goal' cannot be ascribed to A-Life in general. (It follows that A-Life as a whole could not be dismissed merely because one rejected strong A-Life; similar remarks apply to weak and strong AI, as Searle allows.) Nevertheless, Langton is not alone in making such claims.

One of the A-Life researchers who agree with him is Thomas Ray, an ecologist specializing in tropical forests. Indeed, Ray goes even further than Langton: he believes he has already implemented primitive forms of real—albeit virtual—life. His computer models of co-evolution in the virtual world 'Tierra' have led to the foundation of the 'Digital Reserve' (Ray 1992, 1994). This is a virtual memory-space spread across a worldwide network of computers, which allow their spare capacity to be used at idle times. Tierra is one example (another is described in Section III, below) of A-Life work described by its proponent as the creation of actual, if primitive, life forms.

The creatures (Ray's word) inhabiting the Digital Reserve, like those within Tierra itself, are strings of self-replicating computer code. They can mate (exchange genetic instructions), mutate, compete, and evolve. For example, some code strings evolve which lack the instructions responsible for self-replication, but which can 'parasitize' the code of other creatures in order to replicate themselves. This is a successful evolutionary strategy because fitness is defined in terms of access to computer memory—and a 'species' with shorter strings can fit more individuals into a given memory-space. The creatures let loose in the Digital Reserve move from one computer to another in their search for unused memory-space. (Because they are implemented in a virtual computer, simulated by some actual computer, the software creatures cannot 'escape' into computers not on the Reserve network, nor infest the everyday workings of those that are included.) Ray insists that the Digital Reserve is an experiment in the creation of new forms of life.

Those, like Langton and Ray, who regard strong A-Life as a real possibility defend their counter-intuitive view by making two interconnected claims. First, that the virtuality is limited: computers, after all, are material things, and need energy in order to function. Second, that the criteria for life are essentially abstract, or functionalist, saying nothing whatever about the nature of its (admittedly necessary) material grounding. To show that they are mistaken, one must show that at least one of these claims is false.

Since the first claim is indisputable, the focus falls on the second. I suggested, above, that all but one of the items on the typical list of vital properties can indeed be viewed as abstract, informational concepts. The one obvious exception is metabolism. The proponent of strong A-Life must therefore show that virtual systems can genuinely metabolize. (The alternative strategy—dropping metabolism from the list of vital criteria—is discussed, and rejected, in Section IV.)

In the next section, I distinguish three senses of metabolism. The first two (weaker) senses are found in the arguments of some proponents of strong A-Life, for on each of these interpretations some A-Life artefacts would count as genuinely alive. The third, strongest, sense is not. It is drawn rather from biology, and posits a form of bodily identity which (I shall argue in Section III) is not attained by virtual creatures.

Irrespective of questions about A-Life, the strong sense of metabolism is more interesting than is sometimes thought. Besides referring to the biochemical processes (whatever they may be) that maintain an organism's growth and function, it denotes various general properties that those processes must necessarily possess.

II. THREE CONCEPTS OF METABOLISM

What, exactly, is metabolism? It locates life in the physical world (no angels on pinheads). But it does not denote mere materiality. A volcano is a material thing, and so is a grain of sand, but neither of these metabolizes. Rather, metabolism—in the minimal sense of the term—denotes energy dependency, as a condition for the existence and persistence of the living thing.

If energy dependency were all there was to it, then strong A-Life would be possible. For, as both Langton and Ray are quick to point out, virtual life satisfies this criterion. Strong A-Life is utterly dependent on energy. Electrical power is needed to execute the information processes that define 'this' creature, or 'that' one. Pull the plugs on the computers, stop the electrons inside from jumping, and cyberspace is not merely emptied, but destroyed. Strong A-life, having once existed, would have died.

However, 'metabolism' is normally used to mean more than mere energy dependency. Two further senses of the term can be distinguished, each associated with notions of using, collecting, spending, storing, and budgeting energy. These activities are characteristic of life. (Active volcanoes involve huge amounts of energy, without which they would not exist. But they don't use it, collect it, store it, or even spend it, except in a weakly metaphorical sense—and they certainly don't budget it.)

A second (stronger) sense of metabolism supplements mere energy dependency with the idea of individual energy packets used to power the activities of the creature, its physical existence being taken for granted. Each living system has assigned to it, or collects for itself, a finite amount of energy. This is used up as it engages in its various activities. When the individual's energy is spent, either because it is no longer available in the environment or because the system can no longer collect or use it, the energy-dependent behaviour must cease and the creature dies.

Some very early efforts in A-Life (around mid-century) already involved the idea—and the reality—of individual energy packets. Grey Walter's (1950, 1951) mechanical 'tortoises', Elmer and Elsie, were simple robots that used their energy to engage in physical behaviour. They moved around the floor by means of electric power, every so often abandoning their current activity in order to recharge their batteries. The second definition of metabolism would also cover those more recent A-Life robots which are broadly comparable to Grey Walter's tortoises, some of which even have distinct energy stores devoted to different types of activity. Such robots could, therefore, be termed alive insofar as this (second-sense) criterion is concerned.

But A-Life robots are not germane to the question whether strong A-Life is possible. For 'strong A-Life' does not refer indiscriminately to just any A-Life artefacts, including robots and physical systems grounded in exotic biochemistries. Rather, it refers to virtual creatures inhabiting virtual worlds. As remarked above, virtual creatures exist only in computer memory, manifested to the observer on the VDU screen. They 'exist' in the sense that they consist of a particular (perhaps continuously varying) distribution of electric charges at various (perhaps widely scattered) locations inside the machine (these locations may change, as the relevant instructions are swapped from one part of the machine to another for execution or storage). In this sense, then, they may be said to have physical existence. But that's not to say that they have bodies (see below). Nor is it to say (what is required for the second sense of metabolism) that they store and budget real energy so as to engage in their activities and continue their physical existence.

Many virtual creatures are intended by their human creators as computer simulations of real life. That is, their manifest behaviour on the VDU screen (caused by the underlying electronic processes in computer memory) has some systematic relation to, or isomorphism with, certain features of living organisms. And some of these model metabolism (understood in the second sense), at least in a crude manner. Examples abound of programs that simulate individual animals with distinct energy levels, raised by eating and rest, and reduced by activities such as food-seeking, fighting, and mating. A few of these even assign different sub-packets of energy to various drives, so that at a particular time a creature might have energy available to mate, but not to fight. (For a very early example, where a simulated rat has to choose between seeking warmth and food, see Doran (1968).)

However, the 'packets' and 'sub-packets' here are not actual identifiable energy sources or energy stores, but mere simulations of these. At any given time, the program may dictate that the creature will seek food, but this merely means that some numerical variable has fallen below a threshold value, so triggering the food-seeking instructions. To be sure, energy is needed to execute the instructions. But this comes, via electric plug or battery, from the general undiscriminated energy source on which the whole program is passively dependent. If the program simulates more than one creature, this energy source is equally available to all, given the relevant program instructions. Metabolism in the first sense is achieved, but in the second sense it is merely modelled.

Suppose that separate energy sources, distinct real energy packets, were to be supplied (in the computer) for each simulated creature. What then? The second sense of metabolism would have been satisfied. If our concept of life involved this sense of the term, strong A-Life would be conceivable.

However, one must note two important features of the second definition, as given above. First, it speaks of the creature's 'physical existence', not of the creature's 'body'—nor even of its being a 'unitary' physical system. Second, and crucially, it speaks of that physical existence being taken for granted.

Clearly, then, the second sense of metabolism is not the biologist's concept of it. For no biologist ignores the fact that an organism's physical existence is an integrated material system, or body. (Apparent exceptions include slime moulds, within whose life cycle the multicellular organism splits into many unicellular 'amoebae', which later coalesce into a multicellular creature. But at every point, even at the amoebic stage, there is one or more integrated material system. Whether one chooses to call a reconstituted multicellular structure the 'same' organism, or body, is not important here.) Furthermore, no biologist takes the existence of a creature's body for granted. On the contrary, one of the prime puzzles of biology is to explain how living bodies come into existence, and how they are maintained until the organism dies. We therefore need a third, still stronger, definition of metabolism if we are to capture what biologists normally mean by the term.

The third sense of metabolism refers to the use, and budgeting, of energy for bodily construction and maintenance, as well as for behaviour. Metabolism, in other words, is more than mere material self-organization. That occurs (for instance) in the Belousov-Zhabotinsky reaction, where mixing two liquids results in the spontaneous emergence of order (visible whorls and circles)—but no one would here speak of life: too many of the other vital properties listed in Section I are missing. Rather, metabolism is a type of material self-organization which, unlike the Belousov-Zhabotinsky reaction, involves the autonomous use of matter and energy in building, growing, developing, and maintaining the bodily fabric of a living thing. (For present purposes, we may apply the term 'body' to plants as well as animals.)

The matter is needed as the stuff of which the body is made. And the energy is needed to organize this matter, and new matter appropriated during the lifetime, into something that persists in its existence despite changes in external conditions. Metabolism, in this strong sense, both generates and maintains the distinction between the physical matter of the individual organism and that of other things, whether living or not.

Metabolism in this third sense necessarily involves closely interlocking biochemical processes. A multicellular organism must, and a unicellular organism may, sometimes grow. (I take it that multicellular organisms start off as unicellular ones; normally, this is a single spore or fertilized egg, but multicellular slime moulds 'grow' by the aggregation of many unicellular creatures.) And even a unicellular organism must (sometimes) repair damage. Since living matter cannot be created from nothing, growth and repair require that new molecules be synthesized by the organism—which molecules themselves make up the organism. Moreover, the living system (subject, like every physical thing, to the second law of thermodynamics) continuously tends to disorder and the dissipation of energy. Hence metabolism must involve continual energy-intake from the environment.

The simplest conceivable living things might take their energy directly from the environment whenever they needed it. (They would satisfy only the first sense of metabolism, not the third.) Perhaps the very earliest organisms actually did this. But this would leave them vulnerable to situations in which no 'new' energy was immediately available. (Analogously, computers that rely on the plug in the wall are vulnerable to power cuts.) If, by chance, the organism became able to store even small amounts of excess energy for later use, its viability—and Darwinian fitness—would be enormously increased. Once evolution got started, this fact would be reflected in the evolution of metabolism.

Inevitably, then, all metabolic systems (other than the very earliest, perhaps) must not only exchange energy with the outside world but also do internal energy budgeting. Excess energy is stored, so that reliance on direct energy collection is avoided. If (what is likely) the inputted energy cannot be conveniently stored in its initial form, it must be changed into some other form. In other words, living organisms must convert external energy into some substance ('currency') that can be used to provide energy for any of the many different processes going on inside the organism. This is 'the first fundamental law of bio-energetics'. (Apparently, only three convertible energy currencies—one of which is ATP, or adenosine triphosphate—are used by terrestrial life (Moran et al. 1997: para. 4.2).)

Additional, purely internal, energy exchanges are required as the collected energy is first converted into substances suitable for storage and then, on the breakdown of those substances, released for use. Very likely, these processes will produce waste materials, which have to be neutralized and/or excreted by still other processes. In short, metabolism necessarily involves a nice equilibrium between anabolism and catabolism, requiring a complex biochemistry to effect these vital functions.

Bodily maintenance is normally continuous. But the underlying metabolic processes are more active at some times—of the day, year, and life cycle—than at others. Sometimes, they are drastically slowed down, or (perhaps) even temporarily suspended. In hibernating animals, for instance, metabolism is kept to a minimum: respiration and excretion occur at a very low rate. Even in the case of seeds or spores frozen, or entombed, for centuries, some minimal metabolic activity may have been going on. But what if it has not? It's not clear that this strong concept of metabolism assumes that active self-maintenance must be absolutely continuous, allowing of no interruptions whatsoever. If biochemical research were to show that metabolism is occasionally interrupted, in highly abnormal conditions (such as freezing), so be it. Indeed, we already speak of 'suspended animation': a spore may be currently inactive, but if it retains the potential to metabolize in suitable conditions we don't regard it as 'dead'.

What counts as the body is not always unproblematic. We've noted that it must be a material unity supporting various vital properties. Normally, each and every part of the bodily fabric is built and maintained by metabolism. This is as true of trees as it is of tortoises. Often, however, we restrict the term to the higher animals—or even to human beings alone.

This more restrictive use of 'body' recognizes the fact that (normally) many parts of the human body are sources of perceptual information and/or are under voluntary control. But what of physical prostheses? These include a wide range of examples. Some, such as cardiac pacemakers, are 'involuntary' muscle-controllers of whose (successful) activities the human host is unaware. Some are artificial sensory organs, such as retinas and cochlear implants, whose activities cannot be controlled (except to be turned off) but furnish information that the person can consciously use. Others, from simple peg-legs to the many types of jointed artificial limbs, are replacements for motor organs; these involve varying levels, and methods, of voluntary control. Yet others are implanted electrical circuits, integrated with the neuromuscular anatomy so that (for example) a paraplegic person can excite their various leg muscles at will.

None of these is part of the body according to the criterion of metabolic emergence. But some involve close connections to specific aspects of metabolic function. And many are crucial to the dynamics of interaction between the person and their environment. Moreover, motor and sensory prostheses, like ordinary tools, may come to feel like part of the body, from the user's point of view. Admittedly, an artificial hand will not hurt if it is pinched. But its amenability to voluntary control may be continuous with, and even to some extent experientially indistinguishable from, that of genuine bodily parts. Some philosophers stress the embodiment of cognition, and gloss ordinary tools—such as chisels, walking sticks, and microscopes—as extensions of our phenomenological world. They might be tempted also to say that prostheses are, or with practice can become, part of the body. Nevertheless, lacking metabolism they are not strictly alive. (Hair and nails are not alive either, although they once were.)

III. STRONG METABOLISM AND STRONG A-LIFE

The previous section showed that the first sense of metabolism is satisfied by all A-Life systems, and that the second could conceivably be satisfied by certain types of A-Life simulation. But what of the third, strongest, sense? Could this be found in any A-Life creatures, so allowing us to regard them as living things? If so, would these creatures necessarily be robots, or could they also include virtual life?

A-Life robots as currently envisaged do not fit the bill. These are typically 'situated' robots, engineered (or evolved) to respond directly to environmental cues. Some don't look at all lifelike (Cliff et al. 1993). Others resemble insects in their physical form, and may have control systems closely modelled on insect neuroanatomy (Brooks 1986, 1991; Beer 1990). Certainly, such robots are in a significant sense autonomous, especially if they have been automatically evolved over many thousands of generations (Boden, forthcoming). And they undoubtedly consume real energy as they make their way around their physical environment. Unlike classical robots, they are embedded in the world, in the sense that they react directly to it rather than by means of a complex internal world-model. But being embedded does not necessitate being (truly) embodied. I argued in Section II that a body is not a mere lump of matter, but the physical aspect of a living system, created and maintained as a functional unity by an autonomous metabolism. If that is right, then these robots do not have bodies.

Conceivably, some future A-Life robots might be self-regulating material systems, based on some familiar or exotic biochemistry. Just how exotic that biochemistry might be is unclear. In principle, it need not even be carbon-based. However, it may be that carbon is the only element capable of forming the wide range of stable yet complex molecular structures that seem to be necessary for life. And Eric Drexler (1989) has argued that even utterly alien (non-carbon) biochemistries would have to share certain relational properties with ours. They would have to employ general diffusion, not channels devoted to specific molecules; molecular shape-matching, not assembly by precise positioning; topological, not geometric, structures; and adaptive, not inert, components. In effect, Drexler is offering a functionalist characterization of biochemistry (the chemistry of metabolism), one that can perhaps be instantiated in many different ways. Metabolism has also been characterized in even more abstract, thermodynamic, terms (Moreno and Ruiz, in press).

Whatever the details, artefacts grounded in exotic biochemistries might well merit the ascription of life: not strong A-Life confined to cyberspace, but real, metabolizing, life. There is nothing in A-Life at present that promises such alien creatures. (It is, however, conceivable that human biochemists have already created artificial life forms—though not robots—without realizing it, by unwittingly 'creating the conditions under which [metabolizing systems] form themselves' (Zeleny 1977: 27).) In any event, such artefacts are irrelevant to our main question. If novel robots and biochemistries were to be engineered or artificially evolved, they would count as successful A-Life rather than strong A-Life. The question thus remains as to whether the third sense of metabolism rules out strong A-Life.

Metabolism in this strong sense, as we have seen, involves material embodiment—embodiment, not mere physical existence. It also requires a complex equilibrium of biochemical processes of certain definable types. It cannot be adequately modelled by a system's freely helping itself to electricity by plug or battery, or even by assigning notional 'parcels' of computer power to distinct functions within the program. Virtual creatures might have individual energy packets, and some form of energy budgeting, but these would be pale simulations of the real thing. Even 'biochemical' A-Life models are excluded from the realm of the living, if they are confined to cyberspace.

This forbids us to regard as truly living things a 'species' of A-Life that has recently attracted considerable attention—and whose main designer Steve Grand insists that its virtual denizens are primitive forms of life (Grand, p.c.). I am thinking of the cyberbeings conjured up by running 'Creatures', a computer game, or more accurately a computer world, built by the use of A-Life techniques (Grand et al. 1996). It is a far richer virtual world than that of other computerized 'pets'—such as 'Dogz', 'Catz', and the electronic Tamagochi-chick that the user must rest, exercise, and clean. What is of special interest here is that Creatures includes a (crude) model of metabolism, as well as of behaviour.

The human user of Creatures can hatch, nurture, aid, teach, and evolve apparently cuddly little VDU creatures called norns. Up to ten norns can coexist in the virtual world (future increases in computer power will make larger populations possible), but even one solitary individual will keep the person quite busy. One of the user's tasks is to ensure that all the norns can find food when they are hungry, and to help them learn to eat the right food and avoid poisons. Another is to teach them to respond to simple linguistic inputs (proper names, categories, and commands), different norns receiving different lessons. Yet another is to help them learn to cooperate in various simple ways. In addition, the user must protect them—and teach them to protect themselves—from grendels, predatory creatures also present in the virtual world. The human can evolve new norns likely to combine preferred features of appearance and behaviour, since mating two individuals results in (random) recombinations of their 'genes'.

A norn's genes determine its outward appearance and the initial state of its unique neural-network 'brain' (at birth, 1,000 neurones and 5,000 synapses), whose specific connection-weights change with the individual's experience. The genes also determine its idiosyncratic 'metabolism'. Each creature's behaviour is significantly influenced by its (simulated) biochemistry. This models global features such as widespread information-flow in the brain, hormonal modulations within the body, the norn's basic metabolism, and the state of its immune system.

The virtual biochemistry is defined in terms of four types of biochemical object. First, there are 255 different 'chemicals', each of which can be present in differing concentrations. (These are not identified with specific biochemical molecules: the functions of the 255 substances are assigned randomly.) Second, various biochemical 'reactions' are represented. These include fusion, transformation, exponential decay, and catalysis (of transformation and of breakdown). Third and fourth, there are a number of 'emitter' and 'receptor' chemicals, representing various processes in the brain and body (for example, activity in the sense organs). Taken together, these biochemical categories are used to build feedback paths modelling phenomena such as reinforcement learning, drive reduction, synaptic atrophy, glucose metabolism, toxins (from plants or bacteria), and the production of antibodies.

This general architecture offers significant potential for theoretically interesting advances in A-Life modelling. Its largely untapped complexity, including its ability to model global features of information processing, makes it a promising test-bed. It could be developed, for example, by incorporating recent AI-ideas on the computational architecture underlying motivation and emotion (Sloman 1990; Wright et al. 1996; Beaudoin 1994), which have as yet been modelled only in very preliminary ways (Wright 1997). Even now, without such additions, Creatures is undeniably seductive. All but the most hard-headed of users spontaneously address the norns as though they were alive, and some mourn the demise of individuals (each of whose 'life history' is unique) despite being able to hatch others at the touch of a button.

For all that, Creatures is a simulation of life, not a realization of it. There is no actual glucose, and no actual chemical transformation; the system is not even a chemically plausible model of specific molecular processes. Moreover, the simulated metabolism is concerned with controlling the norns' behaviour, not with building or maintaining its 'bodily fabric'. (Still less does it regulate the VDU creature's underlying, electronic, physical existence.)

Admittedly, the 'foods' and 'poisons' are associated with simulated metabolites and metabolic processes. At present, however, these affect the norns' behavioural, not bodily, integrity. They don't froth at the mouth when ingesting poison; and they don't have 'hearts' that stop beating, or 'flesh' that rots without oxygen. Certainly, some future development of Creatures might include a much richer metabolic simulation. The user might even be able to help a favourite norn to acquire a suntan, or to feed and exercise so as to develop its 'biceps'. Nevertheless, there would be no real metabolism, no real body—and no real life.

What if the 'foods' were to be associated with real energy, which was used only to run the electronic processes underlying the VDU manifestation of the individual norn? This would be an example of the type of A-Life system discussed above (in relation to the second sense of metabolism), in which the creature's continuing physical existence depends upon its being able to commandeer specific packets of real energy. In such a case, since the norns can evolve, they might even evolve new ways of attracting real energy and of using it (for instance) to repair their electronic grounding when damaged. Nevertheless, the points remarked above still stand: this imaginary scenario concerns the creature's physical existence, not its metabolically integrated body, and it takes that physical existence for granted. The construction of the computer, and of the parts/processes within it that constitute the norn's material being, was effected by artificial construction, not by autonomous metabolism.

In short, if we regard metabolism (in the third, biological, sense) as—literally—vital, we must reject the claim that norns, and their cyber-cousins, are simple forms of life. Even energy-gobbling and self-repairing norns, evolved without human direction, would not metabolize in this strong sense.

IV. CAN WE DROP METABOLISM?

Someone might suggest at this point that we adopt a weaker sense of metabolism when defining life, or that we drop the criterion of metabolism altogether. In that event, some of the virtual artefacts envisaged by Langton, Ray, or Grand could properly be regarded as alive. Such suggestions cannot be instantly dismissed. One cannot define life, define metabolism, and conclude that strong A-Life is—or is not—possible in a way that will immediately convince everyone. On the contrary, the concept of life is negotiable.

There are two reasons for this. First, there is no universally agreed definition of life. It's not even obvious that what one should do, in this situation, is to try to justify (a priori) a list of necessary and sufficient conditions, since our everyday concept may not name a natural kind. I noted one example of definitional disagreement in Section I, where I remarked that evolution is 'sometimes' added to the typical list of vital properties. Indeed, it is regarded as 'the' fundamental criterion by many biologists, and by some philosophers—such as Mark Bedau (1996). Taking evolution (or, in Bedau's terminology, 'supple adaptation') to be essential has several philosophical difficulties, as Bedau himself admits. One is that creationist biology becomes logically incoherent, not just empirically false. Another is that evolving populations, rather than individual organisms, must be taken as the paradigm case of life. This conflicts with ordinary usage. It also sits uneasily with the concept of metabolism: we saw in Section II that even the weakest sense of this term is defined with reference to the physical maintenance of individual things. (By the same token, including metabolism in the list of vital criteria underscores our usual assumption that individual organisms are paradigms of life.) Nevertheless, Bedau argues that evolution is so important in theoretical biology that it should be regarded as the very essence of life. Others, by contrast, argue that evolution—and reproduction, too—is a merely secondary feature of life, and that one can envisage living things incapable of either (see below).

Second, even if everyone today defined life in the same way, they might tomorrow have good reason for defining it differently. Scientific discoveries might lead to an (a posteriori) theoretical identification of the real essence of life, and hence to a change in the way that non-scientists use the term. The suggestion that evolution be taken as essential, for example, is grounded in modern biology. Before Darwin's theoretical work, it would have been unreasonable to propose this (even though many of his predecessors believed that living things somehow evolved). Again, one of the research aims of A-Life is to study 'life as it could be', not merely 'life as we know it' (Langton 1989: 2), which might eventually lead to a different, more inclusive, definition. Indeed, one new 'essential' vital property has already been suggested: Langton (1990, 1992) conjectures that all living things satisfy a narrow range of numerical values of the 'lambda parameter', a simple statistical measure of the degree of order and novelty in a system. It's not obvious that this sort of discovery is impossible. In short, the list of vital properties can change.

It might appear, then, that the possibility of strong A-Life hangs on mere definitional fiat. Given that there are several senses of metabolism, why not simply choose the weakest, or the strongest, so as to allow or disallow strong A-Life respectively? More radically, why not drop metabolism entirely? If we can consider adding evolution, surely we can consider dropping metabolism? We could retain a commitment to physicalism: no angels on pinheads allowed. And metabolism would still be recognized as a universal characteristic of the sort of (biological) life we happen to know about. But it would no longer be seen as essential.

To see the situation in this way is to confuse fiat with negotiation. I said, above, that the concept of life is negotiable, not that it can be defined just anyhow. Both scientific and philosophical judgement must be involved in favouring one definition rather than another. And both types of judgement imply that to drop metabolism from the concept of life would not be a sensible move. That is, the analogy we are asked to draw here—between adding evolution and dropping metabolism—is too weak to be persuasive.

There are strong scientific reasons for adding evolution to the definition of life, even for making it the most fundamental criterion. Specifically, evolutionary theory has enormous explanatory and integrative power, interconnecting all (or most) biological phenomena. Even in molecular biology and genetics, evolutionary explanations provide many insights. And most biologists who resist the reductionist approach of molecular biology, taking the form of whole organs and organisms as their explanandum, see it as not merely universal, but fundamental. A minority do not. For instance, Brian Goodwin (1990), Webster and Goodwin (1996: part 2) and Stuart Kauffman (1992) argue that biological self-organization is a more fundamental explanatory concept than evolution—and that the two processes can sometimes pull in different directions (see also Wheeler 1997). But even these theoretical mavericks allow that Darwinian evolution selects, and so (superficially) shapes, the range of living things that survive, given the (deeper, wider) potentialities afforded by self-organization. In short, all serious biologists—I do not include creationists—acknowledge that evolution has considerable explanatory force. This is why Bedau is willing to accept the admittedly counter-intuitive implications of taking evolution to be necessary.

That's not to say that everyone will judge the strong reasons for adding evolution to the definition to be strong enough. In particular, those who stress metabolism as a criterion are likely to insist that we should continue to take individual creatures, not evolved species, as the paradigm of life.

Consider, for example, the argument of the biologists Humberto Maturana and Francisco Varela (1980: 105–7). Their definition of life as 'autopoiesis in the physical space' is broadly equivalent to the third sense of metabolism defined in Section II (broadly, but not exactly: see Boden, in preparation). They remark that the concept of evolution logically presupposes the existence of some identifiable unity—that is, of a living thing self-generated and self-sustained by autopoiesis. But their refusal to regard evolution as essential is not a merely semantic point, following trivially from their preferred definition of life. Rather, it is a biological hypothesis. They point out that a living, self-organizing, cell could conceivably be incapable of reproduction. Even if it could be split (either accidentally or autonomously) into two autopoietic halves, there might be no self-copying involved. Self-copying requires some relation of particulate heredity between the mother and daughter systems. Furthermore, without such (digital) heredity, there can be no evolution (Maynard Smith 1996: 177). So the first living things might not have been capable of evolution.

My own view is that to regard evolution as an essential criterion of life is unwise. For the reasons outlined above, it would be better regarded as a universal characteristic, though one offering enormous explanatory power. It's not surprising that many biologists take evolution to be a defining property. But this definition, interpreted strictly, generates too many counter-intuitive—and biologically paradoxical—implications. That is, I don't find Bedau's arguments compelling. Even so, one must allow that he and others like him have a respectable case to make.

The same cannot be said of someone who proposes to drop metabolism as a defining criterion of life. There is no persuasive argument for rejecting our intuitions about its necessity. We have just seen that metabolism is even more fundamental than evolution, since non-reproducing organisms are conceivable and may once have lived. And Section II showed that metabolism, in the third sense, is essential for self-organizing bodily creatures that take in energy from their environment. Or rather, it is essential if that energy is not always immediately available, and it is useful if the energy is not always immediately needed. As for explanatory power, metabolism provides this. Biochemists have identified a host of specific molecular reactions involving general types of metabolic relation (such as breakdown and catalysis), and satisfying general principles concerning the storage and budgeting of energy (the 'laws of bio-energetics' mentioned in Section II). In short, scientific advance in biology and biochemistry reinforces our everyday assumption that metabolism is crucial, while also enriching the concept considerably.

To outweigh this combination of scientific theory and everyday usage, powerful countervailing considerations would be needed. But none exist. The only reason for proposing that we drop metabolism from our concept of life is to allow a strictly functionalist-informational account of life in general, and A-Life in particular. The same applies in respect of suggestions that we weaken the notion of metabolism, abandoning the third interpretation and substituting mere energy dependency (with or without individual energy packets). The only purpose of this recommendation is to allow virtual beings, which have physical existence but no body, to count as life. These question-begging proposals have no independent grounds to buttress them.

Significantly, it is even difficult to imagine what such independent grounds could be like. Perhaps some future science might discover strange wispy clouds, distributed over a large space yet somehow identifiable as (one or more) unitary individuals, and having causal properties analogous to those of living things—but lacking metabolism? In that case, we would have to think again. The concept of life remains negotiable. However, this futuristic scenario is well-nigh unintelligible. What are these 'causal properties analogous to those of living things' that do not require bodily unity? And how, in the absence of metabolism, could the clouds satisfy any self-organizing principle of living unity? The fact that science fiction writers have sometimes asked us to consider such ideas does not show that, carefully considered, they make sense.

Similar remarks apply to the speculative idea of a 'cosmic computer' (or 'computers') distributed across the atmosphere, supposedly supporting information processes that evolve and adapt much as Ray's virtual creatures do. Many philosophers argue that life is a necessary ground of cognition. If that is so, then nothing can be regarded as intelligent which is not also alive. And if life requires some metabolizing bodily unity, then the 'cosmic computer' is irredeemably suspect.

The argument of this paper suggests that such ideas are not just implausible, but irredeemably incoherent. Without independent grounds for doing so, we should not drop metabolism from the concept of life. Nor should we weaken our (third) interpretation of it. On the contrary, we should acknowledge it as a fundamental requisite of the sort of self-organization that is characteristic of life. In sum: metabolism is necessary, so strong A-Life is impossible.

REFERENCES

Beaudoin, L. P. (1994), 'Goal-Processing in Autonomous Agents', PhD thesis, Birmingham: School of Computer Science, University of Birmingham.

Bedau, M. A. (1996), 'The Nature of Life', in M. A. Boden (ed.), *The Philosophy of Artificial Life* (Oxford: Oxford University Press), 332–57.

Beer, R. D. (1990), *Intelligence as Adaptive Behavior: An Experiment in Computational Neuroethology* (New York: Academic Press).

Boden, M. A. (forthcoming), 'Life and Cognition', in J. Branquinho (ed.), *The Foundations of Cognitive Science at the End of the Century* (Lisbon).

—— (in preparation), 'Autopoiesis and Life'.

Brooks, R. A. (1986), 'A Robust Layered Control System for a Mobile Robot', *IEEE Journal of Robotics and Automation*, 2: 14–23.

—— (1991), 'Intelligence Without Representation', *Artificial Intelligence*, 47: 139–59.

References

Burks, A. W. (1966), *Theory of Self-Reproducing Automata* (Urbana: University of Illinois Press).

—— (1970), *Essays on Cellular Automata* (Urbana: University of Illinois Press).

Cliff, D., Harvey, I., and Husbands, P. (1993), 'Explorations in Evolutionary Robotics', *Adaptive Behavior*, 2: 71–108.

Doran, J. E. (1968), 'Experiments with a Pleasure-Seeking Automaton', in D. Michie (ed.), *Machine Intelligence III* (Edinburgh: Edinburgh University Press), 195–216.

Drexler, K. E. (1989), 'Biological and Nanomechanical Systems: Contrasts in Evolutionary Complexity', in C. G. Langton (ed.), *Artificial Life* (Redwood City, Calif.: Addison-Wesley), 501–19.

Goodwin, B. C. (1990), 'Structuralism in Biology', *Science Progress*, 74: 227–44.

Grand, S., Cliff, D. and Malhotra, A. (1996), *Creatures: Artificial Life Autonomous Software Agents for Home Entertainment*, Research report CSRP 434, Brighton: University of Sussex School of Cognitive and Computing Sciences.

Grey Walter, W. (1950), 'An Imitation of Life', *Scientific American*, 182/5: 42–5.

—— (1951), 'A Machine that Learns', *Scientific American*, 185/2: 60–3.

Kauffman, S. A. (1992), *The Origins of Order: Self-Organization and Selection in Evolution* (Oxford: Oxford University Press).

Langton, C. (1986), 'Studying Artificial Life with Cellular Automata', *Physica D*, 22: 1120–49.

—— (1989), 'Artificial Life', in C. G. Langton (ed.), *Artificial Life* (Redwood City, Calif., Addison-Wesley), 1-47; repr., with revisions, in M. A. Boden (ed.), *The Philosophy of Artificial Life* (Oxford: Oxford University Press, 1996), 39–94.

—— (1990), 'Computation at the Edge of Chaos: Phase-Transitions and Emergent Computation', *Physica D*, 42: 12–37.

—— (1992), 'Life at the Edge of Chaos', in C. G. Langton, C. Taylor, J. D. Farmer, and S. Rasmussen (eds.), *Artificial Life II* (Redwood City, Calif.: Addison-Wesley), 41–91.

Levy, S. (1992), *Artificial Life: The Quest for a New Creation* (New York: Pantheon).

Maturana, H. R., and Varela, F. J. (1980), *Autopoiesis and Cognition: The Realization of the Living* (London: Reidel).

Maynard Smith, J. (1996), 'Evolution—Natural and Artificial', in M. A. Boden (ed.), *The Philosophy of Artificial Life* (Oxford: Oxford University Press), 173–8.

Moran, F., Moreno, A., Montero, F., and Minch, E. (1997), 'Further Steps Towards a Realistic Description of the Essence of Life', *Artificial Life V* (Proceedings of the Fifth International Workshop on the Synthesis and Simulation of Living Systems), 255–63 (Cambridge, Mass.: MIT Press).

Moreno, A., and Ruiz, K. (in press), 'Metabolism and the Problem of Its Universalization', *BioSystems*.

Putnam, H. (1967/1975), 'The Nature of Mental States', in H. Putnam, *Mind, Language, and Reality: Philosophical Papers, II* (Cambridge: Cambridge University Press), 429–40 (1st pub. 1967).

Ray, T. S. (1992), 'An Approach to the Synthesis of Life', in C. G. Langton, C. Taylor, J. D. Farmer, and S. Rasmussen (eds.), *Artificial Life II* (Redwood City, Calif.: Addison-Wesley), 371–408; repr. in M. A. Boden (ed.), *The Philosophy of Artificial Life* (Oxford: Oxford University Press, 1996), 111–45.

—— (1994), 'An Evolutionary Approach to Synthetic Biology: Zen and the Art of Creating Life', *Artificial Life*, 1: 179–210.

Searle, J. R. (1980), 'Minds, Brains, and Programs', *Behavioral and Brain Sciences*, 3: 417–57.

Sloman, A. (1990), 'Motives, Mechanisms, and Emotions', in M. A. Boden (ed.), *The Philosophy of Artificial Intelligence* (Oxford: Oxford University Press), 231–47.

Webster, G., and Goodwin, B. C. (1996), *Form and Transformation: Generative and Relational Principles in Biology* (Cambridge: Cambridge University Press).

Wheeler, M. (1997), 'Cognition's Coming Home', in P. Husbands and I. Harvey (eds.), *Fourth European Conference on Artificial Life* (Cambridge, Mass.: MIT Press), 10–19.

Wright, I. P. (1997), 'Emotional Agents', PhD thesis, Birmingham: School of Computer Science, University of Birmingham.

Wright, I. P., Sloman, A., and Beaudoin, L. P. (1996), 'Towards a Design-Based Analysis of Emotional Episodes', *Philosophy, Psychiatry, and Psychology*, 3/2: 101–37.

Zeleny, M. (1977), 'Self-Organization of Living Systems: A Formal Model of Autopoiesis', *International Journal of General Systems*, 4: 13–22.

Index

42nd Parallel 139
4'33" 80–2

AARON 1, 142, 146, 152, 154, 158, 190, 37
abstract art 104, 108, 132, 25, 64
Acconci, Vito 83, 85, 88, 89
aesthetics, *see* values
affordances 4, 8, 56–62, 72
African Virgin Mary 76
agents, 13–15, 154, 164–174
Alexander, Igor 20
A-Life, *see* artificial life
Allais, Alphonse 82
analogue computers 136
analogue processes 136
analogy 166, 182
architecture 14–15, 72 108, 168–70, 213
art, concept of 6, 9–10, 36, 55, 84, 85, 87, 157–8, 206–8
art-envy 4, 5
artificial intelligence 35, 61
artificial life 21–4, 61, 175, 177, 180, 185, 188, 235–8
Art in the Mind 83
Arts and Crafts Movement 50
art system 155, 210
artworld 75, 76
Ascott, Roy 125, 147, 153, 212, 227
Ashby, William Ross 145, 177, 180, 183
Austen, Jane 17, 37
authenticity 14, 17–18, 23, 155, 156, 193–209
authorial responsibility 151–3
autodidacts 3, 6, 41–9
Automatic Mathematician 172
autonomy 13, 14–16, 22, 130, 144, 151, 175–94, 235, 244
 see also self-organization
Autopoiesis 145, 157, 180, 183
autopoiesis 23, 179, 250–1

Bach, Carl Philipp Emanuel 201
Bach, Johann Sebastian 100, 201, 203, 205
Bacon, Francis 25
Barry, Robert 84, 85, 88, 89
Barthes, Roland 101
Bauhaus 108, 109
Bedau, Mark 248
Beethoven, Ludwig van 205
Bell, Julian 16
Bense Max 112, 128
benzene ring 168, 172
Berenson, Bernard 94–97, 102, 105, 114
Bergson, Henri 177
Bianchi, Francesco 95
biochemistry 245, 246
Biomorphs 144
biophilia 118
Bird, Jonathan 92
Bosch, Hieronymus 53, 55, 56, 64
brain-damage 182, 189
Breton, Andre 139
Broken Kilometer 78
Brown, Paul 93, 105, 113–4, 119, 143, 187
Brown, Richard 19, 136, 137, 178
Burlington, Lord 808
Burnham, Jack 128

CA-art (df.) 137
CAD 15
Cage, John 80–2, 84, 85, 88, 89, 125
Calder, Alexander 109
Candy, Linda 215
Carroll, Lewis 103, 164, 173, 223
C-art (df.) 135
cartoons 31, 76
cellular automata 22, 126, 143, 180
CG-art (df.) 141
Chagall, Marc 224
Chance and Order 128
Chopin, Frederic 195, 197–8, 202

CI-art (df.) 146
Cloaca 76
Cohen, Harold 1, 18, 93, 113, 126, 142, 152, 158, 205
Coleridge, Samuel Taylor 165
collage 65, 73, 87, 147, 227
Colloquy of Mobiles 112, 135, 213
ColorField painters 10, 25, 131, 158
combinational creativity 166–7
computational economy 103, 116
computer-aided art 13
computer-aided art (df.) 137
computer art 7–21, 25, 93, 111–114, 125–163
taxonomy of 134–150
computer art (df.) 135
Computer Arts Society 113
computer-assisted art 8, 13–15, 137–9, 164–174
computer-assisted art (df.) 137
computer creativity 9
computer-generated art (df.) 141
computer models of creativity 1, 24
conceptual art 2, 5–6, 12, 25, 70–91, 109, 135, 215, 226
connectionism 36, 106, 126, 136, 143, 165, 178, 183, 204
connoisseurs 94–97
consciousness 10, 20, 23, 36, 190
Constructivism 108, 131, 133
Conway, John 113
Cope, David 18, 37, 142, 156, 157, 197–200
Copycat 166
Costa, Lorenzo 95
crafts 3–5, 8, 9, 50–52, 72, 89
creativity 29–40
combinational 2, 6, 21, 31–2, 36–7, 41, 85–88
exploratory 2, 5, 7, 21, 37–9, 41, 44, 85, 99–101, 203–4
three forms 1–3, 29–40
transformational 2, 6, 33–4, 42, 6, 90, 107, 171–3, 229
Creatures 245–7
Cubism 54, 55, 66
cybernetics 125, 145, 147, 153, 177
Cybernetic Serendipity 112, 113, 214

Dada 104, 108
Daedalus 145

Dali, Salvador 55
Danto, Arthur 75
D-art (df.) 136
Darwin, Charles 249
Davies, David 85
da Vinci, Leonardo 135, 145
Dawkins, Richard 144
death of the author 20, 98, 101, 227
defiant autodidacts 44, 45
Delvoye, Wim 76
de Maria, Walter 78, 79, 81, 85, 88, 89, 216
dematerialization of the art object 79, 216
depersonalization of art 109
see also Constructivism, modernism
Derrida, Jacques 98
Descartes, Rene 145
De Stijl 108
Dibbets, Jan 139, 145
dice music 101, 138, 147
digital art (df.) 136
digital computers 112, 147
Digital Reserve 237
direct perception 59
disgust 72, 76, 89
distributed cognition 12
Donne, John 97, 105
Double Negative 79
Drawbots 114–22
Drexler, Eric 245
Dubuffet, Jean 25
Duchamp, Marcel 75, 76, 87, 89, 108, 112, 125, 153, 191, 216
Duprat, Hubert 140
Durer, Albrecht 64, 94

earthworks 81
ecological psychology 58
Edmonds, Ernest 11, 113, 125, 126, 131–4, 148, 158, 211
education 3, 41–2
effort after meaning 197, 198
Ele-art (df.) 135
electronic art (df.) 135
Eliot T.S. 97, 105
embodiment, 126, 153, 155, 222–4, 239–44
emergence 126, 157
Emily Howell 205
Emin, Tracey 76, 216

Index

EMI, *see* Emmy
Emmy 18, 37, 142, 154, 156, 157, 193, 197–200
emotion 9, 18, 157, 196–200, 213, 247
enactive theories of perception 56–62, 65, 67
energy currencies 242
Eno, Brian 128
Evo-art (df.) 143
evolutionary art 7–8, 21–4, 38–9, 114–22, 152, 185–7, 228–31
evolutionary art (df.) 143
expressionist aesthetics 9

family resemblances 105
fitness function 8, 38, 115, 117, 119, 134, 144, 152, 153, 186, 230
flocking 21, 178
Flockinger, Gerda 55
fluorescent rabbit 6
Fodor, Jerry 103
Following Piece 83
fonts 66, 196
forgeries 94, 201
Fountain 75, 77, 87, 89, 108
Fowles, John 101
Fra Angelico 9, 24
fractals 8, 118
freedom 2, 16, 17, 55, 133, 175, 181, 185, 187, 190
Freud, Sigmund 92, 139
functionalism 236
Fun Palace Project 213

Gabo, Naum 108
Galapagos 144
Game of Life 113
Gardner, Martin 113
G-art (df.) 138
Gauguin, Paul 107
generative art 12–13, 22, 128–9
generative art (df.) 138
  taxonomy of 134–50
genetic algorithms 144, 185
Genetic Images 144
Gibson, James 56–62, 64
Giorgione 16, 105, 114
GOFAI 143, 181, 182, 189, 197, 204
Goldberg, Ken 12, 145
Goldsworthy, Andy 140

Goodwin, Brian 250
Gould, Glenn 100
Goya, Francisco 76
Gozzoli, Benozzo 96
Grand, Steven 245–7
Grau, Oliver 148
Grey Walter, William 145, 239
Guernica 17, 52, 53, 198
Gulliver's Travels 76

Haacke, Hans 138, 140
haikus 197
hallucination 182
hand-axes 4
handmade art/craft 50, 87
Haydn, Joseph 101, 138, 147
H-creativity 30, 41, 82
Heizer, Michael 79–80, 81, 85, 85, 88
Hepworth, Barbara 75
hermeneutics 55
heuristics 172
Hiller, Lejaren 128
Hirst, Damien 76
Hitchcock, Alfred 98, 101, 107, 111
Hofstadter, Douglas 152, 166, 196, 197–9, 202, 203, 204
Hogarth, William 76
homeostasis 15, 23, 175, 176, 178, 183, 190
Homeostat 177–8, 180, 183
Huebler, Douglas 139
Humboldt, Wilhelm von 97
hybrid systems 17, 189
hypnosis 182

I-art (df.) 146
Ihnatowicz, Edward 112, 135, 136, 145, 212
Illiac Suite for String Quartet 128
Illich, Ivan 44
improvisation 170–1
indicative theories of perception 53–6, 65, 67
Infinite Permutations 143
integrity 14, 16–17, 182, 187–90
intentionality 10
interactive art 11, 19–21, 25, 134, 146–54, 175, 183–4, 210–34
interactive art (df.) 146
interactive CD-Roms 19
International Klein Blue 110

Index

Internet 12, 18, 125, 145, 148, 221, 227
see also network art
Isaacson, Leonard 128

JAPE 37
jazz 99, 168, 170–1
jewellery 5, 22, 39, 52, 55, 62, 63, 140
Johnson, Bryan 101, 138
Johnson, Samuel 97, 105
jokes 37
Jonas, Hans 177
Jones-Smith, Katherine 118
Joplin, Scott 197, 203
Judd, Donald 77
Jurassic Park 21

Kac, Eduardo 6
Kandinsky, Wassily 108
Kant, Immanuel 177
Kaufmann, Stuart 250
Kekule, Friedrich von 168, 172
Kepler Johannes 44
Kinetica 158
kinetic art 111, 115, 126, 136
Klein, Yves 110
Koons, Jeff 14, 226
Kroto, Harry 45
Krueger, Myron 215

land art 81
Langton, Christopher 236, 237, 248
Laposky, Ben 136
Latham, William 144, 186, 193, 229
laws of bio-energetics 242, 251
Layard, Henry 97
Leach, Bernard 55
Le Corbusier 108
Leger, Fernand 109
Leighton, Lord 56, 64
Les Arts Incoherents 82
Les Demoiselles d'Avignon 99
Letter Spirit 66
Lewis, C. S. 98
LeWitt, Sol 14, 78, 79, 84, 89, 100, 106, 109, 139
Libeskind, Daniel 72
life 21, 22, 157, 235–54
Light-Space Modulator 108, 112
Lippard, Lucy 79
literature 97–8, 101, 105
Littlewood, Joan 213

Living Room 148, 220
Llewellyn, Nigel 92, 96
Lloyd Wright, Frank, 14, 15, 35, 168
Lord, Andrew 65–7
L-systems 126, 143

Mackintosh, Charles Rennie 55
Magnusson, Thor 12
Mahler, Gustav 203
Malevich, Kasimir 108
Mancini, Giulio 93
Marche Funebre pour un Grand Homme Sourd 82
Martin, Kenneth 128, 139
Maturana, Humberto 177, 250
McCormack, Jon 125, 130, 142, 143, 149, 158
mechanical art 135
mediaevalart 101
memory 165
metabolism 23–4, 235–54
metabolism (df.) 238–44
Metzger, Gustav 140
Michelangelo 75
Mignonneau, Laurent 147, 220
Milton, John 97, 105
Mimetic Starfish 19, 137, 178–9, 183, 189
minimalism 77, 79
mixed media 17, 188, 224
modernism 98, 107, 113, 187
Moholy-Nagy, Laszlo 108, 112
Mohr, Manfred 128
Mona Lisa 19, 59, 226
Monet, Claude 144
Monteverdi 197
Moore, Henry 78
morality 199–200
Morelli, Giovanni 16, 92–3, 102, 105, 114
Morris, William 50, 51
Mozart, Wolfgang Amadeus 45, 99, 101, 138
multiplayer games 12
music, 18, 37, 74, 80–2, 87, 128, 132, 137, 156, 170–1, 193, 196–8
Musicolour 135, 213

Nake, Frieder 128
Naturphilosophie 177
Naumann, Bruce 83, 85

Nees, George 128
Net Work 145, 180, 183
network art 12, 18, 127
Neumann, John von 126, 236
newsensory capacity 115, 153
Nineteen 132
Noland, Kenneth 131
Noll, Michael 128

Ofili, Christopher 76
O'Hear, Anthony 8,198, 199, 202
Oldenburg, Claes 77–8, 79, 80, 81, 84, 85, 88
ontology of art 12, 154
orientation detectors 179, 230

painting as activity 16
Palladian villas 14, 38, 168, 172
Paradise Lost 105
parallel distributed processing 105, 178, 189
Parker, Charlie 99
Pask, Gordon 112, 125, 135, 136, 147, 213
P-creativity 30, 41
PDP 105, 178, 189
perception 4, 8, 50–69 *passim*, 103, 105, 117, 189
performance 204, 214, 226
performance art 83, 85, 87, 100, 126, 135, 146, 155
Perkin, William 45
personal signature 7–8, 21, 92–124
  sources of 98–107
Photoshop 6, 13, 137, 228
Picasso, Pablo 17, 99, 106, 198
Placid Civic Monument 77
Plant Growing 221
poetry 30, 34, 43, 89, 97, 105, 165
Pointillism 136
Pollock, Jackson 64, 118–9, 138, 155, 216
post-impressionism 216
postmodernism 20, 98, 113, 153, 218, 223, 227, 228
pottery 4, 5, 45, 52, 55, 57, 62, 65–7
PPCs 176, 178–9, 183
Prairie Houses 14, 15, 35, 38, 168
process art 128, 139
Prophet, Jane 145, 180

prostheses 243
Putnam, Hilary 236

qualia 199

R-art (df.) 144
Rauschenberg, Robert 82
Ray, Thomas 237, 248, 252
readymades 76, 108, 125, 216
reflexes 13, 16, 62
Reichardt, Jasia 112
relevance 7, 77, 88, 89, 103, 120
Renaissance art 14, 24, 54, 55, 94, 100, 101, 102, 104
Ricks, Christopher 97
Riecken, Douglas 196
Riley, Briget 54
Rinaldo, Kenneth 145, 157, 180, 183
robot art (df.) 144
robots 7, 11–12, 39, 61, 93, 110, 114–126, 153, 157, 180, 183, 224, 230, 239, 244
Rodchenko, Alexander 108
Romanticism 6, 7, 41, 50, 96, 98, 99, 101, 107, 109
Rothko, Mark 9, 10, 16, 18, 25, 131
Rotoreliefs 108, 112
Roue de Bicyclette 108
Rousseau, Douanier 56, 64
Rowlandson, George 76
rule-drivensystems 128–9, 133, 151
Ruskin, John 50, 51

Sacks, Oliver 171
SAM 112, 135, 147, 212
Sandlines 143
Schoenberg, Arnold 74, 87, 206
Schoffer, Nicholas 11
sculpture 75–80, 76–8, 87, 115, 126, 136, 173, 185, 213
Searle, John 237
self 182
self-organization 23, 126, 157, 175, 176–80, 179, 181, 190, 235–54
semantic networks 165
Senster 112, 136, 137, 145, 147, 148, 212
sexual selection 4
Shakespeare, William 30, 65, 99
shape grammar 168

Sims, Karl 144, 212
situated robotics 180, 181, 183, 244
Slade School of Art 113
slime moulds 241, 242
Sommerer, Christa 147, 220
space grammar 168
Sperry, Roger 178
Stelarc 135, 145, 214, 226
Still, Clyfford 131
Stochastic Music Program 128
Stratton, George 178
strong A-Life 23–4, 157, 235–8
styles in art 2, 32–5, 37–9, 66, 99–101, 104–106, 152, 168, 203
surprise 1–2, 31, 38, 41, 50
Surrealism 2, 104, 139
Sutcliffe, Alan viii
swarm grammar 143
Swift, Jonathan 76
systems art 109

Tamagochis 246
Tatlin, Vladimir 108
taxonomy of computer art 134–50
 summary 150
Taylor, Richard 118
TeleGarden 12, 145
telematic art 227
Tenniel, John 223
The Broken Kilometer 216
The Crucible 52
The Flock 145, 157, 180
The FrenchLieutenant's Woman 101
The Hole 77 *The Matrix* 156
Theory of Mind 182, 183, 207
The Rake's Progress 76
The Unfortunates 101, 138
The Waste Land 105, 44
Tierra 237
Todd, Stephen 193, 229

Tourette's syndrome 171
transformational creativity 2, 6, 33–4, 42, 6, 90, 107, 171–3, 229
Trans Plant 147, 221
trompe l'oeuil 11, 148
Tuning Pask's Ear 136
Tura, Cosimo 95
Turbulence 143
Tureck, Rosalind 100

uniqeness 87, 109, 154, 156, 205
Universal Zoologies 149
unpredictability 154, 155, 185, 190, 219–22, 228
unschooled autodidacts 44, 45

values 4, 9, 22, 24–5, 37, 39, 43, 56, 71, 88–90, 150, 218–25, 229
Varela, Francisco 177, 250
Vasari, Giorgio 94
Vauconson, Jacques de 76
Velasquez, Diego 25
Vertical Earth Kilometer 78, 216
Viner, Darrell 115
virtual art 127, 148, 155
virtual instruments 137
virtual life 23–4, 157, 235–8
virtual reality 11, 22, 62,148, 155, 188, 217, 220, 223–5
visual reorganization 178
VR-art 127, 148, 155
VR-art (df.) 148

Webster, Andy 136
Whitelaw, Mitchell 230
Whitman, Walt 189
Wittgenstein, Ludwig 105

Xenakis, Iannis 128

Lightning Source UK Ltd.
Milton Keynes UK
UKOW050914121012

200467UK00003B/4/P